"It matters not how strait the gate…"

~ William Ernest Henley ~
Invictus

J.B.M.   L.G.M.

S.S. President Hayes

June ~ 1926

En Route to Sumatra

How Strait the Gate

Lane Middleton

United Writers Press
Asheville, N.C.

How Strait the Gate

by Lane Middleton

Published by:
United Writers Press
Asheville, N.C. 28803
www.UnitedWritersPress.com

Cover images courtesy of the author
Cover and interior design by United Writers Press

Printed in the U.S.A.

Contents

I offer these reflections in memory of my mother, Totsy. Her life spanned nearly a century, and her legacy was an assortment of vignettes that recall the people she either courted or dismissed. Her influence on those around her was never casual, and she contributed style and sparkle—and sometimes turmoil—to a world from which she expected privilege and plenty. Her unsuspecting devotees jockeyed for space under her enticing little thumb, and then wondered why they were vaguely uncomfortable. The benefits often were not quite as advertised.

She and I took turns being the irresistible force or the immovable object in our own relationship. But at the end, for a moment, we were in step and in tune.

PROLOGUE

My mother died this afternoon. It is Tuesday, April 14, 1998, in Charleston, South Carolina. Even at the impressive age of 93, she wasn't yet specifically ill, but she'd lately become wraith thin, and I've suspected for some time that she was about to move on. Like her appetite, an indignant awareness that she was no longer fully compos mentis had been fading, and I wonder if perhaps it was an inborn determination to defy this assault on her self-respect that delayed her keeping her appointment with her Maker these recent months. It seems she stopped fending off His calls when she finally forgot to be indignant.

I awoke early this morning to the sound of the telephone ringing. It was the nursing home.

"Your Momma's pressure's barely there, Miss Lane," said the matter-of-fact voice. "Maybe you oughta look in on her before you go to work."

And sure enough, by the time I arrived an hour or so later, aeons of lifelessness already stretched between loud, raspy breaths. With blood pressure too low even to register, what was the source of these fierce surges of energy? What wellspring of strength—or willpower—had not yet run dry? As I bent to kiss her, I searched her unseeing, half-open eyes for any sign of distress. But her brow was smooth, even as her soul fought free of this mortal coil. She looked almost young.

Unsure what to do with myself, I sat on the edge of the chair by the open window—awkwardly, as if poised to flee—and reached for the newspaper someone had left on the table at the foot of Totsy's bed.

"The weather should be nice on Saturday, Mommie." I tried to sound conversational—even casual—but hardly knew my own voice. "The paper says it's going to be a lovely day for the funeral."

Why did I say that? Nobody's told me this is the end. But it is, isn't it? It didn't occur to me, either, that it might have been tactless to mention her funeral. She'd planned her own graveside service well in advance, and I thought she might like to know the weekend weather promised to be balmy. She would never doubt that people would come to bid her farewell—rain or shine—but now she needn't worry that their shoes and hats might get wet. Totsy could always be counted on to be practical when the chips were down.

Suddenly I felt at an utter loss. I realised my hands were shaking. My jaw ached. *Have I been gritting my teeth? What's the matter with me? I know perfectly well what's coming. She seems fast asleep, so how is it her eyes are slightly open? Is she really dying? Last night the doctor said she was "stuporous." Does that mean she's in a coma? Haven't I heard somewhere that comatose patients are sometimes aware of their surroundings? So does that mean she knows I'm here? Does she even want me to be here, like this, when she isn't at her best? Normally she would refuse point-blank to be seen in deshabille. Can she hear me? What should I say? Shall I pretend and try to reassure her she's going to get better? Or shall I face it square on and tell her it's time for her to go, that we love her, but that we'll all be fine? Do people really linger at Death's door until they're sure everybody can manage without them? Of course, we'll manage. Death is a universally apocalyptic event, but everybody manages. Don't they?*

Briefly, instinctively, I was embarrassed by my mother's vulnerability and by my own inadequacy, for her soul's nakedness in the torpor of near death, and at my being witness to so intensely personal and private an experience. But then it struck me. In the face of imminent mortality, such delicacy was really nothing more than false modesty, and would surely blind me to what was taking place in our midst. If birth is a miracle, then so must be death—and the price of being shy about the whole thing might be to miss a fleeting glimpse of God.

A warm breeze floated over my shoulder. Letting out a great sigh and grasping the remnants of my tattered courage, I abandoned the formality of my chair and knelt on the floor by the bed. No longer politely frightened, I gathered my mother to me as gently as if she were a baby, and at last a dam of treasures—my heart's careful secrets—broke in a torrent of relief. I promised her she would be missed, but that Heaven would be the brighter for her arrival; that there were others there who were impatient to see her again. And though I could almost hear her angel beckoning, I knew her heart heard my every whispered word.

There's no need to wait any longer, Mommie ... Do go on now ... Truly it's all right ... You must be so tired ... and we'll be okay, I promise ... Anyway, everybody there is longing to see you ... Daddy and Blakie ... and Ma and Pa and Marion ... I expect they've been getting ready for you for days now ... You'll be awfully busy, I know, but you won't forget to give all of them my love, will you? ... My very dearest love? ... And please tell them how much I miss them ... Oh, how terribly much I miss them ... Go on, Darling ... You're such a sweet girl ... I love you so ... Go on now.

I've been dreading this moment for ages, primarily because her death would extinguish the guttering hope that I might one day have a real friendship with her. Totsy prided herself on our "unusually good relationship," while from my perspective, we've always tried to hide—or sidestep—our mutual disdain; our self images fundamentally disapproved of each other. But as I watched her spirit being welcomed into eternity, a frisson of excitement raised the hair on my arms, and I began to suspect she was delaying her au revoir until she was sure I had awakened from a kind of mortality of my own, some 14 years ago. In 1983, at not quite 23 years old, my son Blake died of a brain tumour. And assuming he was lost to me forever, a lassitude had seeped slowly into my soul until its weight threatened to crush me.

Now today, with a clarity as bright as lightning, Totsy was letting me know that her essence would always be somewhere within my reach. And following that stunning revelation came the joy of knowing that Blake must therefore still be here too. I'd spent a lifetime wanting to be close to my mother, but she knew better. Her supreme gift was to be the vessel from which the sun would pour back into my life and open my eyes to otherworldly truths that would at last ease the anguish of losing my child.

Immobile on the window sill sat a bird, a vivid fat cardinal, who kept watch like a little sentinel as I held close my precious charge and listened to her silent breast. Though she lay still as stone, she seemed to wander away into the afternoon light that bathed the room. I imagined she might turn and wave, or blow me a kiss—as she always did when we parted—as if she were about to embark on the trip of a lifetime, and would soon be back to tell me about it, with the embellishments du jour.

Attended at her Alpha and Omega by the two women closest to her in the bonds of blood and love, my mother's life circle—beginning in her own mother's embrace at her birth and ending in mine at her death—was now almost complete. Her last breath, soft against my cheek, seemed somehow to be a sweet kiss of life. And it was all the more electrifying because it took me so totally unawares, crashing its way through the barricade of angry cynicism that had long ago become the sole lynch pin to my increasingly frail equilibrium.

My mother's small hand lay cool in mine, the skin papery and translucent. Looking into her quiet face, into her filmy hazel eyes, I felt a heavy calm, a forgotten harmony, like a field become verdant after a drought and drawn softly back into the earth's seasons. Two bright tears spilled onto her forehead—I'd no idea I was weeping—as eddies of today's sorrow slowly evaporated at the horizon where it met tomorrow's sky. The cardinal fluttered and flew out into the courtyard, up to the top of the yellow ginkgo tree.

When my thoughts return to that unknown crossroads of a few hours ago, my heart lurches with the sort of anticipation that spurs on the eager traveler. I had tried to prepare myself against a numbing sorrow, but instead, I'm giddy with euphoria and a consuming need to describe the wonders of this day to Emmeline and John: Blake's younger sister and brother. What follows here is my attempt somehow to make them understand what has just happened to their grandmother—and to me—other than the plain fact of her dying. I must somehow describe how we both were swept along by a great force that flung wide the chained inertia of my spiritual life, as it slowly dimmed the lights over her temporal one.

HOW STRAIT
THE GATE

Book I
Historic Perspective

I wish I'd known my Middleton grandparents better. I'd like to have been able to sort out for myself—with my own points of reference—the significance of various snippets I've heard about them over the years.

Born in Charleston in 1867, Julia Porcher Blake wed William Dehon Middleton when she was 29 years old and he was 34. To their seven children *[six boys—the second of whom "was carried off by pneumonia" at six months old—and a girl]*, as well as to their multitudinous grandchildren, they were known as Madam and Paps. And in the mannered convention of the times, they usually addressed each other as Mr. and Mrs. Middleton. Favoured with unusual longevity, they died in 1942 and 1953, respectively, at ages 80 and 86.

Paps was a short, dapper man with a soft voice and a neatly sculpted goatee. They say he was an individual of easy and amiable temperament, of charm and wit and admirable intellect. He was born in Pickens County, South Carolina, in 1862, soon after the start of the American Civil War. By the end of that savage national slaughter, his father *[my great-grandfather Arthur]* was almost destitute, but with 10 children still to raise, he gathered up the family and moved to Daisy Bank, a rice plantation near Georgetown.

Soon finding it impossible to sustain a business at once so costly and uncertain—the field hands were, of course, no longer field hands—the Middletons continued on to Atlanta, Georgia, where

Arthur worked for a short time with a London-based insurance broker. Eventually, he brought his large brood back to South Carolina. They settled permanently in Charleston, where he and a neighbour, Addison Ingle, founded Middleton Ingle Insurance Company in 1900, with offices on State Street. Arthur's son *[my grandfather Paps, who was now 38 years old]* soon joined the fledgling enterprise, as did in due course two of his own sons, Arthur and Will *[Daddy's older and next younger brothers]*. My Uncle Will didn't retire, incidentally, until he was nearly 90, by which time he had become known affectionately as the Dean of Charleston Insurance.

We were living in Beaumont, Texas, in 1942, when Paps died. I was only four years old, yet I vividly remember Daddy's receiving the call from one of his brothers in Charleston, with the news of their father's unexpected death. Tightly gripping the receiver, Daddy listened in silence for several moments before slowing hanging up.

"Paps died a few minutes ago," was all he said, as he sank abruptly into the nearest chair and sat staring ahead, his blue eyes dull and empty. No one moved or spoke.

I understood part of this drama. My father's daddy had just died. *So why isn't my own daddy crying?* My eyes welled. *Aren't you supposed to cry when something bad happens? Is it wrong to do that? Why can't I go hug him? Why doesn't someone go over there and hug him?*

Looking intently at him for some sort of sign, I sensed I was expected to resist the impulse to get on his lap and pat his hand or his face. In the unnatural stillness of our living room, stirrings of infantile panic rose in my chest. My father was obviously sorely stricken—hunched over, so pitifully alone—yet it seemed we were supposed to stand by and watch while he suffered. *Why?* I examined my mother's unhappy face. Still no one moved. My chin quivered uncontrollably as I rubbed away tears that paused at the end of my nose.

Eventually, after clearing his throat several times, Daddy got to his feet and went into the kitchen. With trembling hands, he carefully poured himself a beer, and the four of us sat down to supper. And carried on as if nothing had happened.

Such was my initiation into my family's primary pathology. The only way anyone knew to cope with a crisis, however grievous, was simply to ignore it. I wasn't made of such stern stuff, however, and by reacting passionately to passionate situations throughout my life, I've often traveled a deserted and very shadowy road. Furthermore, because my numerous infractions of our neurotic code have invariably proved more interesting than anyone else's, they've been conveniently susceptible to family scrutiny and analysis. And, of course, to family judgment.

But that's another story.

When Madam died in 1953, we were living in London. Totsy and my brother and I had spent most of World War II in Summerville, South Carolina, while Daddy commuted regularly from New York to Europe on behalf of his employer, Socony Vacuum. But apparently we seldom ventured into Charleston— barely 25 miles away—for I remember being taken there only once, when I was about five years old, to visit Madam at 12 Water Street.

It was mid-afternoon when we arrived, and she was resting in her bedroom with the indoor shutters pulled to. The atmosphere was sepulchral. She motioned me to come and greet her, and I approached the bed with considerable trepidation. But after giving me a brief hug, she re-tied the ribbon at the end of one of my braids and, then, looking at me closely, she smiled and unpinned the little Victorian brooch on her bed-jacket and attached it to the shoulder of my pinafore. It was my first piece of "real" jewelry—a small, brightly enameled gold pansy with a wonderful minuscule diamond in its centre—and I was, for once, rendered completely speechless.

Madam had the unfortunate—and perhaps unjustified—reputation of being humourless and unsociable. And while therefore not remembered for a particularly sunny disposition, her seldom smile *is* still famous for what the family collectively calls the Blake teeth. Blake teeth are square and even and very close together. Several of us have inherited those teeth. And in every such case, we seem to have one or two more of them than is usually considered really necessary.

After scrutinising a singularly representative group of us one evening, a dinner guest remarked, "You know, y'all look just like Japanese generals!" and then laughed his head off. We looked at each other and laughed, too. It was true.

Anyway, aside from the mouth full of Chiclets, Madam could easily have been Queen Victoria's plump little twin, complete with mobcap and long full skirt, bouffant sleeves to her wrists, and hand-tatted lace high around her throat. Among the last of an endangered species, she never signed a personal cheque. Nor did she ever visit a beauty parlour. But in keeping with the prevailing fashion, her brownish hair was worn swept up, with corkscrew curls teased from the chignon to bounce at her ears. Left unattended, her hair was actually "as straight as the wall," but she used strips of linen rag to wind it into tight little twists every night before going to bed.

Like so many of her ilk, Madam believed all respectable social discourse should be devoid of any reference to domestics, diseases, and descendants. The "three d's," as she called them. But the best illustration, ever, of her overweening prudery, occurred late one

Saturday afternoon when she was on her way downstairs after her ritual nap.

One of Daddy's college classmates, who'd been invited to supper, came bounding up past her looking frantically about and jostled Madam as he rushed by.

"What is it?" she called after him, her tone severe and peremptory. "What do you want, young man?"

The lad was manifestly agitated. Skidding to a halt as he rounded the corner at the next landing, he sheepishly admitted he was looking for the bathroom.

Outraged at being subjected to such blatantly lamentable breeding—*How dare he allude, however delicately, to something so private, so unseemly, as a call of nature?*—Madam first poked through her reticule for some smelling salts and then banished him from the premises. Permanently.

⚜

My father's 40-year career with Mobil Oil began in 1920, when the company was still known as Standard Oil. He was 19 years old and had just been graduated from The Citadel, formerly The Military College of the South. His position as shift worker at the local refinery on East Bay Street was offered him through the good word of one Robert Hurd, a friend of the family, whose daughter Patty had recently married Daddy's older brother Arthur. Hurd was also an associate of John D. Rockefeller, Jr. *[son of the founder of the original Standard Oil Company]*, and the seemingly casual connection abruptly transformed my father's languid stroll along the parochial path into a sprint down the middle of the metropolitan highway.

Daddy recalled that during that brief initial Charleston phase of his epic tenure in the oil industry, Paps would drive his navy-blue Packard uptown to the plant every day around noon to bring him a sandwich in a brown paper bag.

"It really made me feel kind of foolish for Paps to turn up like that at lunchtime every day as if I were still a little kid," he remarked, affecting chagrin. In reality, I suspect he relished his father's attention. They were an undemonstrative family, and the small, rather late-in-the-day gesture probably went down very nicely.

Over time, the company's name evolved from Standard Oil to Socony Vacuum to Socony Mobil to Mobil Oil. And having merged earlier this year with the Exxon Corporation to become ExxonMobil is now the largest industrial organisation in the world. If my father had lived to see this sensational development, I imagine his only reaction would have been to exhale a note or two of his characteristic off-key whistle through a smile of bashful—and incredulous—satisfaction.

More tired than ill—certainly he was weary of putting on a good show—Daddy called it quits on April 12, 1986. The most courtly of men, he remained patient and affable even in the unkind throes of mild dementia. Our personal relationship had always been outwardly uncomplicated. In fact, there was usually so little conversation between us, you might even suppose it was superficial. But our mutual regard was both profound and extravagant, and his obvious, and often irrational, pride in me was my mainstay when a tendency toward recklessness would threaten to drive me off course. The way he and I approached the everyday world seemed sometimes to set us somewhat apart from it, but it was in this perverse isolation that we were best able to recharge our non-everyday batteries.

Daddy's funeral was very much to the point—a brief but fond farewell at his graveside—and I believe he'd have found the reception afterward equally to his taste. He'd always said that when he was "at last gathered to [his] fathers," he wanted his mourners "*not* to mourn, but to drink a lot and have a helluva party!"

We did. We enjoyed ourselves hugely as we toasted him again and again, interrupting each other with old memories and recalling his helpless merriment over his own jokes and stories. He often laughed so much himself—face scarlet and eyes streaming—that he'd give up before reaching the punchline and feel for the white linen handkerchief that was always slightly falling from his breast pocket.

He was a man liked and honoured by members of every stratum of society. He would clasp the hand of prince and labourer with equal firmness, incline his head in the same bow of respect to intimate and stranger, acknowledge child and peer alike with his impartial, blue-eyed benediction. His sweetest trait was the simplicity of his generosity. And, in return, he asked only that he be allowed to be himself without pretension of any kind.

We missed him without sadness, our spirits buoyed by his spectre, our hearts insulated with love of him. And we knew we would not see his like again.

A few days after the funeral, I stopped to visit with Totsy on my way home from work, and was astonished to find her vivacious and gay. Breathlessly, she told me that earlier that morning during the bittersweet task of going through Daddy's drawers and cupboards— or, as he would put it, his "impedimenta"—she had come upon a locked deed box that she didn't recognise. Unable to find a key that fit but filled with curiosity, she stopped what she was doing and took the box down the street to Jantzen, the locksmith. And within minutes, she was holding a sheaf of memories that lent her smile the softness of a bride's.

The collection of over 200 letters and telegrams from her young love—tied with narrow satin ribbon or lengths of lace into a dozen or so bundles—had been written between July, 1924 and their wedding in February, 1926. In that interim, Totsy attended Ward Belmont, a women's junior college in Nashville, Tennessee. And Daddy worked at the Standard Oil plant on the outskirts of Charleston while still living at home at 12 Water Street.

Having forgotten the letters even existed, Totsy was barely able to contain her excitement at the prospect of reliving their courtship through this old documentary, penned in Daddy's near-illegible hand. Her unselfconscious pleasure quite brought tears to my eyes, and following her upstairs to be shown her dear discovery, I felt the ghost of the girl who had so enslaved my father's heart.

They were first introduced at a Citadel hop, during the time her father *[my grandfather Pa]* was Commandant and Professor of War and Military Tactics there. Though Daddy had been graduated from The Citadel two or three years before Pa joined the faculty, he still occasionally went to the homecoming dances. And like himself, Totsy had apparently been smitten from the moment they met.

"For several weeks after that dance, I wondered why he didn't call on me." Her famous dimples would form whenever telling the story. "I just knew we clicked. And it never crossed my mind that, of *course,* he'd think twice before approaching the commandant's daughter!"

Everyone would laugh as if on cue.

"Well, the turning point came one Friday afternoon when Pa was reviewing the Corps of Cadets on the parade ground. I'd been told that Blake was among those invited to the weekly ceremony. And looking back, it was almost as if I suddenly couldn't stand the suspense any longer and decided to take matters into my own hands.

"I really don't know what got into me. But instead of waiting on the sidelines, I walked across the parade ground toward Pa, and stopped just behind him. He didn't notice me at first. But when he did catch sight of me, he blurted out, 'Well, for the love of sweet Jesus! Look who's joined us!' Why, you could hear his Alabama voice all the way across the field!"

Knowing my grandfather as I did, I'm sure Pa was charmed by the interruption, albeit during an event traditionally conducted with sacred formality. The quintessential flapper, spit curls framed Totsy's face, which sported a beauty spot and bright red lipstick. Her dress, too, was red, with the skirt cut well above the knees of her black-and-white-striped stockings. A cigarette, in its gold-rimmed parchment holder, may even have dangled from her fingers. Needless to say, she smoked in those days. The 1920s symbol of female suffrage and emancipation was every bit as important an accessory as were feathers and fringe, and she flaunted the paraphernalia with innate effect and expertise.

This unscheduled bonus to the Parade drew involuntary smiles from even the most conservative among the guests. And encouraged by the commandant's own small breach of protocol, Daddy at last tossed caution to the winds and telephoned Totsy that evening.

"By the by, Margaret Lane, the circus is in town this weekend," he said, after presenting himself in somewhat stilted fashion. It wasn't until after they were married, incidentally, that he began calling her "Totsy," the nickname given her originally by her 11-month-older sister Marion, who referred to her as "that little tot."

"And now I think of it, speaking of the weekend," Daddy added cautiously, "the wrestling favourite is scheduled to fight tomorrow afternoon. Might I persuade you to go with me? To both events? I should be delighted if you'll allow me to pick you up at two o'clock."

Without bothering to question even for a moment her hero's idea of romantic entertainment, Totsy agreed enthusiastically. Needless to say, she and her handsome cadet fell in love—hook, line and sinker. And, as the saying goes, the rest is history.

As the summer of 1986 approached, and she neared the end of her slow-dance down memory lane, Totsy mentioned to me that she'd been reading only three or four of Daddy's letters every night, eking out the pleasures of remembrance for as long as she could. She said that rationing herself to just a few at a time made it easier to recapture in her mind's eye and heart's delight the face and voice of the darling man who had won her hand 60 years before.

Small wonder she fairly glowed. And what a treat for me to become acquainted, if only anecdotally, with the woman who was my mother before she decided to become une grande dame.

But she also asked me to be sure, when the time came, to have the deed box and its precious contents buried with her. I was startled. Even without reading them, I knew the letters would be rich and fascinating. And I hastily appealed to her vanity by pointing out that they could provide invaluable insight should any of us wish to learn more about herself and Daddy than we already did merely by virtue of being related to them—as well as about that era in the South of their youth.

Reluctantly she agreed to leave the box in my care. And aside from extracting a random few to be placed in her hands by the funeral home at the time of her own death in 1998, the bulk of the letters will remain in their box, above ground.

Years earlier Daddy had expressed a similar sort of wish, but his notion of proper burial accessories involved a certain carved gilt-wood bird of prey—his "shrike," he dubbed it—which he bought in London in 1956 from Mallet's of Bond Street. Thomas Chippendale never signed his work, but an expert could occasionally hazard an educated guess, and the dealer at Mallet's had identified the griffon as bearing all the characteristics of Mr. Chippendale's genius.

For 30 years, the sculpture had hung—as if in mid-swoop—on the wall directly facing you as you entered my parents' drawing room. And now, in a flight of fancy of his own, Daddy said he wanted to await the Day of Judgment with the bird placed alongside him in the coffin. "It'll protect me in the life to come," he declared, a touch of the Pharaoh in his tone. Did he really mean it? I've never been completely sure.

Moderation did rule in the end, however. But frankly, the beautiful golden creature might have been better off if it had indeed been allowed to rest quietly with Daddy in the west graveyard of St. Philip's Episcopal Church in Charleston. It has instead, unfortunately, become the focal point of my brother's mid-western living room. I say unfortunate, because Blake and his second wife, Joan, can only be described as Philistines de premier ordre.

With no true appreciation of its intrinsic significance, they "dress up" the bird at party time by pressing a paper hat onto its head and a Beanie Baby fish into its rapacious beak, oblivious—or, probably more accurately, indifferent—to the fact that their manhandling is slowly but very surely wearing away its 250-year-old gilt.

Poor Daddy. I wonder if people really do roll over in their graves.

It seems a subtle sort of irony that the talisman my father wished to accompany him when he quit this earth was an objet d'art. You might think that being an intellectual—a man who lived primarily within his own thoughts—he'd have preferred, as eternal companion, something along the lines of an anthology of early poetry to a predatory bird. Yet it was my mother—the self-styled materialist—who believed her entrance into the hereafter might go more smoothly if she were pressing to her heart the indelible words of her beloved's devotion.

I suspect my grandfather Paps' classics library was the foundation of my father's education and catholic tastes. Daddy seldom set foot outside South Carolina until he was in his mid-20s, but judging from the eloquence and esoteric content of his letters written around that time, he was already well-read and erudite far beyond the institutional resources likely available to him. Certainly The Citadel, his alma mater, cannot claim credit for the broad range and discipline of his early literacy.

The reason I have read but a few of his letters to Totsy is that it's a tedious process, requiring a good light, a strong magnifying glass, and lots of spare time. Daddy's cursive script was barely distinguishable from the hieroglyphs on the Rosetta Stone—the most arcane code ever yet to engage scholarly analysis. And after putting up with endless poking of fun as a young man, he finally resorted to printing everything save his signature, which remained forever indecipherable. His letters from Europe in the 1940s were usually propped prominently on the mantlepiece, with the implied invitation to all and sundry to "have a go."

Once, in the 1950s, Miss Folley forgot to type Daddy's name beneath the oblique scrawl at the close of a business letter. *[Edna*

Folley was his devoted secretary in London.] Thanks to the engraved letterhead, however, a reply was duly received at the Socony headquarters at Caxton House on Tothill Street in Westminster. But instead of to Mr. J. Blake Middleton, the letter was addressed to the redoubtable Mr. J. Bleecker Childester.

On the following pages is a transcription of three of Totsy's treasured billets doux.

----

12 Water St.
Charleston, SC
Nov. 2, 1924

Lane, beloved –

I mailed your letter on my way to the works on Monday and after I had finished what I had to do up there, I dropped in at the bowling alley to see what was in progress, and was inveigled into making a very unsuccessful maiden attempt at bowling and was directly sore the day after, as I rolled five games, and didn't get home till about midnight. Tuesday we had a holiday—election day—but I, being very industrious and hard working, spent a very unprofitable (for myself, anyway) morning, till about 12:30, up at the plant. I was thoroly put out, too, because I had wanted to go hunting, but just couldn't make it. On my way down from the plant, I stopped in at Ball's Supply to pay a modest little bill, and began talking to one of the boys about fresh water fishing, and very foolishly let him show me rods, reels, etc., and they proved so enticing, and the artificial minnows so alluring (I might have been the fish they were intended for) that against my better nature and judgement, I bought a whole outfit, and now, methinks, I shall be obliged to run my Lizzie on Goose Creek water until the 15th, payday.

Even as the conquering hero returns home, I proudly came back, and was so entranced with all my new equipment and impedimenta, so to speak, that I spent the rest of the morning, and the afternoon, up to about 3:30 (allowing time out for a very hasty dinner), in the yard, practicing casting the artificial minnow, being very greatly hindered by the two puppies, who despite my whoopings and hollerings at them, persisted in dashing madly after the minnow every time I would cast it out and pull it back to me, on the ground. I called up Monty [Montague Ball, a lifelong friend], and we together squandered the rest of the afternoon up until about 7:30, in a fruitless endeavor to catch some fish up at Bee's Ferry. I didn't get home till about 8:00.

Wednesday, rather than starve to death, I was forced to undergo the monotony of another day's work, and about 3:30, Roy came up to me and suggested that we go over to Walterboro that afternoon right after work, and go to the Fair over there and see the Ku Klux Klan (of which you so heartily disapprove) ceremonial. So right after work we started off on that wild goose chase. And Lane, contrary to my expectations, I had a sorry time at the Fair at Walterboro. In the first place, the boy who drove us over poked along most exasperatingly, and it's quite maddening, I think, when one is accustomed to getting where he's going and not lingering by the road side anymore than is absolutely necessary, to have everything even trucks go dashing by. In the second place, it was cold as everything and I was miserable, as I had not had the foresight to take an overcoat, the afternoon being so warm when we left Charleston. I didn't even have enough pep to ride on anything, even the Whip, nor did I have sufficient self confidence to risk even a dime throwing balls at things, and not enough confidence in Lady Luck to risk a dime on a wheel, or a chance to win a doll baby.

The one redeeming feature of the whole trip was the Klan, and they were the stuff. I do wish you would change your mind concerning them. About 300, I dare say, in full regalia, paraded thru the Fair grounds, some of them on horses, the officials, I suppose, and went thru the ceremony of initiating about a dozen new members. It was very impressive and inspiring, and quite an orderly assemblage, and I'm heartily in favor of them.

And now Lane beloved, you have my doings around in both outline and detail, and I must stop and dress as I'm going to see "Captain Blood," and the show starts at 8:30. Goodnight, Margaret Lane, sweetheart seems to me that I've always loved you, and I know I always shall.

Blake

P.S. I've tried, intentionally, to send this letter with tobacco smoke. I love you, Lane - JBM

----

12 Water St.
Charleston, SC
Nov. 3, 1924

Lane, beloved

I've recently become besotted on the subject of cross word puzzles they come out every afternoon in the paper, with the correct solution coming out the next day and I've just finished the successful completion of a very long and complicated one. I was very much involved in it at the supper table tonight, to the great irritation of my mother and father, and the great scorn of my brothers and sister, because of my asking them questions like the following "What means 'pro potion,' ending with 'io' and having five letters?" and such like intricate things. Those cross word puzzles, by the bye, are very instructive. I've learned tonight that "Leamia" (a word that I had never heard of before) was a mythical vampire who devoured young children—quite gruesome.

I chuckled heartily and repeatedly at your recital of your efforts to decipher my letter of last Sunday, and I'm sorry that so many things I said were unclear in meaning. 'Twas quite unintentional, I assure you, but it seems that in writing like that, I was unintentionally clever, for I'm told it is the acme of genius to write that which may be read and re read, with each time a different possible meaning.

And now, young lady, how do you like my longhand? It seems very unnatural for me now, to be writing this way, after having printed everything I've written for a long while, and my printing everything has quite a history. It started this way. Up at the works, where I would write orders of what I wanted done at night while I wasn't up at the plant, many were the caustic comments on my caligrophy, & inevitably, before I left the plant I was hailed back to my battery of stills, and made to translate. And several times I've been called up at home, with the inquiry, "Say, Blake what in the hell was that you wrote in the book about so and so? I can make out some of it, but what the rest of it is, the Lord alone knows," & I would be forced to rack this old cerebellum and try to remember what I had written. And frequently, going back after what I had written was cold, so to speak, I, too much to my mortification have been unable to read what it was.

To eliminate all that, I started printing, but now my former elegant and legible printing has become degraded almost to the point of illegibility. I have thought frequently of taking lessons on the typewriter, but have so far refrained, as you are the only person I write to, and so far you have not complained too strenuously about my writing. I appreciate your asking me, in such a delicate way, to swap over to longhand once, so that you might try that and see if the effort to read it is less than the effort of reading my printing. I don't think I shall until you do complain, & when you do, I'll either get a stenographer, or delve into the mysteries and intricacies of manipulating an Underwood.

So now you know all the details. All that I retain of my longhand is my signature, and that I have to keep, to sign my very small and infrequent checks, whenever I'm in dire need of the coin of the realm, which seems to be continuously, as my perennial state seems to be broke. The dilapidated state of my pocket book, however, was quite forgotten in my delight at receiving your most recent letter last night when I got home I quite forgot everything, I think, including the very poignant pangs of hunger that had escorted me all the way from The Bluff, except that I had a letter from you, & a picture. Lane, I don't know when I've been so glad to get a letter before, or enjoyed one so much, because it was such a peach of one—I fair did enjoy it thoroly.

And now I'll have back at you. The meaning of what I've at times written you is certainly not more doubtful than your spelling ("prophesied" not "prophesized" and "deciphering" not "deshipering," for your information) which is atrocious. I shall have to take you in hand and see that you are well versed in the fundamentals before you aspire to "The Appreciation of Music," etc. But I have this advantage over you. I at least know what you mean. And Lane, you do deserve a medal, a big brass one, for your priceless remark about politics the "Yankees and the Democrats," and their dispute. Concerning politics, I'm very ignorant myself, and I'm delighted to find someone who apparently knows less than I do but, my dear child, it's "Yankees & Rebels," & "Republicans & Democrats." Your innocence is quite refreshing.

Will [Daddy's next younger brother] has just come down with our young niece. Patty & Arthur [Daddy's elder brother] took dinner here today, & perforce had to bring the young hopeful. Immediately after dinner she began yelling lustily and "Uncle Will" went upstairs and brought her down to pay me a visit. Our maid came in while I was looking at her, and admired her and talked to her, and finished up with this remark "Mr. Blake, 'e sure do favor 'e pa."

Margaret Lane, sweetheart, I must stop now. My hand is tired. I've enjoyed writing you to night more than anything I've done in a long while, because I've had lots of time, nothing to worry me, and I feel almost as tho I had been talking to you I'd give anything if only I could. Sweet, sweet girl, write me soon and tell me that you love me.

Blake

----

12 Water St.
Charleston, SC
Nov. 14, 1924

Lane beloved

I had just started writing you when the radio that Lewis [Daddy's youngest brother] was listening to went wrong, and I had to stop and get it going again my family finally left to go to bed, and I got to bed myself about 12:30 I was in a temper, and very much insulted because of their deploring my too little stock of knowledge concerning rheostats, condensers, vario couplers, and "sich like." Yes, verily, "a little learning is a dangerous thing." I haven't the faintest thought of looking at it again until I finish this letter, and if my excellent humor, engendered in my manly breast by two letters from you this afternoon, endures, I shall beset it once again.

Along with your letters, I got one from R.M. [Robin, Daddy's third younger brother], a peach of a long one, and from his remarks, the proverbial wandering Jew hasn't a thing on him, as he seems, weekly, to fold his tent like the Arabs, and silently steal away. From his letter, he seems, tho, to be much more optimistic and better satisfied than formerly, and still very much in love with Emily Elliott. And speaking of letters, while one of yours was lacking in length, 'twas, I think, the most satisfying and charming one I'e ever gotten from anyone and the other one was a dear. I do wish tho, Lane, that I could see you, damned if I don't, more than anything I know of if I were twins I couldn't wish it any harder. I've been thinking of something I saw on a Post Card once "Ain't it funny, that some folks you never miss, and some you miss an awful pile and the ones you'd never miss you always see and the ones you miss you see once in a while."

And Lane, apropos of calling me "Angel" you can call me anything you please and I shall be equally pleased, regardless of your Daddy's despairing glances over that particular name. And speaking of names, who, if I may be so bold as to inquire, is "Johnny," and what excuse can he offer for existing? I can't help it, but the old pangs of jealousy always gnaw at the old heart strings, almost to the point of breaking them, whenever you tell me of some other boy most unpraiseworthy on my part, I know, but nevertheless true, because Lane sweetheart, you are mine, and the Lord willing, shall always be, forever to have and to hold, to love and care for, and ne'er shall belong to anyone else, even the tiniest bit.

And Lane, beloved, even tho I long for your letters, let me tell you something before I forget don't dare write me during your exams. I'll know, you see, that you are loving me, and I'll be satisfied. And don't be as the Foolish Virgins and be totally unprepared against the bridegroom's coming rather a far fetched simile, but 'twill serve because it will entail much burning of the midnight oil, and won't be at all good for you. And Lane child, do please, for the sake of your very kindly and lovable Daddy, pass them all, for he will be so disappointed if you don't, and I must admit, I shall too. And you know that I'm not one of the particular variety of person who worships the greatly cultured and all that sort of thing, but I'm speaking from personal experience. To go to school and flunk everything is a fearful waste of time and a source of regret afterward, to yourself and your family. But let me cease I didn't mean to lecture so but I would have you profit by my shortcomings and subsequent regrets. And Lane sweetheart, I must stop. I love you, and you alone, more than I've ever loved anyone before, or shall love any again, should you stop caring for me.

Blake

P.S. I've not reread this. Pardon mistakes. I'm sending you some of the feathers from one of the ducks—I thought they were so pretty & wanted you to see them. JBM

My parents were married on February 13, 1926, in DeLand, Florida. Totsy's parents *[Ma and Pa]* had briefly owned property there, though no one in the family today remembers either why, nor what happened to it.

A lifetime later, at some point during preparations for my own wedding, Totsy mentioned that *her* wedding dress had been a powder-blue wool suit. I stared at her. She explained that their ceremony was a small, informal affair, and that she had thought it foolhardy to pay an exorbitant sum for a long white gown she knew she'd never wear again. But a *suit?* For her *wedding?* I knew she was sensible about money, but she also was a slave to style and fashion, and restraint in such matters was disconcertingly out of character.

On returning to Charleston after the wedding, they rented a house at the corner of Church and Tradd streets for a few months before taking the *SS President Hayes* to the Dutch East Indies: Daddy's first overseas post. For four years he headed the Socony refinery in Palembang *[the capital city of South Sumatra]*, and their recollections of those faraway places were colourful and glamourous.

Something of a comedown, they repatriated in 1931, to Cleveland, Ohio, where my brother Blake was born on August 15, 1932. Two years later they were transferred to Toledo, and I eventually arrived on May 9, 1938. The migration then turned south, to Beaumont, Texas. World War II was readying itself, but the United States had not yet joined the melée.

After the Japanese attack on Pearl Harbour at the end of 1941, Daddy took a bedsitting room in New York City near the Socony headquarters at 26 Broadway, and began traveling regularly to Europe on business. Totsy and Blake and I moved to Summerville, South Carolina, and until the end of the war, the three of us lived in the guest cottage belonging to Totsy's aunt and uncle, Margaret and Ed Saunders. *[Margaret was my grandmother Ma's younger sister.]* The cottage was compact and cosy, with a galley kitchen, a bathroom you could hardly turn around in, a bedroom that Totsy and I shared, and a combination living room and dining room where Blake slept on a couch.

Christmas Eve 1943 still stands with rare charm in my memory. Ma and Pa, who lived not far from the Saunders, had come by during the afternoon on their way into Charleston "to do some last minute shopping," and said they'd call in again for a cup of cider before going home.

A good while later I heard footsteps along the porch, and the screen door open and close. Then there was silence. I paid no attention. Sitting on the bedroom floor, surrounded with ribbon and paper, I was busy trying to tie bows around my small Christmas offerings. Brother Blake was laying a fire in the living room—reading the newspaper as he went, word for word, before wadding it up to stuff under the kindling. And Totsy was in the kitchen, trimming celery and peeling hardboiled eggs.

Suddenly a cry disrupted our Norman Rockwell-type tranquility—a loud but not unhappy cry. I scrambled to my feet, and ran into the living room to see Totsy frantically tugging off her apron as Daddy rushed toward her, reaching for her, tripping over his suitcase—both of them laughing, with tears in their eyes. And Ma and Pa looking on, tightly holding hands. Hardly able to believe our own eyes, Blake and I pushed to find room within our parents' embrace, and clung to them. Everyone's face was damp with tears and kisses. The so-called last minute shopping had, of course, been a drive to the airport. Daddy had flown home from Naples to surprise us for Christmas, and at that soft moment in the cottage, we all felt we would never again want for anything.

As far back as I can think, this storybook reunion sparked the most electric spontaneity I ever saw between my parents. And, as Totsy would say, I value the memory more than gold and rubies.

<hr />

Using the Charleston vernacular of the times, we addressed Totsy's parents as Ma and Pa, pronouncing the "a" as in "cat." Their given names were Charlie Paul Lane—Ma was christened, unaccountably, for one of her uncles—and Albert Gallatin Goodwyn. Pa was generally known as Colonel, and his pet name for Ma was Colleen, though all other adults called her Charlie. I'm the second female Charlie Lane, and I feel uniquely privileged to be Ma's namesake. She was an angel.

She was also a keen gardener, with a rare talent for grafting new varieties of camellias. Her gifts to me on my fifth birthday were a variety of buds and blossoms floating in a shallow crystal bowl, and a white velveteen cat. Feeling very grown up, I put the camellias on my bedside table, and christened the cat Isobel, in memory of a male kitten given to me a year or two earlier by Izzy Jackson.

Izzy and Rae Jackson were my parents' closest friends from Beaumont, Texas, in the days when I assumed all cats were girls. Extraordinarily longsuffering, the original Isobel allowed himself regularly to be dressed in doll's clothes—including a traditional Charleston poke bonnet that tied under the chin—and to be crammed into the basket on Brother Blake's bicycle when he ferried us down the street every morning to my nursery school. Thus stirred the beginnings of what eventually became the moniker of which I am ferociously proud: The Crazy Cat Woman.

Pa made no bones about how much he liked me. I gather I was "hard-headed and unruly," and I suspect he considered us kindred spirits. I've been told of an occasion during the early 1940s—doubtless one of many—when I charged into the kitchen at Pinewood *[their house in Summerville]*, letting the screen door slam behind me. The windows rattled and the porch shook.

"Who slammed that door?" Pa hollered from the head of the stairs.

"I did!" I hollered back as I belted through the house and out the other side.

"Oh," he said mildly, the automatic rebuke stillborn.

Another time, he was kibitzing in the doorway while Totsy and my nanny Christina were trying, amidst much thrashing about, to pin me down in the bathtub so they could wash my hair.

"What character!" Pa observed proudly, as I slithered out of their grasp and ran off, wet as a fish and covered with suds. "The child has such character!"

And he eagerly grilled me when he came to pick me up after my first day at kindergarten.

"Did you have fun? What did you have for lunch? What did you learn?"

"Yes, thank you," I am said to have dead-panned. "Crab sandwiches. They were okay. And we learnt voice modulation and music appreciation and self-control. What have you and Ma been doing?"

"My, my," he said under his breath as we got into the car. "That's some schedule for one morning. But thank you, too. We've been missing you."

I wish I could tell him I'm still working on the "self-control" part.

With Pa's coaching, I memorised the following wordy little verse before I could read, and though I hadn't the first idea what it meant, he told me I was a genius just to be able to enunciate it. I didn't know what that meant, either, but it didn't matter. Pa was my all-time best fan.

When promulgating your esoteric cogitations or articulating your superficial sentimentalities on psychological and philosophical observations, beware platitudinous ponderosities.

It is my enduring and cherished memory that those doting grandparents refused me nothing and indulged me everything, even to the point of submitting daily to my "pretend" French lessons. I can't begin to guess how I conceived such a game—as far as I know, I'd never even heard French spoken—but while Ma's diligence was always awarded A-plus, I judged Pa to be a malingerer, deserving only reproof. Of course, he played along with hangdog contrition and elaborate promises to apply himself in the future. And, of course, I had the most lovely time being in charge.

Protected by the serene ignorance of a sheltered and uneventful childhood, I assumed everyone grew up as I did, with a pair of conveniently-at-hand old people, who loved me extravagantly and unconditionally, who loved each other openly, and without whom my world would have been a pale place indeed.

Book II
Sibling Sensibilities

By the time I was seven or eight, my brother had perfected an extensive repertoire of strategies that guaranteed his permanently having the upper hand. The most effective of these was threatening to "tell Mommie you know what" if I refused to polish his shoes, for instance, or to hang his bathing suit over the clothesline to dry. Or to sharpen his pencils before he started his homework.

What's "you know what," I wondered uneasily—and rhetorically. I knew it would be futile actually to ask, and he got away with real mischief until it occurred to me that even if I *had* committed some fell crime, Mommie probably couldn't have cared less.

Every night after supper, when it came time for me to go upstairs and get ready for bed, Blake would leap out at me from the dark, bellowing. I always knew what was in store as I tiptoed past his hiding place. But I never got used to it, and always reacted as if a snake had just bitten me. He also often warned me that I was "achin' for a takin'" or "cruisin' for a brusin'."

I knew he was only savouring the cool new jargon, but I invested a lot of sycophantic energy trying to ingratiate myself—just in case. We never did come to blows. He would have considered it terribly infra dig to stoop to that level. But he did like to snap the end of a rolled-up wet towel at my legs and hear me squeal.

Like many children's, my forearms bore a luxuriant coat of blonde down—a simian feature that inspired yet another of my brother's character-building measures. Without warning, he would grab one of my arms and double it back onto itself, pinning wrist against shoulder, while I wriggled and struggled to get away. He would then spit into the palm of his free hand, which he would rub briskly in circles on my arm.

This action knotted the hairs networking across the elbow crease so that when I tentatively extended my arm again, whole tufts would be yanked out, quite painfully, leaving numerous bare patches. These Blake would examine and then solemnly diagnose as "a really bad case of the mange." And howl with laughter.

Our four maternal first cousins—Pat, Pam, Mit, and Susie Shattuck—lived in Mount Pleasant with their mother during most of World War II, which was being fought in Japan by their father. We six children often spent weekends together at Pinewood.

One morning at daybreak, Young Mit and Blake ambushed Susie and me and tied us back-to-back over an ant hill just outside the kitchen door. Before abandoning us to our fate, they warned us in no uncertain terms that if we made a ruckus and woke up the rest of the household, they'd drag us from our beds the next night, and lash us down over the new shoots of a stand of bamboo behind the guest cottage. Susie and I exercised exceptional self-control. We'd heard her soldier-father's war stories of fiendish Japanese torture and were convinced the bamboo saplings would grow straight through us overnight and we'd perish impaled. So we squirmed until breakfast and scratched all summer.

Our fine big brothers, whom we stubbornly worshiped in spite of their cavalier excesses, also tried to corrupt us with reefers made of dried-out rabbit tobacco rolled up in bits torn from the funny papers. There was much choking and watering of the eyes, but Susie and I wheezed like veterans.

A few years later, when we were living in Connecticut, I was again at Blake's mercy, now of a more sophisticated variety. Often his high school friends would come over after school, and at the first sign of my wanting to hang around with them, Blake would remind me to close my mouth. I realise how innocuous that must sound, but this was before several years of orthodontics managed to modify what Pa had described as "the best buck teeth in the county." In fact, such then was my natural dental configuration that I generally found it easier to leave my mouth open than to attempt to drape my lips across the protuberant overbite. So, whenever my brother would draw attention to my set of those damnable Blake teeth, I'd slink away horribly self-conscious, silently cursing heredity.

I must admit I really don't think Blake would have been a normal teenager if he *hadn't* taken advantage of the spectacle of his pesky little sister staring slack-jawed at his 15-year-old friends. Apparently, sisters are given to brothers for the express purpose of providing homegrown targets for novice machismo dart throwers.

My Uncle Mit Shattuck was the tallest, strongest, handsomest man I'd ever seen, and by far the most fun to be around. He could mimic an entirely believable cat-and-dog fight, vocalising the most realistic snarls and growls and howls and screams, and would perform at the slightest urging.

We bedeviled him mercilessly to play with us whenever he was at home on leave, and the boys' fascination with his grisly war trophies—such as the German soldier's helmet with a bullet hole at the temple—was contagious even to us sissy girls. Sixty years on, I still occasionally dine out on his riotously funny tale of recuperation at Walter Reed Army Hospital from surgery for glaucoma.

All the officers on Mit's wing of the hospital had eye problems, so the story goes. The real malaise among them, however, was earth-shattering boredom, and they'd start their own Happy Hour every afternoon right there in the ward, long before the sun was even remotely over the yardarm. As night fell, one of their number—who already wore a glass eye—would produce a slim case containing a set of imperceptibly graded, increasingly bloodshot spares. These the man would substitute one for the next over the course of the evening to match his real eye as it became increasingly bleary—until at last a tiny Confederate flag peered out of that eye socket at the group of now insensate, very silly soldiers.

I handled two turns of crushing childhood disappointment with unchildlike stoicism. The first occurred when we were spending the summer of my sixth birthday at Edisto Beach in South Carolina. Splashing from dawn to dusk in the gullies at the edge of the surf, my pigtails never dried out properly and became sticky and matted with salt and sand. At the suggestion I might like to have a new "do" that would dispense with tangles and rubber bands, I jumped into the barber's chair—with my back to the mirror—and waited to look like Shirley Temple.

Three minutes later, I was spun around so that I could admire the new me and found myself glaring at a little girl I scarcely recognised. What remained of my hair looked as if the barber had combed it with an eggbeater. He hadn't even bothered to loosen my pigtails before hacking them off behind my ears. And they lay like dismembered limbs on the floor behind me, still tied in their soggy, faded grosgrain ribbons.

I was very young but not *too* young to know the fear of being a laughingstock. I collected my shorn locks off the unswept floor, stuffed them into the front pocket of my overalls, and crept home, trying to be invisible. My apprehension proved justified.

"Never mind, Lane," people said, looking down at me, hardly bothering to stifle their laughter. "It'll probably grow back. Yeah, it'll grow back—if you can be patient for a coupla years."

The second blow fell when I was twelve. We'd recently moved to England. And thinking I might have a future in the world of dance, Miss Cartwright—my teacher at the Cone-Ripman School of Ballet in London—arranged for me to audition with Sadlers Wells Ballet School. I later learnt that my parents were slow to agree to this audition. The chances of my becoming a star in the firmament of international ballet were virtually nil, and they didn't think I'd thrive in the chorus line. But while hoping against hope that the Wells would turn me down, they decided nevertheless to let me take my chances.

The practical portion of the audition went well enough—I executed the entre chats and tours jetées without a hitch—but then I was told to remove my toe shoes to allow an inspection of my bare feet. Yet again, my genetic makeup was to be my undoing. Even though I was only 12 years old, it was already possible for an expert to predict with some certainty that I was destined to a life of foot problems—a prediction that has since become a dismal and chronic reality, and one that instantly disqualified me from further consideration by the prestigious ballet company.

Pointless anymore to dream even about the corps de ballet, much less about becoming prima ballerina, my hopes of a vocation in a tutu became moot in a single afternoon. I threw my toe shoes—little traitors that they were—in the trash, and never danced again.

The humiliation of these two watersheds was the bitterest gall. Both times I closeted myself in my bedroom and didn't come out for days. No tears. No claims of injustice. No nothing. My pride was in shreds, but I stewed in silence.

Book III
The Barn

Early in 1946, my parents began house hunting. Daddy no longer had to travel regularly to Europe now the war was over, so he canceled the lease on his New York flat and resigned himself to joining the ranks of commuters to the city from the suburbs. Connecticut was the right suburb, according to those in the know. So in order to be roughly midway between his office and the general area where we hoped to find our Shangri La, we moved temporarily into the Heathcoat Inn in Scarsdale, New York.

Late one Sunday afternoon, as we were driving through the outskirts of New Canaan, Daddy pulled up alongside a FOR SALE sign outside a white-painted brick farm building set right at the edge of Valley Road. It was plainly still a working barn, but it had broad, classic proportions that immediately inspired the draftsman in my father and the decorator in my mother. Within a few days, they'd bought the structure and several surrounding acres and immediately set about converting it into what became known as ... The Barn.

We could be found there every weekend for months afterward. Totsy and Daddy inspected the gutting and remodeling and drew plans for the landscaping, and Blake and I explored the woods and swam in the Silvermine River. I swam in the Silvermine River, that is, until the time I spied a water moccasin paddling alongside me. I already hated the feel of the slimy muddy river bottom—and braved it only so Blake wouldn't make fun of me—but that snake was the last straw.

Our neighbours a little way up the hill were Marge and Steve Valentine, who often came with Dodger, their cocker spaniel, to join us when we picnicked on the riverbank. And down the hill on our other side lived Marion and Cliff Burroughs. Cliff was an architect. And Marion, with her hair in braids tacked down across the top of her head, looked exactly like the woman in the ad for Swiss cough drops. From a child's perspective, the Valentines were lots of fun and the Burroughs were just a couple of staid old fogeys—fogeys who were no doubt well into their early 40s.

By October, the renovations were far enough along for us to move in, and though for a while it was like living on a construction site, you could tell the end result was going to be worth the inconvenience. The dining room—formerly the cow stalls—opened through French doors onto a flagstone terrace now bordered with evergreen shrubbery. Beyond, a smooth sweep of lawn ended at a low wall made of local stone, cut and assembled by an Italian stonemason, whose name was—most appropriately—Rocco. And below the wall, rough grass spread down to the river.

To take full advantage of the view of the woods and valley at the back of the property, the hayloft upstairs became the living room, with ThermaPane filling the 20'-long rear elevation. Evidently that vast double sheet of glass had been improperly installed, because at around midnight during an eggnog party on New Year's Eve 1947—the coldest winter on record—there came a sound like the report of a pistol.

Running beneath the window was a narrow balcony on which snow had built up several feet against the outer pane, causing it gradually to contract. Meanwhile, the interior pane expanded slightly from the warmth of the living room fire. And though the glass didn't shatter and collapse into the room, the opposing thermals caused a jagged diagonal fault across the entire expanse, critically destabilizing it.

The next morning Daddy telephoned the contractor. My father was never known to raise his voice, but his message was unmistakable: *Fix it or else!* And by some managerial sleight of hand, the huge window was replaced that same afternoon.

Next to our parents' bedroom was a large dressing room with a daybed under the window, and deep walk-in closets along the opposite wall. At the back of Totsy's lingerie drawer was a locked compartment in which she kept a loaded .32 revolver. In today's world, having a handgun within reach might not be such a bad idea, but in the 1940s, aside from occasional reference to the Mafia, crime seemed barely to feature even in the newspapers. And in the wilds of New England? Maybe it was *because* we were in the wilds of New England. Anyway, just knowing the gun was there was darkly exciting.

Their bathroom was the last word in luxury. Daddy owned a full set of cutthroats, all seven of which he sharpened every Saturday morning. And with the trendy appointment of "His" and "Hers" basins, he could perform his straight-razor toilette without interruption. The other upstairs bathrooms, Blake's and mine, each had a laundry chute that disgorged into a bin next to the washing machine downstairs at the utility end of the garage—doubtless one of Daddy's inspirations—that made it easy for us to pick up after ourselves.

A giant sugar maple filled the view from one of my bedroom windows and cast speckled shadows everywhere during its fiery autumn metamorphosis when the sun filtered through the yellow and red leaves. On school mornings, Totsy would sit on the edge of my bed and murmur sweet nothings until I surfaced. On one such morning, I focused rather more quickly than usual when she remarked softly, more to herself than to me, that my "nice straight eyebrows" were my best feature. And I remember thinking, at barely 10 years old: *If my eyebrows are no kidding my best feature, why not just shoot myself right now and get it over with?*

Mr. Bodycott, the carpenter, performed wonders with old pine, sandpaper, and beeswax, leaving his signature trim and flooring throughout the house. The kitchen was especially gorgeous—even by today's standards, 50 years on—with a polished pine breakfast table and pew-type benches built into a pine-paneled alcove. Rose-pink Formica countertops matched vinyl floor tiles, and groups of large, unframed laminated prints of Redouté roses hung on every wall. We even had a garbage disposal unit and a small trunk-type freezer. *Nobody* had garbage disposals and freezers in 1946.

The Silvermine Valley sparkled in the winter like Fairyland in snow-covered silence, and Blake and I felt we'd won the lottery whenever the morning radio announced our school was among those being closed that day because of snowbound roads. Commuters, too, were subject not only to disrupted schedules on these occasions but also to being seriously stranded.

One February morning, Daddy telephoned Totsy just after stepping off the train at Grand Central Station. He normally left the house before six o'clock, believing resolutely in getting to the office well before the telephone started ringing at around nine. But today it was nearly 11 o'clock when his train pulled into the station.

"I'm coming on home right now, Tot," he told her. "We're in the middle of a blizzard here, and everything'll probably be at a complete standstill by lunchtime. I'm not even going to stop in at the office first."

In fact, the return trip to New Canaan took until past nightfall, and Daddy's little maroon Austin car, parked as usual at the station, was by now packed solidly under a snowdrift. He knew it was useless to try to dig it out. It was snowing too hard and the roads would be impassable anyway. But the telephone lines were still up, so he called home and asked Blake to come and get him.

Muffled to the gills, and balancing an extra pair of skis over his shoulder, Blake trudged out into the dark storm, and the two of them finally fell, exhausted, through the front door just before midnight—laughing, stamping snow off their feet, and reaching for mugs of cocoa.

※

When we lived in New Canaan, we had a little dachshund named Baroness von Engel Kraut *[Baroness von Angel Cabbage]*. She was one of the red variety and was spirited and smart and sweet. In the winter, when you threw her out into the snow first thing in the morning, she would sink all the way out of sight except for her tail, which looked like a rudder as she wove around under the frozen white blanket before racing back into the kitchen.

Ma and Pa adopted Engel when we moved to England in the fall of 1950, when Britain still required all immigrating animals to be quarantined for six months. The rigidly enforced law had kept the British Isles free from rabies for over 100 years—a laudable and highly prized statistic—but it would have been unthinkable to incarcerate Baroness along with the proletariat.

The following spring Totsy returned to Charleston for a visit, and her account of her reception at the airport is the essential animal lover's story.

You remember, in those days you could wait on the tarmac just outside the terminal building and then walk on out to the plane after it set down? Well, there they were, Ma and Pa and Engel, all running toward the plane as I hurried down the steps. And after all the usual hugging and kissing and how are you's, Engie trotted off ahead of us as we went to get my bags. She was being perfectly cordial, you understand—I mean she was running around in circles and wagging her tail and smiling and all that. But I sensed she didn't really recognise me, and I began feeling terribly sorry for myself. I guess I hadn't realised how much I'd been looking forward to seeing her again—and, of course, it had never remotely occurred to me she might not even know me anymore, for Heaven's sake!

But then suddenly she stopped dead in her tracks, and stared directly ahead, pointing like a bird dog. You know the way I mean? The way they hold one foot up and their tail straight out behind them? Well, she stood perfectly motionless like that for a second or two—she seemed to be really concentrating—and then, very abruptly, she wheeled around and leapt straight up into my arms, almost knocking me over.

"Mother! It's you!" she barked, wriggling and yelping and curling her lips and licking my face. "Omigod, Mother! I'm so sorry I didn't register at first. I knew I recognised your voice from somewhere, but just couldn't quite remember. Where have you been all this time? How long has it been? Oh, Mother, I've missed you so much! It's wonderful to see you! Are you fine? I can't believe it! How long are you going to stay? Are you back for good? Where's the car? Let's go home! Tell me everything. Oh, this is so much fun, I can't stand it!"

Book IV
Leaving the New World Behind

D addy was appointed Director of Socony Vacuum-England in May of 1950, which meant that living happily ever after in The Barn was not to be. He left for London, almost immediately, to get settled in his new position and to do some real estate scouting. And when the school year was over, Totsy and Blake and I returned to Summerville, where we camped for several weeks in the guest cottage at Pinewood. Totsy loved telling people that "Ma and Pa bought Pinewood from the Roeblings. The Roeblings who built the Brooklyn Bridge, of course."

The property was about two acres of woodland, on which stood the large, two-storey white clapboard house with columns and porches and a widow's walk, and the self-contained dependency at the end of the drive.

The grounds were typical of the Summerville area—cultivated but informal, and densely populated with camellias and wild azaleas. The air was spiced throughout early summer with the heavy perfume of several Magnolia grandiflora that periodically shed their green-bronze leaves. Confederate Jessamine wound its way up tree trunks and spilled over walls and fences everywhere, drenching the air with its exotic fragrance. Pungent tea olive bloomed on and off all year round. Banana shrub flowers, cupped warm in your hands, smelled like fresh banana bread. And there was, of course, the unforgettable, wondrous gardenia.

The house itself was somewhat down-at-heel—no doubt because Southerners still claimed to be "too poor to paint and too proud to whitewash"—but it was gracious and hospitable, with Audubon and Catesby prints on the walls, lovely family furniture upholstered in faded chintz and worn linen, seasonal flowers everywhere, and the welcome of comfortable kindliness from my grandparents. I have never since felt so at home anywhere else in the world.

Daddy soon wrote with the glad news that, for our London home, he had settled on the top-floor flat at 37 Grosvenor Square in Mayfair.

"The only problem I foresee with our fine accommodations," he concluded, the underlying tone dripping with contempt, "is that we shall be forced every day to look at a colossal bronze statue of Franklin Delano Roosevelt. Unfortunately, the statue directly faces our side of the square."

My father was a dyed-in-the-wool, latterday Southern Democrat, whose blinkered political stand could be summed up by his annihilating assessment of the presidential candidates of 1968. At election time that year, he refused to go to the polls at all.

"The trouble with democracy is that they let all those people vote," he declaimed. "After giving it a lot of thought, I've decided George Wallace is just plain too liberal for my taste. And, frankly, no one else is worth even considering. Anyway, voting only encourages them."

His scorn for religious missionaries was no less absolute. "Just give 'em $10 each, and tell 'em for God's sake, to stay home and mind their own business. They need to leave all those people alone."

It was generally understood that he intended an element of levity in his drastic political determination, but he viewed the paltry nature of available candidates as an unforgivable affront to the voting public. And his antipathy to our World War II president remained unequivocal. For a man of principle and kindness, Daddy was maddeningly intractable when it came to his philosophy that being strong meant never changing his mind.

From his perspective, Henley's *Invictus* said it all.

> Out of the night that covers me,
> Black as the pit from pole to pole,
> I thank whatever gods may be
> For my unconquerable soul.
>
> In the fell clutch of circumstance
> I have not winced nor cried aloud.
> Under the bludgeonings of chance
> My head is bloody but unbowed.
>
> Beyond the place of wrath and tears
> Looms but the horror of the shade,
> And yet the menace of the years
> Finds and shall find me unafraid.
>
> It matters not how strait the gate,
> How charged with punishment the scroll.
> I am the master of my fate.
> I am the captain of my soul.

Totsy and Blake and I stayed at Pinewood until August, when it was time for Blake to matriculate at Williams College in Massachusetts and for Totsy and me to leave for England. Both of these new beginnings occurred on August 15, which happened also to be Blake's 18th birthday.

I felt sorry for him for a long time afterward. From being big man on campus at New Canaan High School—president of his class, captain of the football team, winner of the public speaking contest three years in a row, and recipient of the prestigious Harvard Award—Williams must have seemed like scholastic boot camp.

Not only was he living away from home for the first time in his life—home itself was now worlds away.

He would never have admitted to being lonely nor to having trouble keeping up with the high-powered academic pace at Williams, for which he had been ill-prepared. Instead, true to form, he simply squared his shoulders and went doggedly forward. I wouldn't be surprised if it was at this point that the hairline creases around his mouth began prematurely to form, with the result that even when his face is in repose, he appears to be antagonized and on the verge of giving vent to soft-spoken but scathing sarcasm. Consequently, in most of his adult relationships, the other person scurries around trying to please him, to make the withering look go away. But the scurrying antagonizes him, too—quite understandably—so it's hard to make any real headway.

Blake joined Alpha Delta Phi fraternity, forged a few longtime friendships, studied hard, graduated well, and a few weeks after graduating in 1954, he married an excellent person named Nancy Daniels from Milwaukee. I was disappointed not to be allowed to leave school and go to America for their wedding, but what I've never been able to understand, at all, was the fact that Daddy stayed in England, too; only Totsy represented the Middleton contingent. Years later, when I asked Blake if he had any idea what had been going on at the time, he just shrugged and tightened the corners of his mouth, as he always does when he wants to change the subject or just doesn't want to talk at all.

He and Nancy were divorced after 30 years.

———

On the same day that Blake started at Williams, Totsy and I boarded the Queen Mary—the flagship of the Cunard White Star

Shipping Line—and spent five days on the high seas, steaming from New York to Southampton. I wish I could repeat that cruise; at only 12, I wasn't old enough to appreciate such an experience. And a few years later, when I made the return voyage—this time on the Queen Elizabeth—everybody was deathly seasick. So I missed out all round on the incomparable glitz of traveling in an era that is now forever lost and gone before.

My first few days in England were tantamount to a crash course in British anomalies. We docked at Southampton on August 20, 1950, and Daddy took us to stay the night at St. Margaret's Priory in Sussex. The heavily beamed Elizabethan house had been adapted as a bed-and-breakfast, and had cut flowers in every room, hand-hemstitched bed linens, strong sweet tea with milk, crumbly arrowroot "digestive biscuits" *[cookies]*, fireplaces with inglenooks, stone hot water bottles in beds with hand-stuffed horsehair mattresses, uneven creaking oak floors, and damp draughty corridors.

And there was toilet paper that you extracted—sheet by crisp, skimpy, non-absorbent sheet—from a metal dispenser on the wall next to the commode *[or, as I soon learned, "loo"]*. It looked and felt exactly like heavy-duty waxed kitchen paper. The heels of my saddle oxfords clicked indignantly on the polished oak floor as I stomped back down the long narrow corridor to our bedrooms. The one bathroom in the house, apparently to be shared by all the guests, seemed blocks away.

"What's this?" I demanded, waving a sample of the discouraging curiosity at my parents. "Where's the regular toilet paper? What am I supposed to do with this stuff? What do they expect us to do? Don't they at least have any Kleenex?"

Totsy looked inquiringly at Daddy. He looked at both of us. "I imagine you'll find lots of things are different here," he began hesitantly, and then shrugged, evidently deciding to let us figure it all out for ourselves. Little old New Canaan seemed all of a sudden to acquire a kind of glow.

The next morning, the company chauffeur—the lugubrious Mr. McMuldrow—drove us into London to the Dorchester Hotel in Park Lane, where we lived for several weeks while our flat around the corner in Grosvenor Square was being spruced up. And it was there, at Flat 14, that the first signs of our lives' transformation could have been spotted—if anyone had been looking.

Totsy began being served breakfast in bed every morning, an indulgence that soon became as crucial to her self-image as the prestige of her surname—at least in Charleston it was prestigious—and one that was to continue for the rest of her life. While she brushed her teeth and tidied her hair, Rosa *[her Yugoslav handmaiden]* would open the curtains, straighten the bed, and spread a cloth against newsprint smudges over the monogrammed edge of the top sheet. Totsy would then get back into bed and allow Rosa to hand her the breakfast tray, on which would be coffee, fresh orange juice, toast with a little pot of Oxford Vintage Seville Orange Marmalade, and a carefully folded copy of the *London Times*.

If she'd ever thought of it, I'm sure Totsy would have held the occasional levée. Her frothy nightclothes always outclassed most people's formal evening dress, and she loved "receiving." As far as she was concerned, nothing was more fun than presiding over a hand-picked, trapped audience.

She also took to keeping a stash of Godiva chocolates and a bottle of Taylor's '27 port under her bed, vindicating the tiny decadence by explaining that she often woke up in the middle of the night, "and if I can't have a piece of candy or a sip of port right that minute, I just go to pieces."

Totsy determined to make the most of the revolutionary change in her status, from insignificant housewife in the backwoods of Connecticut to hostess-with-the-mostest in one of the most glamourous cities in Europe. Now on the threshold of dignified middle-age, and avidly aspiring to the beau monde, she decided that her childhood nickname had outlived its usefulness, and began using her given name, Lane, when introducing herself.

But it didn't work. Totsy she was and Totsy she would apparently always be.

Interestingly, though, there evolved a curious secondary phenomenon. As her reputation in London spread as everybody's "charming American friend," her nickname, too, began to assume its own customized significance. And anyone taking the liberty of using it seemed, by enviable association, to have acquired a coveted membership in some recherché new club.

It was right about now that Totsy began overhauling *my* image, too. And based on her early observation that anyone using the Queen's English seemed naturally to possess breeding and intelligence, she first targeted my speaking voice. Those early Charleston kindergarten elocution lessons had by no means brought my voice and diction to the level typical of my English peers', and on reaching British shores, there was no denying my colonial provenance.

No time was lost in arranging for a modern Henry Higgins to stamp out all audible indicators of this unpardonable flaw. His remedy for the lazy mouth was the tongue-twister, and I can still spout the following frivolous formula with hardly a pause for breath:

One old Oxford ox opening oysters.

Two tortoises, totally tired, trying to trot to Tadbury.

Three tall tigers tippling tenpenny tea.

Four fat friars fanning fainting fleas.

Five frippy Frenchmen foolishly fishing for flies.

Six sportsmen shooting snipe.

Seven Severn salmon swallowing shrimp.

Eight Englishmen eagerly examining Europe.

Nine nimble noblemen nibbling nonpareils.

Ten tinkers tinkering upon ten tinder boxes with ten tenpenny tacks.

Eleven elephants elegantly equipped.

Twelve topographical topographers typically translating type.

Number 37 Grosvenor Square is at the corner of Grosvenor and South Audley streets, and contiguous to the Indonesian Embassy. Fortunately, our Regency-style building had been neither damaged during the war nor subsequently "improved," as was happening all over. This meant that although the kitchens were antiquated, the bathrooms were still paneled from floor to ceiling with gray Italian marble and fitted with the heavy porcelain and solid brass appliances of the 19th century. The fireplace mantels and surrounds were of unfashionable but magnificent red marble. And all the rooms had panoramic views of London, which was as yet unblighted by the modern skyscraper.

Dressed in their gold-and-green doormen's uniforms, the portly Messrs. Jones and Nutter stood like fixtures at the massive opaque-glass entrance doors, pleased to carry parcels, hail taxis, hold umbrellas, and interminably to discuss the weather. From the splendid worn Aubusson carpet in the entrance hall, to the rattling cage-type lift lined with mirrors and polished brass, it was pure old-fashioned, matter-of-fact luxury. We heard through the grapevine that Frank Sinatra and Mia Farrow bought our flat in 1966, a few years after my parents left London—a choice addition to Totsy's list of names-to-be-dropped whenever at all possible.

Diagonally across from us was the square block that was to become the site of the present American Embassy, a colossal structure whose severe façade is relieved only by a giant gilded American bald eagle. As soon as construction was concluded in early 1960, *TIME Magazine* photographed Totsy standing at our seventh-floor drawing room window, her hand resting casually on an open book on the sill, watching with studied approval as the great eagle was hoisted by crane and affixed high on the front of the new building.

As Grosvenor Square is predominantly of the Georgian flavour, the blatantly modernistic design of the Embassy incited much controversy. But both my parents were of the faction that stoutly defended Eero Saarinen, the prizewinning Finnish architect, on the principle that as long as they are of premier quality, different periods of architecture placed in close proximity can, by dint of contrast alone, be superbly complementary.

The Blitz laid most waste to the City *[referring to the business and newspaper section of the East End]* and the docks, but Central London was also badly scarred, and even by 1950—the year we arrived—buildings everywhere still nursed the open wounds of war. I tended to dawdle on my way to late-afternoon ballet lessons as I walked past the skeleton of Number 24 Grosvenor Square, at the corner of Upper Brook and North Audley streets. The German bomb had struck clean, from roof to pavement, sheering off the two outside walls of the tall Georgian house, but leaving eerily intact the interior circular staircase. The filigree iron railing was warped and bent, and the treads—still clinging tenuously to their fractured supports—soared four storeys within a stairwell lined with water-stained William Morris wallpaper. Thriving in the rubble was a thicket of weeds and wildflowers, and the remains of a Venetian chandelier still dangled by a single wire from what was left of the moulded plaster ceiling.

Restless ghosts seemed to wander about in the gossamer fog that often settled throughout this broken shell of a house, and it was easy to imagine voices and footsteps and food smells wafting up from the basement kitchen. I felt protective of the family whose genteel privacy was now on view to idle passersby. In 1954, *The London Times* printed a touching literary homage by an anonymous "Visitor from America" to this inanimate casualty of war. And, like my nameless countryman, I prayed a silent prayer that its defenseless occupants had somehow survived.

For years after the war—perhaps even to this day—United States Embassy and military personnel were quartered in various locations in Grosvenor Square, known as "Little America." Every evening at sunset, Daddy watched through our drawing room window the ritual lowering of Old Glory on the Admiralty rooftop, directly across the square from ours. Looking through his ultra-precision German binocular, he never failed to be impressed by the pair of Marines who, though entirely oblivious to his inspection, discharged their sacred duty with a precision of coordination and respect that would have done justice to a full-dress parade. Never tiring of the sober display of their young patriotism, Daddy would smile and dab away proud tears.

My father also often wept at the ballet. I think he was not-very-secretly in love with Margot Fonteyn, ballerina assoluta of The

Royal Ballet. At Covent Garden in 1954, during a performance of Prokofiev's *Cinderella*, I glanced up as he reflexively squeezed my hand, which he was holding in his lap. He was smiling, but tears were sliding down his cheeks. Fonteyn was alone on the stage, dancing wistfully with her broom—the wicked stepsisters had already left for the ball—and Daddy ached, visibly, from the pathos evoked by this uniquely graceful woman.

"Doesn't she make everyone else on the stage look like a sack of flour?" he whispered, leaning toward me. Still as limber as a girl, Daddy's 54-year-old contemporary moved as if she were made of swan's down. I could scarcely breathe.

After the final curtain, friends took us backstage and introduced us to the dancers. Fonteyn had taken off her toe shoes, and a pearl-coloured jacquard kimono skimmed over her leotard. Her long dark hair, which had hung loose during the ballet, was now skewered into a glossy knot on top of her head, Japanese-style. In one hand she balanced a cup of tea. The other was trapped in my father's vise clasp as he stammered his admiration.

"Ah, thank you, Mr. Middleton." She smiled as he fell silent, and gently withdrew her hand so she could sip her tea. "You're too kind," she said, looking into his very blue eyes. "But really, all I had to do was to make the prince want to kiss me." Her voice was soft and cultured, her manner poised yet personal. Evidently, the admiration was mutual, and Daddy looked as if he were about to swoon.

Later that year I went with both my parents to see Fonteyn in *Fire Bird*. Stravinsky's modern dissonance was still relatively unfamiliar to the classics-attuned ear, and the evening began more as an education in atonality than an experience in the transports of Russian ballet. Halfway through the unapologetically strident *Overture*, Daddy prodded my arm. "Do you think they're still warming up?" he asked, very quietly.

I didn't need to look at him to know he was grinning.

Then from the wings, as if out of nowhere, Fonteyn sprang like a shooting star onto the stage, her body encased in a tutu of quivering, shimmering flame-red sequins, her panache headdress of stiff red feathers glinting and dazzling as they caught and refracted the light. With tightly crossed ankles she rose onto her points—her feet, barely touching the floor, becoming a blur as they tap-tapped, too rapidly, too fast to see—and stretched her arms upwards, wrists and fingers entwined and reaching, rippling and wisping like leaves in the wind.

Of course. Now I understand. Now the music makes sense …

Prokofiev's *Romeo and Juliet* also affected me profoundly. I saw it in 1970—several years before Fonteyn retired, but well after my parents had returned to South Carolina—and I still much regret that Daddy wasn't able to share the experience with me. In the *Cinderella* we'd seen together years earlier, David Wall had been Fonteyn's prince. But here, her Romeo was Soviet-born Rudolf Nureyev—19 years her junior, and smooth and powerful as a tiger. Like the fabled Nijinsky, who they said would alight from his impossible flights across the stage only when the music told him to, Nureyev's leaps and turns seemed to defy the laws of time and gravity. Apparently, nobody ever told the Russians that "white men can't jump."

Once again backstage when the ballet was over, this time I tingled as Fonteyn gazed adoringly at her partner. I passionately believed the rumours of their romance. By now, I was 32 years old—but still starry-eyed—and anything less passionate between them was unimaginable.

Daddy's assignment in England was to coordinate the construction of an oil refinery in Coryton, Essex, on the Thames

Estuary. His colleagues in London represented the last of 1,000 years of chivalry—of men whose demeanor silently declared, "There'll always be an England!"—and I know they valued his friendship as much as he did theirs.

As an American, my father was atypical in his reserved demeanour and sophistication, and he was universally welcomed by the cosmopolitan coterie of businessmen in Socony's English subsidiary as one of their own. On his retirement in 1960, they presented him with a silver Pegasus: a replica of the Socony Flying Red Horse logo, on the silver-clad ebony base of which is engraved an eloquent—but conspicuously wanting in its punctuation—statement of their esteem and affection.

The magical wingèd creature now rests on the bureau bookcase in my drawing room.

JULIUS BLAKE MIDDLETON
The last ten of whose forty year's service with the
Mobil Group of International Companies
was spent in England to the great benefit and pleasure
of his colleagues there.
LONDON 1950-1960

John Gridley, one of Daddy's co-directors and best friends, was a man whose charm and natural gift of oratory saved the day on May 27, 1954. Queen Elizabeth, the Queen Mother, had accepted an invitation to open the new refinery that day, and as de facto host, my father had the honour of greeting and introducing the royal visitor. However, as he bowed over Her Majesty's hand, lightning seemed to strike. His mouth went dry and his brain went blank, expunging every word of his brief speech of welcome and preventing even the feeblest attempt at improvisation.

Seeing his friend overwhelmed by stage fright, Mr. Gridley quickly stepped forward and tactfully welcomed the Queen Mother himself. I was sitting with Totsy in the front row of guests and couldn't fail to notice that in spite of the nimble rescue effort, the script had taken a painfully wrong turn. My heart pounded, and in an agony of compassion, I watched Daddy as he sat down abruptly and clasped and unclasped his hands.

Not long afterward, and on a much lighter note, Daddy informed Totsy that she was soon to be approached by the President of the Grangemouth Dockyard Company in Scotland and the Directors of Socony Vacuum. The *Vacuum Pioneer* was the first Socony tanker whose home port would be in England, at Daddy's Coryton Refinery.

"They tell me they'd be honoured if you'd christen the *Pioneer*, Tot," he said, "and they've asked me to find out if you'd like a ruby-encrusted Flying Red Horse brooch as your honorarium?"

He waited, his face impassive, as Totsy strived politely to explain that she wouldn't be caught dead wearing a horse-shaped logo made of rubies.

"That's okay." By now he was laughing, and fumbling for his handkerchief. "I've already told them I knew you'd much rather have the clock and that pair of sconces you've been drooling over lately at the Fair."

Those particular rarities from Ayers Antiques of Bath were currently for sale at the annual Antiques Dealers' Fair at Grosvenor House in London. And having already become subjects of Totsy's critical scrutiny and the objects of her fondest yearning, both treasures were, of course, acquired forthwith on her behalf.

The launching ceremony was held in Scotland. Guests and dignitaries traveled on the Heart of Midlothian Express from London to Edinburgh, leaving King's Cross Station on Wednesday, December 17, 1952. Luncheon and dinner were served on the train— with menus the Orient Express would have been pleased to claim— and the Caledonian Hotel in Edinburgh hosted the group after they arrived the next morning. Below is the article reporting the event as published in the Spring 1953 edition of the *Vacuum News*.

"The launching took place at 3:15 precisely ... Mrs. Middleton's timing was perfect ... she named and commended the ship as she broke the bottle *[of reserve wine]* at exactly the right spot. Owing to the fragility of *[the clock and sconces]*, photographs of them were handed to Mrs. Middleton, the gifts themselves being installed in her London home later the same week.

"In her speech, Mrs. Blake Middleton touched every heart; with charming poise and diction she achieved a perfect blend of sincerity, grace and effectiveness in conveying her pride in the occasion, and her gratitude for the lovely presents. After dealing most gallantly, and with some humour, with some rather involved technical data, she ended with a happy reference to the gifts she had just acknowledged, by expressing her most sincere wish that as her sconces lit the way, and her clock ticked off the hours, so should Vacuum Pioneer have bright passages and happy days.

"Mr. Middleton thanked everyone, very quietly, for all the kind things [that had been] said of and done for his wife ..."

With the following note to her father, Totsy enclosed her launching speech.

December 30, 1952

Darling Pa

I am enclosing a copy as I remember it of my acceptance speech which I made at the reception after the launching when I was given my beautiful gifts. I send it to you only because it was so kindly received by my friends and because you like speeches and because, being one of the pleasantest occasions of my life, I so wish that you and Mother could have been there.

Devotedly, T.

Totsy's launching speech:

"I am thrilled with my gifts. Even if Blake does say that, with me, it's the gift that counts and not the thought, I do assure you that this has been a very proud day for me.

"I take pride and pleasure in being allowed this delightful privilege of christening the Vacuum Pioneer and. As an American, I choose to feel that I am one more small link between my country and the greatest maritime nation in history.

"I am proud to sponsor a ship owned by the best oil company of that nation, built by I'm sure the finest shipbuilding concern in Great Britain, and carrying, to my great relief, a main engine of the North Eastern Marine triple-expansion superheat and reheat design! (laughs)

"I hope you all will come soon to see these lovely gifts at our flat in London. And at the risk of being sentimental, may I hope that the years to come the years that will be ticked off by my beautiful clock, the years that will be lighted by my lovely candelabra may I hope that these years will bring only good fortune to her officers and men, and to our lovely ship, herself the Vacuum Pioneer.."

I have inherited these honoraria. Of its kind, the clock case is incomparable and is illustrated in the *Antiques Encyclopaedia* as a definitive example of early 18th century rococo gilt carving. The three-branch ebony sconces are encrusted with ribbons and flowers of ormolu, and are said to have belonged to Mrs. Fitzherbert—a Papist, and favourite mistress of George IV, the Prince Regent. "Prinny" ascended the throne in 1830, when all hope was abandoned that his father, King George III, was fit to rule. An underground passage links Mrs. Fitzherbert's house to the Royal Palace—now known as the Brighton Pavilion—in Brighton, Sussex. It is believed that after divorcing Caroline, his queen, the Regent secretly married his paramour. It was illegal in those days for royalty to marry Roman Catholics. Perhaps it still is?

Another gem that eventually came my way was Daddy's 1981 Buick Riviera. It is dark green and has wire wheels and heavy gleaming chrome. When I took possession in 1993, the odometer registered barely 17,000 miles, clocked mainly on trips to the nearby grocery store on East Bay Street, and infrequent sorties to "the country"—a beautiful property on Wadmalaw Island, some 20 miles south of Charleston, that belongs to Daddy's brother and sister-in-law, Will and Frances.

I loved the Buick and had long had my eye on it, so I felt seriously conspired against when I discovered quite by chance, a year or two earlier, that Totsy had bequeathed it outright to my brother. *Couldn't she at least have allowed us to draw straws?* I was rolling up my metaphorical sleeves to duke it out with Blake when he declared he didn't want the car at any price. "It's a gas-guzzler," he said, obviously bored. "It floats all over the road like a battleship.

And it certainly wouldn't do well in the Minnesota snow. So sure you can have it. I want a car I can depend on." His tone suggested I was simpleminded even to consider keeping it.

The battleship simile was prophetic. The Buick does creak like an old wooden boat. And initially, I worried that if Blake felt such scorn—he was a Navy pilot, and therefore someone who should surely know these things—then maybe there really was something wrong with it. But even so, I sprang for an expensive paint job and dealt with the dry rot and rust of disuse. And since then, I've felt my "simple-mindedness" exonerated when observing Blake's subsequent inspection of the refurbished version with silent but unmistakable approval.

Even without its "PURRRR" custom license plate, the car has high recognition value. The mechanics and car-wash types who look after it have all developed a personal attachment to it. And even Totsy, when I drove her to the movies not too long ago, said she was "so glad it's still in the family"—as if it were a significant piece of period furniture.

※

Of my father's English friends, I believe Miles Reid was his best beloved. Miles and his wife Frances lived in Farnham, Surrey, in a Jacobean house flanked on all sides with deep herbaceous borders. We sat outside among the bees and butterflies for tea one autumn afternoon when I was on an exeat from school, and I was much taken aback to see that Frances' hair had turned pure white since our last visit. She was cheerful as always, and since no one else mentioned her hair, I kept my questions to myself. But I was unaccountably worried. She was one of those few-and-far-between adults who contribute immeasurably to a child's general experience.

She made me feel I was a valued equal, and I didn't want anything to happen to her.

Totsy wrote the following week that Frances had been put in hospital, but even now she said nothing about cancer—the word then was a death knell—and I was afraid I'd be thought a pest if I asked what was really wrong. Within days Totsy wrote again, this time to say Frances had died. *But she had rosy cheeks just the other day. And she was smiling. Since she looked so well, how could she die?* I knew I'd lost a future confidante, and was shaken to my very core.

Daddy once remarked that he'd been curious at Miles' frequently addressing him as "Blake, my dear," until he understood the term was merely the contraction of "my dear friend." It appealed to my father that another man would acknowledge deep friendship through endearment, and he also appreciated the echo of a former day when the art of conversation was a serious business. As a nation, the English still converse as if they feel an obligation both to entertain and to edify—a noble duty from which my father felt no one should be exempt.

In spite of thinning hair and a long, tired face, Miles was very good looking. Tall and wiry, he seemed always to be wearing the same sagging, elbow-worn tweed jacket and pair of baggy flannels. His neck was chafed red behind the ever-present stiff white collar, and he walked unevenly as if his hip bothered him.

There was something fascinating and mysterious about him, which I speculated might come from the bleak romance of his having been a prisoner of war at Colditz Castle from 1943 until the Allied victory. It was a chapter in his life he apparently refused to talk about.

A German fortress-cum-prison from which no one had ever escaped, Colditz was the Nazis' first choice when deciding where to send the toughest and most decorated captured Allied officers to wait out the war in Europe. But if anyone asked him about it, Miles would invariably limit himself to a few quips about his fellow inmates—particularly the Italians.

"There weren't many of them. No more than a handful, really. And actually most of the time they were remarkably easygoing. Much more so than us. Or even the Americans, now I think of it. Really not much trouble a'tall, so long as their captors were willing to listen to them sing bits of opera in the evenings. That always seemed to satisfy them. And, of course, the rest of us tuned in too. Being Italian, every one of them had a voice, of course. They were really awfully good, and all they wanted was an audience. Quite fun, really."

For reasons he couldn't—or wouldn't—explain, my father never wrote to any of his former colleagues after returning to Charleston. After several years of receiving no word, Miles voiced sincere hurt at being "forgotten" when he had believed their friendship was fast. And as I reflect on this enigma—for Daddy did unquestionably love Miles—I begin to understand what was at play. Like my father, I'd just as soon break my neck as write even the briefest of letters. For as long as I can remember, it's been the telephone rather than the postal service that has kept taut my lifeline to my English mates. If it weren't for cheap trans-Atlantic rates these days, I too would undoubtedly be accused of abandoning everyone.

I dearly wish I'd had the chance to reassure Miles that when my father gave you his heart, it was yours—whether or not you ever heard from him again. I am the spirit and image of my father in this regard, so I know for a fact that once he had grappled you to his soul with the Bard's hoops of steel, it followed—silence or no—that the bond was forever and a day.

⌘

Every so often on her Friday morning visits to the Caledonian Market—a high-end flea market in Bermondsey, on the Thames Embankment—Totsy would chance upon the delightful Peter Ustinov. He was another regular browser of the Market, and the two became quite friendly as they traipsed up and down the stalls. Ustinov was best known as a stage actor, but he was also an acclaimed author, journalist, and playwright, as well as a liberal benefactor of the Kirov ballet and opera. Indeed, a man of many parts.

As well as being veteran hagglers, Totsy and her amusing friend had beautiful automobiles in common. Ustinov zoomed around town in a vintage yellow Rolls Royce, and Totsy drove an up-to-the-minute, celadon-green XK150. Daddy bought the Jaguar in 1952, soon after the opening of the initial 54-mile stretch of the M1, the first in a network of wide straight motorways that would eventually connect the various metropolitan hubs. Never before could a driving enthusiast open a powerful car full throttle *anywhere* in England, and Totsy shrank at the thought of accompanying Daddy for a spin in his high-powered new toy on the unrestricted new freeway.

"Tsk, pshaw, Tot, you don't know what you'll be missing," he said, crestfallen. "Oh well, never mind." He had a terrific lust for speed and wanted company on this little trial outing. Suddenly, he turned to me. "Ah, Puddin'," he said, eyeing me hopefully, "maybe you and Francis would like to come along?"

We covered the 54 miles in 27 minutes, which I think works out at 117 miles per hour. But even at that speed, scores of far less mighty vehicles left us in the dust. Gone were the days of "knights of the highway," as Totsy had fulsomely dubbed the entire British driving population.

Some few years after returning to Charleston, Totsy was given a citation for making a U-turn on Broad Street.

"Couldn't I pay the fine to you now, Officer, and avoid going to court?" she flirted.

"No, Ma'am, you really oughta go. And, anyhow, you might could even talk your way out of the ticket," drawled the policeman, creatively rearranging the conventional syntax.

In due course, Totsy had the pleasure of meeting The Honorable Joe Mendelsohn at traffic court. She told us later how much she'd admired his thoughtful and deliberate manner when hearing the defendants ahead of her on the roster. When it came her turn, he read the charge and politely asked how she pleaded.

"Well, Your Honour," she began, "since I now realise U-turns are against the law in South Carolina, then, of course, I must plead guilty. But I wonder if I might let you know—in my own defense, of course—that I lived in England for many years, and U-turns are permitted there, you see, as long as you're not obstructing oncoming traffic. So after finally becoming accustomed to English law, I'm really finding it awfully difficult to change my ways!"

Totsy's reasoning was obviously intended to charm—and disarm. A brief titter erupted somewhere in the back of the courtroom.

"That's a pithy argument, Mrs. Middleton," Judge Mendelsohn conceded, adjusting the neckline of his robe and leaning forward with exaggerated attention. "Really, very pithy. But please allow me to explain something to you. When the founding fathers of this great country of ours were attempting to define the new republic, they concluded that while they'd continue to follow the basic tenets of English common law, there were nevertheless a few areas they felt it was then time to reevaluate. Or perhaps even to abolish. And Mrs. Middleton, I must tell you that, unfortunately, one of those few points that went the way of all flesh was ... uh ... U-turns."

Within the English legal system, there are judges, barristers, and solicitors. The function of an English judge is much the same as that of judges everywhere. But when asked if he'd ever figured out the difference between the barrister and solicitor—neither of whom has a comparable American counterpart—my father replied, "Sure. Easy. The solicitor makes the snowball. The barrister throws it."

While they were in Britain, my parents traveled tirelessly and studied their adopted country, acquiring a working grasp of its history and a heart-love for the sheer beauty of the land. They lodged in out-of-the-way inns and stood on the White Cliffs of Dover and the black cliffs at mythical Tintagel. They collected place names like Mousehole *[Moozul]* and Thorpe-le-Soken and double-barreled surnames like Gratton-Bellew and Prideaux-Brune and Bromley-Davenport. They explored the stately homes of England and killed wild salmon in Scotland. They spent a summer in Clovelly—a fishing village pressed into a steep hillside in north Devon, whose unspoilt streets and vine-clad houses put you back into the Middle Ages. And they lamented not buying a little castle that was for sale in St. Mawes.

"There were swans in the moat at that darling little castle," Totsy said wistfully. "They were adorable. Absolutely adorable. And they knew how to ring the bell when it was time for their supper. Can you imagine such a thing?"

Like so many Cornish villages, St. Mawes was built almost entirely of stone and, being buffeted for centuries by gale-force winds off the English Channel, few plants have ever managed to grow above the walls barricading every property. Westcountry hollyhocks and delphinium and stocks and snapdragons are the hardy but stunted versions of the perennials that typically form the tall back row of the famous English herbaceous border.

Totsy and Daddy hiked the moors and downs. Soft soaking rain lured them to the parks. They loved the theatre and museums and galleries and restaurants and became friends with antiques dealers all over the country. They relished the summer pleasure of picking apricots off a warm kitchen-garden wall, and they adopted the practice of serving—as a separate course—buttered baby peas in individual bowls, to be eaten, quite logically, with a spoon.

Daddy took hundreds of photographs with his Leica—the German-made camera considered at the time to be the best in the world—and its innumerable state-of-the-art attachments, each in its own hand-stitched, drawstring chamois pouch. Of these scads of photographs, both my favourites are of signs. One was in rural Cornwall. At the entrance of a branch of the National Westminster Bank—a structure scarcely more imposing than a telephone kiosk— was a handwritten notice indicating the local banking hours:

Noon - 2:00 p.m.
3rd Thursday of the month

The other sign—a billboard at the England-Wales border— welcomed the intrepid motorist with the following laconic announcement:

SUBSTANDARD BRIDGE AHEAD

In 1957, Daddy went through a phase of asking anyone who would listen if they'd read a certain theatrical review that had recently appeared in *The New Yorker*. "It's about that new play *I Am A Camera*," he would explain, "and all it says is 'No Leica.'"

Then he would guffaw until his eyes streamed, and he'd be reaching for his handkerchief.

Book V
Heathfield, Riante Rive, La Sorbonne

Isuffered severe culture shock when we moved to England. It was most unnerving at Miss Faunce's Day School for Girls at Lancaster Gate in London. The lessons were so far beyond my educational horizon that I began to wonder if I were a dolt, a suspicion reinforced by Daddy's frequent and completely straight-faced reminder, "As long as you learn to read and count to ten, Puddin', I expect you'll get along just fine." I was never sure he wasn't joking.

After nearly a year of stumbling conspicuously behind my classmates, an expatriate American friend of my parents suggested that perhaps boarding school might be the answer.

"I know just the place," she told them with autocratic finality. "It's in Ascot. I'm sure it'll work wonders. It has the most impeccable connections, of course, and very strong foundations in the Church of England. I'll arrange it."

Mrs. Scott McComb's endowments to Heathfield School for Girls apparently entitled her every whim to be met without question, because within a week or two, Heathfield invited me to enroll the following autumn term. To this day, I have no idea why a girls boarding school should have been Mrs. McComb's pet project—she was a widow, with an acerbic tongue and, fortunately, no children of her own—nor why my parents would have been influenced by her in any way. Nevertheless, I loved Heathfield and I have been forever glad they took her advice.

In early July, we motored to Ascot for an exploratory visit and to meet the headmistress, Miss Kathleen Dodds. After a perfunctory tour of the campus—dormitories, gymnasium, library, and the Chapel—she offered us tea in her drawing room, where the subject of Ascot week suddenly swamped the conversation. Since Royal Ascot is exclusively about horses and hats—and since I was unaware that either of my parents even *liked* horses—I assumed the insatiable interest here was hats.

Totsy knew all about hats. So did Miss Dodds, apparently, but said she seldom wore them, "because all this hair gets in the way." Daddy must have decided it wasn't worth mentioning his old fishing hats. And I didn't have any hats at all. So with nothing to contribute, he and I drank Lapsang Suchong tea and wolfed brandy-laced fruitcake while Totsy and Miss Dodds put their heads together, so to speak.

Taking stock on the way home, there was mixed-bag consensus. Daddy very much liked Miss Dodds. Totsy very much liked the fact that daughters of celebrities and English royalty numbered among the students. And I very much wanted to know why I was leaving home. "Oh, Puddin', you'll love it. You'll see," was the placatory non-answer. "All those girls from such interesting families? Just wait. You'll love it."

That settled, off we sped to Debenham & Freebody on Wigmore Street to buy a trunk and bedding, and my school uniform—which was *not* designed to launch a thousand ships. In the summer, we wore gingham dresses of varying design and colour combination. They were harmless enough, but during the winter months we were inexcusably dowdy in navy-blue tweed suits, cream Viyella shirts, green neckties, beige kneesocks, and galumphing lace-up shoes.

The only item of any sartorial merit was the camel hair overcoat with its chocolate-brown velveteen collar. Needless to say, the coat was meant to be worn out of doors, but in the lean days of recovery from war, Heathfield had no central heating and often those coats were all that stood between us and frostbite. I never had chilblains—the winter scourge that afflicts so many—but they were common enough among my schoolmates and, from the look of the weepy swollen sores, they must have been hellishly painful.

It was at Heathfield that I was first exposed to the concept of "striking" to protest an injustice. We filed into the dining room one evening and stood at our pre-appointed tables-for-eight. At each of our places was a glass of water, a solitary baked potato on a plate, and a banana on the table next to the plate. We bowed our heads piously while Miss Dodds said a short grace in Latin. *Amen.* Then, instead of seating ourselves, we looked in silence across the tables at each other, and with one accord, all 99 of us turned and filed back out of the dining room. Hungry, but haughty, we went up to our dormitories and prepared for bed.

True, the times were not prosperous—it was only six years since the end of World War II—but we'd been expecting more for supper than a potato and banana to be washed down with water. At assembly the next morning, Miss Dodds took the wind out of our self-righteous little sails by agreeing that the pickings had indeed been somewhat slim the night before. We were unaccustomed to such forthright behaviour in a figure of authority, but we still agreed it had been worth making a show of resistance.

Kathleen Dodds was a classic beauty in her mid-40s, with wide-set dark eyes and masses of chestnut hair which she coiled loosely around her head. She bore no resemblance whatever to the stereotypical English headmistress of the 1950s. Or, for that matter, to any headmistress of any era.

During the holidays one summer, my parents invited her to come up to London for one of their cocktail parties. Seeing her clustered about by every man in the room, one thought of Scarlett O'Hara. Daddy claimed that, at work the following week, several of his Socony colleagues asked what they had to do to be admitted to Heathfield.

⁂

After leaving Heathfield in 1954, I spent a year in Switzerland, at Riante Rive, a small finishing school on Lake Geneva just outside Lausanne. My parents struck gold when they sent me to this establishment.

Formerly considered essential to the launching of young women into society, such schools have now been a thing of the past for at least 30 years. Ordinarily, they would undertake to polish a dozen or so girls in the refined but outmoded manners of their mothers and grandmothers. The finished product was expected to be both soft-spoken and well-spoken at all times; to be able to spar lightheartedly in French; to know when an abbreviated curtsy was appropriate; to be able to open a door and enter a room with perfect decorum; to master the ritual of serving the ultimate cup of tea; and so forth and so on. All with a view to snagging a husband.

But Riante Rive took a daringly avant-garde view of how to prepare us for our future. With our two tutors as expert veteran guides, an excursion to Italy at the end of the school year was the high point of a well-designed and exacting curriculum in the theory of music, the French language, and art history. It was a trip never to be forgotten. Spending nearly a week each in Florence, Rome and Venice breathed life into our earlier, somewhat arid studies of the Italian Renaissance and opened our eyes to a world that most spoilt 17-year-olds didn't know even existed. Year after year, our indefatigable teachers would take on a fresh crop of aimless girls in the hope of resetting the sights of at least a few of them on interests and perspectives beyond the narrow clique they were born into—and in which most of their unsuspecting families expected them safely to remain.

Head Mistress Mlle. Thiébaud taught us French and art history—and taught us well—but it was her assistant, Mlle. Béné, who loved classical music above all else and who recognized in me another soul possessed. She allowed me unlimited access to her vast collection of recordings, and I spent untold hours ensconced next to the woodburning fire in her little study overlooking the lake. I became hopelessly intoxicated by the divine drug. I discovered that listening is almost as much an art form as performing; that *real* listening is an almost-religious communion of ears and brain and heart, one that creates a thirst that only intensifies with drinking; and I quaffed the sounds in great drafts of joy, never to be satisfied, always longing for more.

There were 14 of us students that year, and 11 nationalities. Riante Rive was deliberately of disparate composition. The frustration of isolation by a language barrier is an intensely compelling incentive to master a common medium, and we were driven to even further industry by a sly system known as the carnet d'honneur.

The accursed little book of honour was passed around the communal dining table every evening during soupé Suisse, to be signed by those girls who had managed to speak only French for the past 24 hours, letting slip not a single word of their mother tongue. The penalty for laggards was to forfeit an unchaperoned walk au bord du lac, for instance, or to stay behind during the next ballet outing or some such diversion. Considering our cloistered living conditions, such privations seemed to us unduly severe, but the system served its purpose, and within a few weeks we were all thinking and dreaming in French. And translating backwards into English, Danish, Italian, Spanish—whatever used to come naturally—when writing to our families at home.

Elisabet van Rechteren was one of my two roommates. Like most Dutch nationals—and unlike the rest of us—she was a born linguist, able to move seamlessly from Dutch to English to French to Italian to German without thinking and, at only 16, she was spinning her wheels at Riante Rive until she became old enough to go to university.

My other roommate was a Düsseldorfer named Ute Bagel— a statuesque blonde girl, with a pudding-basin haircut. She was another neophyte disciple of the great classical composers, and she soon appointed herself my keeper, sitting every afternoon by the open window of our second-floor bedroom where she could hear my Czerny piano exercises reverberating from the gymnasium below. She gave me a metronome, which I still have tucked away in the bottom drawer of my desk.

I invited Ute to London for the Easter break that year. My best friend from Heathfield, Jane Fairey, joined us the first weekend, and the three of us got on famously. Thinking to return the favour, Jane asked us to visit her in Hampshire the following weekend. Delighted, we accepted; my parents were particularly pleased to broaden the scope of Ute's trip to England with a taste of English country life. Midweek, however, Jane telephoned to say that she must withdraw her invitation.

"Father's still smarting from the war," she tried unhappily to explain, "and refuses to welcome a German. He can't forgive the Nazis for what happened to Richard." Jane's RAF half-brother had lost both his legs in World War II.

I was fascinated by Sir Richard's implacable ruling. Ute's meagre English was, for once, a blessing. And my own father was deeply aggrieved on Ute's behalf.

"By that same principle," he grumbled, "nor should Sir Richard be willing to have *you* in his house, Puddin'. Because, of course, you were every bit as responsible for the American Revolution as Ute was for World War II. Weren't you? Tsk, pshaw!"

The combination here of politics, personal injury, and historical perspective was beyond compromise. Their views and feelings—too raw and subjective for either of them to set aside—placed the two men in irreconcilable camps. Jane and I each revered the other's father—who themselves usually shared a sincere mutual regard—and our girlhood bond was too valuable to place at risk. We never spoke of it again.

My parents seldom bemoaned the high cost of my teenage maintenance. It was they, after all, who authorised most of my activities, and I can remember only two incidents to which they took any real exception. The first concerned an exorbitant telephone bill one Christmas holiday, which logged daily long-distance calls from me in London at Grosvenor 1996 to Jane in Hampshire at King's Somborne 247. At that point in our growing up, we felt the compelling need to communicate the tiniest details of our burgeoning lives, but we promised to cut back. Even *we* were surprised at the pounds, shillings and pence necessary to keep each other properly au courant.

The second was a bizarre financial accounting at the end of my first term at Riante Rive. This bill totted up my nightly baths, which, hardly surprisingly, equaled the number of days in the term. But what made it bizarre was a charge of $3 per bath, which for the term would have amounted to roughly $270—a sum which, when converted at today's rate of exchange, would be close to $1,000. No wonder my parents were upset. Americans have long considered Europeans sorely wanting when it comes to personal hygiene, but I imagine they attribute the delinquency more to culture than to cost.

I never learnt how the fiscal aspect of this contretemps was resolved, but at least no one asked me to limit myself to two or three tubs a month.

⁑

Then, in 1955, from the proudly insular country of Switzerland, with its vast lakes and majestic mountains, I abruptly found myself in Paris in a large flat on the fourth floor at 108 Rue du Bac, on the Left Bank of The City of Light. I lived there for just over a year with a Jewish family that hosted foreign teenage girls who were working toward their Diplôme D'Études de Civilisation Française by attending lectures at La Sorbonne, the oldest university in the world.

The matriarch of my host family was Violette Stein, whose husband Henri had been killed during the war. Now a widow, with few financial means at her disposal, opening her house to young students not only helped in supporting her own family but offered those students an unveiled, multi-layered view of French culture at its very best. My roommate, the only other boarder that year, was Kristin Sjögren—a classic blonde, blue-eyed Swede—who, like most of her countrymen, was multi-lingual. In mutual accord, however, she and I invoked Riante Rive's former policy of speaking only French. We liked each other, and got on well.

Madame Stein invited Kristin and me to call her "Tante Violette," thereby allowing us to feel at home from the start. We saw very little of her teenage son, Bertrand, a virtual hermit who studied—cloistered in his bedroom—at least 24 hours a day. Her agèd mother, Madame Châtel, also lived with us, but she died in her sleep shortly before Christmas that year and lay in state for two days in her own bed, hands carefully folded on the sheets' lacy trim, her face serene and pale, the room full of flowers and aromatic candles. Dozens of visitors roamed the flat and shared stories about their sweet friend. And other family members, who lived abroad, flew to Paris to kiss her forehead and whisper a prayer and, before taking their leave, to linger at the floor-to-ceiling window next to the bed, which provided a breathtaking panoramic view of their city's exquisite, patterned roofscape. The sight seemed to restore a certain equilibrium.

Horror and sorrow struck in early summer of the following year. The night after breaking off her engagement to her fiancé of two years, Tante Violette's 20-year-old daughter, Marie Claire, overdosed and died in her bathtub. Even now, more than 40 years later, words fail me. All I do know to say is that the flat seemed to echo like a vault. Meals were served and eaten slowly and in silence. I put away my school books and stopped playing the piano. The family suddenly seemed to become strangers to each other. And I wanted to go home.

Aside from the domestic tragedy, my time in Paris was uniquely rich and rewarding in its historic significance and all-encompassing architectural beauty. Kristin had a bicycle, but if my destination was too far to walk, I rode the buses. I cruised the Seine on the Bateaux Mouches. I surveyed the world from the top of the Eiffel Tower and was a frequent visitor during Mass on Sundays at Notre Dame. I haunted museums and galleries all over the city and went to a concert or the theatre almost every night.

I became very attached to Tante Violette's maid, Michelle, who encouraged me to join her when she went grocery shopping at the Les Halles, and patiently indulged my company while she cooked and ironed and sewed and watered the plants and generally kept the large household running smoothly. And, of course, we talked non-stop, which I imagine contributed considerably to the gradual conversion of my Swiss accent to a more indigenous one. My command of the language when I arrived in Paris was fairly secure—to the extent that shortly after arriving, I was asked where in Switzerland was my home. Evidently, Lausanne has a distinctive regional accent that I had "unfortunately" acquired.

I actually studied, too. Our formidable philosophy professor, Monsieur Lusérand, was blind, but to us, his absorbing lectures were delivered in sharp relief and infused with metaphoric colour and texture. It was fascinating, too, to watch him refer to his Braille notes, with dextrous, fluttering finger strokes as he mesmerised his invisible audience. The enormous auditorium was invariably crammed to the rafters and attended by hundreds of devotees of all ages, in every one of whom he inspired unqualified admiration and academic devotion.

The Steins had an old, but regularly maintained Steinway grand piano—a truly magnificent instrument that somehow minimised the intrinsic boredom of standard scales and arpeggios and elaborate fingering that I fought to master. My piano teacher at the Conservatoire de Paris was friendly enough, but he was an uncompromising task-master, who expected uncompromising dedication from his pupils. I was nothing if not eager, and practiced obsessively, with the metronome that Ute had given me perched in front of me on the score rack, ticking away.

And I tried not to despise my own little upright Chickering piano when I returned home to London.

Book VI
Time to Spare, Go by Air

The first time I ever traveled by air was in 1953. I was 15 years old and journeying alone from London to Milwaukee, Wisconsin, where Nancy Daniels lived. Nancy and Blake had met three years earlier when they were freshmen at their respective colleges, Smith and Williams, and Nancy's parents had invited Blake and his family to spend this Christmas with them. I could hardly wait. It promised to be a super vacation—pure Americana, lots of snow, chestnuts-roasting-on-an-open-fire and such—but I dreaded my maiden trans-Atlantic flight.

Brother Blake heard about my cold feet and took the trouble to write to me—the first letter I ever received from him. He reminded me that air travel was safer than crossing the street. He recommended that I request a seat overlooking the wings where turbulence was less noticeable. And he reiterated that I needn't worry about a thing—"except in the highly unlikely event you happen to see flames coming out of the propellers." I was touched by his thoughtfulness, and reassured by his levelheaded reasoning.

Gullible as I was, I never suspected, even remotely, that Blake's so-called thoughtfulness had, in fact, been a very mean practical joke. Airplanes in the '50s *always* appeared to spew flames from the propellers, and I spent the first leg of the trip from London to Shannon frozen with fear that the whole plane was about to catch fire. It was only when we left Ireland that some conscientious stewardess noticed my wide unblinking eyes and thought to explain to me—when she managed finally to determine the cause of my rigor mortis—that orange tongues licking over the wings outside my window was a normal occurrence.

With this new refinement, my brother had now raised sibling antipathy to a science of sorts; he could now amuse himself at my expense even by remote control. Incidentally, since the usual term sibling *rivalry* implies at least a potential for equality somewhere along the line, I've chosen instead to use *antipathy* as more accurately describing the fundamental dynamics between Blake and me.

As I grew older, the wisecracks became fewer and stung less, but his brazen indifference cuts to the quick even now. Over the years, Totsy had expertly trained us in observing the proper hierarchy—Blake as the entitled son and me as the geisha—thereby remorselessly widening the already unbridgeable rift between us. I was expected to feel honoured to wait on Blake, and Blake naturally learned to take such groveling as his entitlement.

For example, at breakfast—whenever he visited us in Charleston—Totsy would solicitously survey the state of his eggs and bacon and the level of orange juice in his glass.

"Your brother needs a refill, Dear, and perhaps some more bacon—while you're up."

The criticism in her tone implied I was already derelict in my servile duties, and I would leap to accommodate Blake's superior status, while at the same time deeply resenting the additional effrontery of his allowing our mother to order me about on his behalf.

He's perfectly able-bodied! Why isn't he helping himself? And offering **me** *more orange juice, for Pete's sake!*

This relentless double standard has inevitably created an enmity that neither of us is secure enough to confront, nor strong enough to break down. Latterly, however, Blake has seemed genuinely to appreciate my looking after our mother. It's been a responsibility that he would sooner have been dead himself than take on, and at least for the present, he has suspended his habitual taciturn posture. But I'll lay you a racing certainty that after the funeral this coming Saturday, he'll never come to Charleston again.

Another flight for the annals—this one in 1956—was from London to Charleston, with stops at Shannon, Gander, New York, and the endless ports of call on the way down the coast. At 18 years old, I was now a seasoned traveler, fazed only by sometimes having to sleep bolt upright in some airport or another. This trip introduced an entirely new perspective. After circling Washington National for more than an hour, the captain's voice crackled over the intercom.

"Ladies and Gentlemen, I'm sure you're wondering about the delay we're experiencing. We're still working on it, of course, but at this moment in time, our landing gear won't lock into place." I looked around, craning my neck. Everybody else was looking around, too—some more wildly than others. "But there's no need for concern," the monotone placebo continued. "When ground control has cleared the runway, we'll attempt our approach."

*Attempt our approach? What does he mean, **attempt** our approach? Godalmity!*

The man sitting next to me was a loud, fat Texan, whose obnoxious manner up to that point suddenly dissolved into unabashed sniveling as he tried to bolster his courage with the contents of his hip flask. I recalled a former statement made by my aviator brother: Even in such dire circumstances as these, an able pilot should be able to bring the plane to a satisfactory landing, tearing up the runway only a little bit. I proffered Blake's theory to my frenzied neighbour, whose hollow-eyed expression told me plainly that I was only adding insult to injury.

"Y'all really gotta lean all the way forward when we hit," the stewardess instructed us, as she herded everyone to the back of the half-full aircraft and padded us about with blankets and pillows. I found her Appalachian twang—and her completely unedited choice of words—more interesting than her instructions.

"You know what I mean?" she insisted. "I mean you *really* gotta put your head all the way down on your knees. No kiddin'."

Then, apparently to kill time until the cabin crew were ordered to secure themselves, she balanced her derrière on the arm of a seat just ahead of her now-terrified charges and proceeded to treat us to an engrossing account of a recent airline disaster. "You guys read about that Piedmont Airlines crash last week? You know, the one where everybody got killed…crew an' all?"

We happened to be flying Piedmont. Maybe this woman was new to the job. At any rate, after enthusiastically ensuring us of our likely doom, it was reasonable to assume she didn't know a whole lot about crowd psychology.

Sitting next to the window per Blake's instructions, I had a wide-scope view as we coasted toward the runway—a runway that starts smack at the edge of the Potomac River. As anyone who has ever flown into our capital would know, when you land at National, the plane's nose appears to be aiming straight into the water. Even when all things are equal.

In this case, nothing was equal. Not only were there no other aircraft anywhere in sight, but the entire landing field had been evacuated except for fire trucks, ambulances, and dozens of men in white coats closely lining the runway. The sight wonderfully concentrated the mind.

As we touched down, my pitiful companion flung his arm tight around me. "Goodbye," he wailed, burying his face in his Stetson.

I squeezed my eyes shut, and we bounced and scraped to quite a respectable halt. Blake was right. We did tear up the tarmac, but no one was injured. A halfhearted cheer went up as our half-witted stewardess opened the exit and activated the emergency chute. It shot down into a sea of foam and we all slid to safety.

"Mommie," I said hoarsely into the telephone after I found my luggage, "I've just been in a crash-landing. We're in Washington. I've missed my connection, so I'm taking the 9:15 instead. I should arrive a few minutes after 10 o'clock. Is that still okay?"

"Of course, Puddin'. Your Daddy and I will meet you then. Goodbye, Dear."

And then there was that other trip to Charleston, years later, which included a lengthy delay in New York before I could make the connection south. Engine trouble, I think they said. I bought a cup of coffee, made myself at home in the waiting area, stowed my overnight case between my feet, and opened my book.

Before long a man sat down next to me and lit a cigarette. I shifted slightly in my seat and glanced menacingly at him. Evidently accustomed to such encounters, he smiled as my scowl morphed into an ogle. He was movie-star handsome, and he knew it. I felt like a mouse in a trap—uncomfortable, yes, but not so much so that I wasn't still interested in the cheese.

Sure enough, he chatted me up, and I responded with dazed uncertainty. I couldn't take my eyes off him. He was tan, blonde, and sculptured. I was a nervous wreck, puce in the face, and perspiring. He affected amazement on learning that I had never been to New York—"except to the airport"—and quickly sought to remedy the situation by inviting me to spend the weekend with him at the St. Regis.

"Cultured woman that you obviously are," he purred, soft-soaping me to a regular lather, "you must allow me to show you 'round town. Actually New York's the hub of the universe. We could take in a play or two—I can tell you love the theatre—and we'll look at the rest of the world from the top of the Empire State Building. And we'll walk through Central Park. And I'll take you shopping on Fifth Avenue. Or anywhere you like. For anything you like. Anything at all. Say yes. Aw, c'mon, do say yes."

By now, he was holding my limp little hand. I licked my lips. My equally parched mind groped for words—words that were apparently stuck, irretrievably, way back somewhere in the dark. None of the obvious reasons to decline spending the weekend in New York with this man occurred to me—my husband, my children, my cats. They never entered my head. Even for a second.

But a life-sized mental image of Totsy did.

"You know, uh," I hesitated, extracting my hand from his, and idiotically winding my already-fully-wound watch, "I'd absolutely adore to, but I'm not sure how I'd explain it. You see, my mother… uh…my parents are expecting me in Charleston later tonight. But honestly I'd really love to. What do you suppose I could tell them?"

I looked up—my most dazzling smile at the ready—only to find the seat next to me empty. Mortified, I searched the middle distance in vain, soon reaching the obvious conclusion that the minute he discovered that his prey answered more to her mother than to her husband, my beautiful serpent slithered silently into the underbrush and vanished.

Shoving my book back into my overnight case, I spent the rest of the layover reflecting ruefully on the perils of temptation and the long arm of maternal law.

Book VII
The Queen, God Bless Her

Brother Blake visited England only twice during the 10 years our parents lived there. His first trip was in 1950, at the start of the Christmas holidays, when he and two Williams classmates made a brief stop in London before setting off in a rented Peugeot to tour western Europe until school started up again in January.

The following Christmas he joined us in the postcard village of Wengen. Now on the ski patrol at Williams, he eagerly anticipated flexing his superior skiing skills on the Swiss Alps. But calamity struck the day after he arrived. Wearing goggles against the sun's blinding reflection off the snow, his eyes didn't adjust in time for him to take evasive action when he cruised into a shadow that fell across his path—and he plowed at full tilt into a protruding rock.

Thinking at first that he was only bruised, he was aghast as he tried to get to his feet to find his pant leg soaked with blood. He'd been aware of the treacherous ground under the snow as he tumbled over and over, but had apparently felt nothing when the steel edge of his ski sliced through his calf muscle to the bone. Now hopelessly hors de combat, he spent the rest of his dream vacation on the chalet balcony, his eyes fixed longingly on the Jungfrau. Like pink spun sugar in the sunrise and diamond dust by the light of the moon, the towering prehistoric mountain is every skier's Mecca. And as far as I know, Blake never indulged himself a single word of complaint at being denied his week's worship.

His second trip to London was in 1953 for the Coronation of Queen Elizabeth II, which took place on Tuesday, June 2. He and Nancy arrived the previous weekend, and they went with Totsy to meet my school train at Paddington Station the day before the ceremony. Every school in the country closed for the week of national celebration—an unprecedented bonanza—and I was thrilled at last to be meeting my future sister-in-law.

Like Blake, Nancy was nearly 21, almost six years older than I. And like me, her only sibling was a brother. So we connected right away—each of us instinctively converting the other into the missing sister—and felt we were ready-made friends. We even appeared at dinner that first night wearing identical seersucker Lanz dresses from Bonwit Teller.

I suspect most English school children were well prepared for this once-in-a-lifetime spectacular. Certainly Heathfield ensured we had a solid grounding. And at just 15, I was old enough to be fairly discerning yet young enough still to be awed by England's pomp and circumstance. My journal of that historic week *[excerpts below]* includes reference to the early affection Nancy and I shared, as well as to my youthful adulation of my brother—with telling allusions to his already-aloof persona.

Nancy herself captured Blake's essence with touchingly resigned yearning.

"You know, I'd give *anything*," she told me, "anything at *all*, if he'd look at me—just *once*—with the same expression on his face as when he's looking at a dog. Or even at an airplane."

I knew exactly what she meant. We all were victims of Blake's parsimony when it came to showing affection.

01/06/53 Monday

Very excited! Arrived à Londres (from Heathfield) met Nancy! And so glad to see Blake and Mom. Daddy was still at his office. Nancy's very sweet; short, straight hair, about 5' 3", hazel eyes, wonderful smile, pretty teeth, thin, little, very friendly, happy, and just pretty OK! Blake's changed sort of quieter and yet more wonderful than ever. Stopped at Harrods, had a bite at the flat. I went to get my hair cut while N & B went to get film for the camera, and I'm never, ever going to let Cynthia cut my hair again. It is excruciatingly awful all endy, uneven and thin.

We met back at the flat and went for a walk; got plumb jammed in Oxford Street; the crowd just jam-packed the place honestly, the decorations, the stands with their fresh paint and coats-of-arms and gay flowers, lovely clean statues and buildings, polished brass everywhere. The people (even at that early hour) sitting with their rugs, food, books, PATIENCE, and each other, all with the same feeling and wonderful spirit, the order, the beauty and tidiness of it all, the splendour and solemnity. Wonderful.

The thing which amazed me most was the way everyone could sit there like that, with the prospect of a cold, grey, rainy night, and still not bat an eyelid, and just read, eat snacks, talk, and keep so marvelously cheerful. Crowns of flowers, gold crowns, streamers connecting houses across the streets, lights, solid banks of flowers, shop windows, gaily coloured little "convenience" huts in the park, the joy in people's faces, the way even the poorest gave up pay for decorations because their Queen was going to pass them. I think the real reward for those patient curbsitters and standers was that in the end, they got a much closer view of the Queen and Procession than some people who had paid £50 for a seat.

02/06/53 Tuesday; CORONATION DAY

Blake woke Nancy up at about 5:30 a.m. and they left at 6:30; they were going to find a place at the edge of Hyde Park or Park Lane where they could wait. Mom and Daddy and I left at 8; we were meeting lots of Daddy's cronies at the Fifty Shillings Taylor Shop Building in Oxford Street. We were lucky enough to be out of the rain. The crowds on the way were simply fantastic many people had slept out on the sidewalks all night in the pouring rain, and we noticed four men carrying a stretcher someone who had probably collapsed from cold and fatigue. During the whole time we were there, we saw three ambulances tearing along, clanging their bells madly.

Our building had every advantage imaginable a lovely party with divine food, two excellent TV sets, drinks (champagne, sherry, etc., delicious), fruit, nuts; and about 15 windows for us to look out of. We walked around, leaned out of the windows, ate very salty almonds and some fruit, looked at magazines, talked to each other and just passed the time until the television was turned on at about 9:30. The one we watched was very good, indeed; clear and distinct, and didn't go blurry once. We first saw the Abbey, and the speaker told us in a beautiful voice and in great detail, exactly how, where and when everything was going to happen during the Service. In spite of the television's not being in colour, we still felt the splendour and beauty of Westminster Abbey and I cannot find the words to describe my feelings.

Even on the television, we could tell that the lighting in the Abbey was dazzling. After leaving the Abbey, the television returned us to the streets and the crowds; they were so patient. When it rained, which it did almost the whole time, all they did was to put up their umbrellas (the few of them who had them), put on their macs and plastic scarfs, and those who weren't so fortunate put newspaper on their heads and no one was willing to leave the horrible gloom of the long wait. One man on the opposite side of the street from us was wrapped up in a big white blanket, which I'm sure must have been absolutely soaked, poor thing.

I'll never understand how the Almighty could let it be such an uncertain, grey, cold day for such an occasion. Every now and then, the sun would try hard for a while and finally peep through the solid mass of grey clouds. Everyone who had cameras would scramble to a window to take advantage of the temporary brightness for their picture-taking. The window ledge going all the way round our building was quite wide and all the windows opened on an axis, so Daddy had the bright idea of sitting in the space provided by the open window, putting his left leg and foot outside on the wide ledge and his right foot on a chair inside to balance himself, so that whenever the sun did condescend to come out for a minute, he could quickly snap a picture. One of his remarks: "Just think of the millions of feet of film that'll be wasted today!"

The crowd outside our window were so lacking in diversion that they even cheered the sun when it came out, as well as a garbage truck that went up and down the route! We thought often of Blake and Nancy, hoping they were OK and not too wet. By now, the troops began to line the Coronation route, creating a welcome diversion. The Army came first, then the R.A.F. The men had their macs all wrapped up neatly in a minute bundle attached to the back of their belts, but it wasn't long before they all were wearing them; they were rather like unevenly-cut waterproof capes. The rain was really bad luck, particularly for the Marines, because the whiting on their belts ran and trickled down the legs of their lovely dark uniforms.

We talked some more, ate some more, and finally got back to our chairs in front of the television when the Queen's coach left Buckingham Palace. When you consider the grueling experience she was about to face, you can't understand how she could look so lovely and composed, so calm and happy. The cheering was wild! Such a young woman with so much responsibility on her shoulders for the rest of her life; she and her proud husband formed a picture we would never forget for the rest of our lives. The Queen reached the Abbey, the Duke continually at her side, and the service at last began. "The hour is come!" The colour, accentuated by all the powerful, brilliant lights, must have been gorgeous beyond belief, and the singing of the choir of 400 was superb.

Briefly, The Order of the Service was like this. First, the recognition of all four corners of the world, then the presentation of the Bible on which the Queen took the oath in which she vowed to serve her people. Then she was divested of all her royal robes and jewelry, and wore a simple, pure white linen smock for the most impressive event: the anointing of her hands, heart and head, which represent her mercy, her love of country and her wisdom. A Zadok the Priest was sung triumphantly. Then was the presentation of the Regalia: the Spur (which she only touches, as she is not a man), the Sword (with one edge blunted to show mercy), the Armilla (or A bracelets to show protection of her on all sides, always), the Stole and Robe Royal, the Orbe, the Ring, the Sceptre (to show power), and the Rod (to show purity, with its dove).

AND THEN SHE WAS CROWNED!

The peeresses all donned their coronets, the Westminster Boys Choir cried out "God Save the Queen" in Latin, the trumpets sounded and the guns at the Tower were shot off. The Queen leaves her chair and is symbolically lifted by the Bishop of Bath and Wells, and the Bishop of Durham into the Throne. Then the paying of homage takes place. First the Archbishop of Canterbury, then the two Royal Dukes (the Duke of Edinburgh who kisses her cheek, the Duke of Norfolk on behalf of the rest of the Dukes), the Marquis of Hereford and the Earl of Snowsberry on behalf of all the Earls; then the Viscounts and finally the Lords.

The Queen delivers her Sceptre and Rod to the Lord Great Chamberlain, and she and the Duke of Edinburgh (each at their little stools before the altar) take communion. Then the Archbishop of Canterbury gives the blessing, first to the Queen and then the congregation. The

Queen enters the Chapel behind the High Altar where she puts on the Imperial Crown and the Purple Robe Royal. She proceeds through the Abbey with the Orbe and Septre, and as she leaves the Chancel, everyone sings the National Anthem.

The Procession reached Oxford Street about an hour and a half later. It had been drizzling steadily the whole time, but with the Procession appeared the sun; the faces of the people in the waiting crowd changed, their patience at last rewarded. First came the Household Cavalry, then the Commonwealth Contingent (including the Air Force, Army and Navy). When the Armed Police came by, the troops lining the route immediately grounded their arms to acknowledge that the State is above the military. There were several terrific bands. I found it particularly fascinating to watch the drummers twirl and swing their sticks, with string tied to their wrists so they won't drop the sticks between each beat. I noticed a long rip in one of the drums; he must have really been letting them have it!

Then the Carriage Procession started, the fourth Carriage being particularly interesting. It was open and it carried Queen Salote of Tonga, who was "really quite a lass," as Daddy's friend, John Gridley, said. She's 6' 3", weighs about 350 lbs, is black as soot, very jovial and was just waving to beat the band. She was the only woman in an open carriage and to top it all, it began to drizzle again, so she pulled out a handkerchief and busily mopped her face and neck. The crowds loved her but, of course, they would, the way she smiled at them and the gracious, friendly way she acknowledged their cheers. "Quite a lass!"

At last, at long last, the long-awaited gold coach arrived, with Queen Elizabeth II truly now a crowned Queen and the Duke of Edinburgh. You can imagine the wild shouts from the people. Here was the young Queen, looking so radiantly happy, passing slowly and majestically in the rich gold coach before the eyes of thousands of her loyal and loving subjects. (Behind the very last troops lining the route came something that caught my eye a typical street cleaner with his little cart and brooms. He was definitely required. I've never seen such a mess: mud, food, fruit peelings, paper of all sorts. But to think they'd get to work on cleaning up the minute the "day" was over really brought me to a halt. Londoners are very tidy-minded as a whole.)

Well, now it was over, and to think that I'd been fortunate enough to be present at such a wonderful and unusual event quite overwhelms me. I'm so grateful.

Book VIII
The London Season

Iaccumulated débuts. I "came out" first at Buckingham Palace, then at the St. Cecelia Ball in Charleston, and finally at the Philadelphia Assembly in Philadelphia. I also went to private dances in Richmond and then back in Hampshire. No one ever thought to explain how I was to benefit from such multiple introductions, but some years later it came to me that at least Totsy had the satisfaction of knowing that I possessed the credentials, if not the inclination, to follow her socially ambitious lead.

My entré into this powerful minority tradition was on March 22, 1956, when I was presented to Queen Elizabeth II. It was the last such occasion at which Winthrop Aldrich, the American ambassador to the Court of St. James, sponsored a dozen American débutantes during the London Season. These royal audiences subsequently scaled down to the more informal garden parties that are still held annually on the lawns of Buckingham Palace, so I made it with the in-crowd by the skin of my teeth. One can only imagine Totsy's relief.

For my Court appearance, she took me along to Christian Dior, whom she referred to as her personal dressmaker. My extraordinarily unbecoming outfit was a slate-blue, ankle-length taffeta dress and duster. I hated myself in it. I felt like lamb-dressed-as-mutton.

The day before the Presentation, the 12 of us were summoned to Winfield House *[the Ambassador's Residence in Regent's Park]* for afternoon tea and a brush-up on royal protocol. We were also urged to pay special attention—if we weren't too bemused by all the goings on—to the paintings lining the Palace halls. What I did notice as I dropped my deepest curtsy in the throne room the next afternoon, was that Prince Philip was wearing heavy pancake makeup. I nearly toppled over in surprise, but there was no mistaking it. It showed as plainly under the unforgiving camera lights as did the Queen's own cheeks of flawless English-rose fame.

Ambassador Aldrich's hospitality concluded that evening with a dinner-dance at the Dorchester Hotel and a dozen eligible English bachelors to squire us. I quite liked the one sitting across from me. His name was Ted Ostrer, and when I learnt that he lived at 47 Grosvenor Square—at the at the opposite end of the block from Number 37, where I lived—I suspected Fate was plotting.

After dancing until we could no longer stand, he drove me in his baby-blue Bentley the short distance back to his flat, where I sat primly on a tuffet at his feet while we sipped old port. My new beau was polite and attentive, and he walked me home through the foggy square just before sunup. And he followed me to Paris a few days later. Which is to say, he crossed the Channel to visit me every weekend for several months. And in due course, he slipped a ring with a large square diamond on my finger one Friday evening as our taxicab drove away from Orly toward the city.

I wasn't even infatuated with Ted—much less in love with him—but I went along with this development as if I'd been preprogrammed like a live Barbie doll. The ring was another matter. I was seriously enamoured of that ring.

I'm not sure of the formal criteria for presentation by our ambassador to the Queen in those days, but Daddy's high profile rôle in Socony's lingering war-recovery effort probably qualified me quite nicely. It was hinted, however, that the clincher absolute was to be found in the fact that one of my more remote antecedents was Arthur Middleton, a South Carolina signer of the Declaration of Independence. *From* England.

To honour a person for descending from a line of insurrectionists does seem somewhat unlikely, but, of course, the English are second to none when it comes to oblique commentary. Their tongue-in-cheek diplomacy was further illustrated one Fourth of July when some British friends of my parents sent them an enormous armful of red, white, and blue flowers. Clearly, they viewed the American Revolution as little more than a blip in the Divine Order of things.

The best-ever example, however, of this good-natured national arrogance was an exchange Daddy claimed to have overheard one afternoon as he waited his turn in the post office on Mount Street. Apparently, the man in front of him—on reaching the head of the queue—politely asked the girl behind the counter the cost of mailing a postcard to the United States. From his speech, Daddy guessed the man was a compatriot.

"Why, it's the same to all the colonies, sir," the clerk replied, reaching the same conclusion, and elaborately raising her eyebrows at the American's distressing ignorance. "It hasn't changed in years."

On June 14, 1956, I shared a thé dansant with Holly Miller *[my godmother's daughter]* in Richmond, Virginia. We wore matching frocks of white dotted Swiss, except that the dots on Holly's were blue, and mine pink. Made with loving care by the local sempstress, the hems sagged, the seams were uneven, my hair wouldn't curl, and I wished I were dead. In spite of old newspaper articles and photographs which recall the evening in some detail, all I really remember—aside from being acutely self-conscious in that frightful dress—is that Holly was the belle of the ball.

A week later, I flew back to England. Jane Fairey was having a dance on the 25th, and it was the one date on the Season's calendar that I actually looked forward to. Usually at such affairs, I felt as much at sea as if I'd been thrown into the English Channel without a life jacket, but this time I'd be in familiar surroundings and would know enough of the other guests not to feel a complete outsider. It was, in fact, a wonderful evening, and I didn't get to bed till dawn.

Somewhere still among my bits and pieces is a clipping from the *Tatler* describing the party and a picture of myself stepping gingerly out of Richard Fairey's private helicopter onto the lawn at Bossington House, on the family estate in Hampshire. Richard was Jane's older brother, and I'd been included in his dinner party before the dance—he lived near Maidenhead, a 20-minute flight away—and he deposited his guests in great style at the edge of the terrace where the band was already in full swing.

This Hollywood touch was even more of an experience than you might think—Richard's legs were missing below the knees. Formerly an officer in the RAF, his plane had been shot down over the North Sea during World War II and, while waiting and praying to be rescued, frostbite claimed his feet and ankles. After the tragic double amputation, he adjusted well to matching prostheses, and eventually a walking cane was the only clue to his terrible injury. He learnt to swim again and drove his cleverly converted Ferrari like a bat out of hell. And he flew that helicopter with every bit of his old skill and derring-do.

Charleston accepted me into its exalted ranks on January 24, 1957, via the St. Cecilia Ball. I was living in Paris then and attending lectures at La Sorbonne, but my parents shipped me back for the Charleston Season, and for several months, I stayed at 83 Tradd Street with my Aunt Frances and Uncle Will. To all the

Middletons of my generation, as well as to our descendants, Frances and Will are known as Fanny and Dads.

Except for the strapless creation of Schiaparelli pink satin that Fanny and I found at Terrell's on Church Street, I have scant memory of The Ball. Totsy had commissioned Fanny to kit me out, and though the gown cost an outlandish $200 (calculating inflation into its original price, it was by far the most expensive garment I have ever owned), Fanny dashed off the cheque with a flourish of patent satisfaction. Perhaps her impulse to splurge on my behalf came from an unfulfilled mother-daughter relationship. Her maternal quiver held only sons and her own mother died when she was only six years old. Who knows? Maybe she just loved me.

We also found full-length kid gloves that exactly matched the dress, which I was instructed never to take off. *What? Why?* Fanny explained that if I became peckish and wanted to sample a pickled shrimp or a crab vol au vent, the time-honoured protocol was to undo the buttons at the wrist and discretely tuck the hand of the glove inside. *Isn't that sort of overkill? Oh, well. Okay.*

Cousin Will photographed me descending the stairs, at the foot of which was a handsome lad named Luke Simons, to whom Will introduced me, and who had been inveigled to be my escort at the Ball. Luke promptly broke the potentially awkward ice by handing me the wristlet of gardenias that he'd brought for me and telling me that his surname was pronounced as if it were spelt with *two* m's. I blinked and smiled and sniffed the flowers and thanked him.

Will then chimed in with the supporting local story that Mr. Ohlandt—"a grocer down the street, right there on the corner of Tradd and Meeting"—always advertised "RIPE PERSIMONS" on his sidewalk stand when that fruit was in season.

I blinked again, took Luke's arm, and off we went.

The only other time I ever wore the pink satin dress was to the Philadelphia Assembly, in the fall of 1957. My hosts in Wawa, Pennsylvania, were Pa's sister and brother-in-law, Priscilla and Frank Griffin. Frank worked for DuPont. Totsy would have you believe he single-handedly invented nylon.

"Till" was tall and fair and an accomplished equestrian. I have a terrific photograph of Daddy, looking to the manner born, astride one of Till's sleek hunters in mid-jump over a fence. She wore jumbo-sized emeralds all the time—even when she was riding or gardening or cooking—and laughed a lot. What better way to be remembered if you were somebody's great-aunt?

When Frank asked her what she wanted for her birthday one year, she said, "Give me a kiss, Sweetheart. I won't have to dust it or insure it."

Membership in both the St. Cecilia Society and the even older Order of the Cincinnati is passed from father to son. The Order was formed in 1783 by officers of the victorious American Army of the Revolutionary War, with George Washington as its first President-General.

The principal purposes of its constitution, which was read at every meeting, were "to preserve Liberty, to cherish the union of the States, and to maintain permanently the cordiality between officers and mutual friends." One of the first acts of the founding meeting was to extend membership to certain grades of French officers, declaring that to do so "sealed in a solemn manner, and in an hereditary way, the friendship of the two peoples."

The new republic had received generous assistance from France in its uncertain bid for independence and wished to "perpetuate the friendships that had been formed, and so happily subsisted, between the officers of the allied forces in the prosecution of war."

When Daddy's death left vacant his membership in the Order, Totsy made no attempt to hide her disappointment—and disapproval—that my brother did not trip over himself in his haste to fill it or even offer it to one of his own sons. Blake despised this sort of thing, which was a double whammy for Totsy, as it directly followed my own scornful refusal to be added to the rolls of either the Daughters of the Confederacy or the American Revolution.

Blake and I were born to a set of archaic privileges neither of us had any intention of exploiting, and I know Totsy despaired of us both.

My parents had at their disposal a fail-safe strategy which they would deploy the moment they suspected I was becoming romantically entangled. Wherever I happened to be, they would simply dispatch me to the other side of the Atlantic. If someone smiled at me in Paris, say, or New York, I was told it was time to vanquish new foes or charter new territory and would soon find myself either staying with Nancy and Blake in California for a while, or back at home in London. If I smiled at someone in Charleston, there would suddenly arise the urgent need for me to learn a new language, and I'd be winging my way to Switzerland practically before sundown.

I met Lindsay Luke on Christmas Eve in 1954. My family had convened from Williamstown, London, and Lausanne to spend the holidays with Ma and Pa in Summerville. Lindsay and his sister Mary happened to be sitting next to us at the midnight service at St. Paul's Episcopal Church, and he and I caroled our way into love at first sight.

Our families soon noticed the obvious, and everybody started objecting loudly that we were "too young to be so serious about each other." Well, of course, we were too young. We were both only 16 years old. But the true basis for my own parents' objection to the teenage attachment was that Lindsay's father, Gordon, had so far been married and divorced several times, and Totsy and Daddy feared Lindsay would follow his father's example. So, back I flew to Switzerland and got on with being finished.

Nearly 30 years later, as everyone was leaving St. Michael's Episcopal Church after my son Blake's memorial service, Lindsay appeared unexpectedly at my side. He hugged me silently, and enveloped me in his heavy overcoat against the winter chill, but it was his dear face that warmed and comforted me. I wanted to stand there in his arms forever.

I must go on record here as saying that Lindsay did not follow in his father's footsteps. He is the stable, decent man he promised at 16 to become. As far as I know, he has been married to the same person for some 30 years, and they have raised two good sons. His agèd mother loves and respects him. And he is head warden of St. Paul's Episcopal Church—the very church where we first met that long-ago Christmas Eve. And where I am to be buried next to my beloved Pa whenever I fall off my perch.

In the fall of 1956, when Ted Ostrer put that ring on my 18-year-old finger, I was spirited to California almost before I could pack a suitcase. Brother Blake was by now a Navy pilot, stationed in San Diego, and I would be living for a few months with him and Nancy in La Jolla.

"You've been abroad too long, Puddin'," I was sternly informed, as if being at La Sorbonne in Paris were somehow my own nefarious doing. "It's time for you to go home and test your native waters."

"Home? California's hardly home," I sulked. "Anyhow, La Jolla's a stupid name for a town."

Ted's problem, as my benighted parents saw it, was quite simply that he was a Jew. But the "abroad too long" business was the facile pretext I was expected to use to explain away my hasty and very churlish departure. I returned the fabulous diamond and flew to the West Coast. And occupied my dejected self for six months by trying to learn to type. And trying to forget that diamond. Uncharacteristically cooperative, I wore my emotional straitjacket like a second skin.

John Sands proposed to me in December of 1957. We were driving through the Holland Tunnel on our way to the theatre in New York City. My elderly Griffin relatives had introduced us several months earlier at the Philadelphia Assembly, and I was now staying temporarily in Manhattan with Izzy and Rae Jackson *[my parents' friends from our days in Beaumont, Texas]*. The Jacksons were hosting a couple of parties for me, and since John's flat was conveniently near theirs on Fifth Avenue, he'd squired me around a bit and we fancied we'd fallen in love.

But, of course, such a liaison was too ludicrous even to contemplate.

"He's *far* too old for you, Puddin'," was the resounding refrain from all quarters. "He's 38, for Heaven's sake! *And* Roman Catholic! Horrors!"

So, of course, the next thing I knew, I was on my way back to London, to Queen's Secretarial College in Stanhope Gate. Earning my Certificate of Competency in shorthand and typing was "sure to take [my] mind off this nonsense."

By the time Francis Kinsman materialized, apparently enough was enough. It was summertime 1958. English through and through, he had been to the requisite Eton and Cambridge. He was also a member of the indisputably waspish Church of England, and his military service had been with the King's African Rifles. At this point, even my parents were fed up with all the trans-Atlantic backing and filling, and no one stepped in to reverse course.

Charlestonians never lose an opportunity to identify with the Chinese, pointing out that both races eat rice and worship their ancestors and eventually come home to die.

"They also set off fireworks at New Year's and can't speak English!" some sassy Yankee is rumoured to have added. Furthermore, the Holy City is said to be a genealogical quagmire. Everybody is rather pompously related to virtually everybody else.

It was therefore considered wonderfully inspired when, on learning of my betrothal to Francis, a great friend of my parents—Judge Lionel Legge of the South Carolina Supreme Court—remarked dryly…

"How suitable for a Middleton to be marrying a Kinsman!"

Book IX
So Long as You Both Shall Live

I met Francis John Morland Kinsman in July of 1958, through a business associate of my father. Will Codrington was a larger-than-life rather resplendent man with a walrus mustache. He was also Lord Lieutenant of Rutland County—a choice bit of the English midlands. Instituted by King Henry VIII, the royal appointment conferred full military authority on the monarch's representative to each constituency. Today, the honorary title is given to the local civilian equivalent.

It was Mr. Codrington's daughter, Jane, who actually introduced us. She had tickets for what turned out to be an historic performance at the Royal Festival Hall of Edward Elgar's *Dream of Gerontius [Dream of an Old Man]*, and she invited three girls and four men to gather beforehand at her parents' London flat. I wore a pink cotton shirt-dress, and my contribution to supper-in-our-laps was a plate of brownies. I wonder why one remembers such minutiae.

Francis and I hit it off fairly well, I suppose, in an un-dizzying sort of way. He mentioned early on that he was an only child and that like so many of his generation he had been brought up "strictly to be seen but not heard." While I was silently deploring this anachronistic practice, he proceeded to wax patriotic about how "incredibly proud" he was to have "stuck it out" with his grandparents in London during the Blitz. *The London Blitz?* I quickly changed mental gears, and was beginning to savour this dramatic note when Francis threw in another tidbit that was so awful, it was downright delicious: His father, a gentleman-farmer near King's Lynn in Norfolk, was teetering on the verge of bankruptcy. I almost gasped aloud. *Why on earth would he think to tell me something like that?*

After my initial appraisal of him, I concluded Francis was an appealingly upbeat type, but I was put off by his general pallor and gaunt aspect. I also noted, to my dismay, that he needed to give his wardrobe a careful once-over. As if discussing national treasures in the British Museum, he proudly informed me that the suit he was wearing had belonged to his grandfather and been cut down to fit his own more slight build. And that his well-polished, peeling patent-leather shoes had also been his grandfather's. This gratuitous information confused me at the time and, even now, I'm not sure whether those heirloom hand-me-downs were evidence of a stiff upper lip in the face of post-war hardship or merely that Francis was completely without personal vanity—pure and simple.

He was taller than six feet and had fluffy fair hair and light-blue English eyes. His small mouth often smiled around not-particularly-even teeth, and a pronounced Roman nose emphasized the narrowness of his chin. His frayed necktie—black, with duck-egg-blue diagonal stripes—told the world that he was an old Etonian. And he mentioned that in keeping with family tradition, he'd gone on to Trinity College, Cambridge, where he read Botany and became an energetic member of the Footlight Players—an amateur theatrical association that I later determined was entirely in keeping with his personality, if not entirely supported by ability.

Francis then set about giving me an overview of his National Service. He was an excellent storyteller, and I was impressed to learn he'd been an officer in the King's African Rifles, in Nyasaland *[now Malawi]. But what king is that?* I wondered. *Don't we have a queen now? And where's Nyasaland?*

Actually, even if I'd dared ask these questions, Francis would never have noticed. In fits of laughter, he was having far too much fun describing one of the enlisted men in his regiment. "The poor chap was an African," he coughed as he came up for air, "who'd had a hex put on him that made him think he was a poached egg!" Witchcraft in Nyasaland was evidently alive and well, and the giggles of this jocular, disjointed man were irresistible.

I was trying to catch my own breath as he continued merrily.

"By the way, a couple of Cambridge chums and I are sharing digs at the moment." Their digs turned out to be a ragged, freezing basement flat in Edward's Place in Kensington. "Julian Ashby and Guy Cooper. You'll like them. Oh, and yes, I've just started as a lowly marine broker at Lloyds. You have to fork over an enormous entrance fee to be an underwriter—I think it's ten-thousand quid—but really all you need to make a go of it is the gift of the gab."

He seemed perfectly at home in his straitened circumstances. To tell the truth, he probably thought of such circumstances as rather bohemian and therefore as rather charming. And if I'd known any better, I'd have immediately placed myself on alert. His thumbnail autobiography revealed a pattern of financial ineptitude of epic proportion, about which its perpetrators remained cheerfully unperturbed.

Francis didn't fit my idea of the knight on the white charger. Based on the men in my family whom I admired, I tended to fancy myself with bronzed athletes rather than with dilettantes doing the soft-shoe shuffle. But he was very good value and we were at ease in each other's company. And when you looked at it in that light, nothing else seemed to matter much.

I didn't know at the time that there was a yawning gulf between *pleasant* and *passion,* nor that such difference was fundamentally significant. We were so young. And youth, by definition, is often so dangerously sanguine.

The Royal Festival Hall was built to coincide with the opening of the 1951 Festival of Britain, and being equipped with the most advanced acoustics technology, it didn't matter that our seats—that night in 1958—were way up in the gods. Soaring echoes hung in the air, and you could hear the softest sigh.

The production of *Gerontius* by the celebrated Bach Choir deserved a word of superlative praise all its own. I'd never before heard the great oratorio, but the music was ethereal and the text so poignant, I bit my lip to keep from crying.

It was taken from a poem, written in his old age by John Henry Cardinal Newman, of a man contemplating his own approaching death, of his fear at meeting God, and of his Angel's words of grace. The part of the Old Man was sung by Richard Lewis, the sublime English tenor of the 1950s, and I could see—even at that distance—that his own face was streaked with tears as he entreated the Old Man's Angel at last to lead him to God. *How can he sing in the thrall of such ecstasy?* I will remember that evening until I die.

Our courtship of just over a year followed a predictable and uneventful course. We met each other's friends at dinner parties and house parties that autumn and took in movies and the ballet and theatre. We even swam a few times the following summer in the pool at Hurlingham Club in Putney, though it was seldom warm enough really to enjoy the water.

I fought to keep a straight face the first time I ever saw Francis dive. And I use the term *dive* loosely. Crouching low, with knees bent and hands cupped at chest level, he could have been Jacques Tati himself as he fell forward—heavily—into the deep end, displacing mountainous waves over the shivering souls scattered in deck chairs around the pool. In case you, my reader, are too young to remember, Jacques Tati was the star of *Monsieur Hulot's Holiday*, which was, for me, the most side-splittingly funny film of all time.

Not only could Francis not dive according to any conventional style or standard, he could barely swim. But he did seem to be having a tremendously good time.

We went to every one of the season's Henry Wood Promenade Concerts at the Royal Albert Hall and spent many an evening at Quaglino's and Annabel's, the "in" nightclubs; Francis was a marvelous ballroom dancer. At the weekends, we walked in St. James's Park and picnicked on the Serpentine. And discussed names for our future children. I realised at some point that he'd never formally proposed to me; everything seemed to happen involuntarily. Something was missing, but it was too subtle, whatever it was, to arrest my attention.

Our favourite restaurant was a bistro on Curzon Street in Soho, within easy walking distance of Grosvenor Square. It was the usual sort of venue for indigent graduates of Oxbridge and the London Season, with the mandatory dripping candle stuck in an empty Chianti bottle on every checkered cloth-covered table and the ambient Italian waiter with a tea towel flung over his shoulder, hovering about and doing his best to spark young love.

During supper there one night, Francis bit onto something hard, and clumsily fished a bullet from his mouthful of spaghetti. Laughing and sputtering, he placed it carefully on the edge of his plate. And then, in a loud and imperious voice, he insisted on inspecting the kitchen. His avocation at the time was the composition of light verse and libretti, and he was hoping to find from this unexpected encounter the stuff of a new skit.

But the restaurant's kitchen was as sterile as an operating theatre, so we entertained ourselves instead by speculating whether we were frequenting one of the mob's hangouts. Our wine that night—lots of it—was on the house.

We were married, in the early evening, at the Grosvenor Chapel on South Audley Street on August 7, 1959. Strictly speaking, it was a Chapel of Ease—an adjunct place of worship intended to take up any overcrowding at the parish church proper, which in this case was St. George's, Hanover Square. But the Grosvenor Chapel was one of the chefs d'oeuvres of Sir Christopher Wren, the architect who best exemplified the English Renaissance. And having sometimes attended Matins or Sung Eucharist there when I was on holiday from school, my heart was set on being married there. Such chapels are licensed for neither weddings nor funerals, but dispensation from the Archbishop of Canterbury was readily granted us in the form of a parchment scroll sealed with wax. On this scroll, in unleavened civility and spidery calligraphy, His Grace's order began with the energetic greeting, "Health!"

Everything went like clockwork. Well, almost everything. Gratified by the august nature of her guest list, Totsy had been mightily disappointed when Princess Alexandra Kent—one of my Heathfield schoolmates—declined "with regret," thereby foiling Totsy's plan to let slip at every opportunity the choice nugget that the Queen's first-cousin had been to my wedding.

Christian Dior had decked me out for the presentation at Court three years earlier, but standards had slumped a bit when it came to deciding on my wedding dress. After lobbying unsuccessfully for a white Irish lawn confection with endless rows of hand-sewn tucks, I settled for an off-the-peg, nylon tulle gown and veil from Harrods. My sop, however, was an understated, but beautiful diamond coronet lent to me by Francis' Great-Aunt Dorothy Hilbery. Dolly and I shared a Taurean birthday, as well as similar annoyances with our mutual in-laws, and we had already became good friends and unspoken allies.

It should be noted—for the record—that Totsy herself sneaked back to Mr. Dior, who outdid himself for her with a narrow little suit of rose-watered silk, and a cloche hat of pastel ostrich feathers.

The London florists Pulbrook and Gould filled the Grosvenor Chapel with peace roses and lavender-blue delphiniums so tall they seemed almost to reach the vaulted azure ceiling. My old choirmaster from Heathfield, Charles Faulkner, hummed noisily and tunelessly from the organ loft as he played the distinctly upbeat incidental music from Grieg's *Wedding Day at Troldhaugen*. And incumbent vicar Father Derry graciously stepped aside so that The Reverend Eric James might officiate. Eric and Francis had been at Eton together.

Our reception was held in the flat belonging to friends of my parents—on the ground-floor of the same building, as it happened, where my former beau Ted Ostrer lived. And, like the Grosvenor Chapel, it was dressed to the nines with peace roses and delphiniums. It may be worth noting here that an entire gross—140 bottles—of extra brut champagne was polished off by a mere 100 well-wishers. I seldom drank even sherry in those days. And as the evening wore on—and the level of decibels continued to rise around me while this illustrious crowd let its hair down—I began to feel more like a spectator than a participant.

At an English wedding reception, it is always the groom who leads the toasts. When the moment was right—that is, when everyone was nicely mingling, and well fortified with the delicious champagne and gustatory delights from Fortnum & Mason— Francis looked around until he located Totsy. After catching her eye, he cleared his throat loudly and chinked his glass with a fork.

"Years ago," he began, as the hubbub subsided, "when I was still far too young to appreciate the wisdom of his words, my godfather offered me some excellent advice. 'Francis, old son,' he said, 'whenever you find yourself thinking seriously about choosing a bride, the first order of business should be to inspect the mother— much as you would the mare when acquiring a foal. This should give you a fair idea of what you might expect as time goes on, eh, what?'"

A crescendo of laughter rippled around the room.

"And as you can all see," Francis continued, as he raised his glass in Totsy's direction and bowed, "I took his suggestion very much to heart."

"Hear, hear!" Our guests called out their approval, as the focus of all eyes was no longer on me, but on my mother—on whom it remained fixed for the rest of the evening, and who proceeded to settle comfortably into her newly designated rôle as the undisputed centrepiece of my wedding reception. The overtly exclusionary relationship spawned at that moment between her and my new husband rankles even to this day.

⁓

Jane Fairey was my maid of honour. She has been my alter ego since childhood, in spite of our being widely geographically divided for the last 20 years or so. She personifies unreservèd love of friend, and I admire her valour of spirit and height of intellect above all others.

We first met at Heathfield. Jane was 14 years old and a boarding school veteran of already two years. I was 13, thoroughly confused, desperately homesick, and seriously behind in schoolwork. My peers could already parse sentences. *Parse* was a term that had so far never crossed my path. And they were well-versed in *Plutarch's Lives*. *What? Who's Plutarch? Did he live more than once?* They could also speak Latin and French like natives—or so it seemed to me—whereas I was master of not much more than rote multiplication tables.

Jane soon noticed my displaced-person demeanour and she adopted me. And even at only 13 years old, I recognized how lucky I was to have such a protector. Moving cautiously in the safety of her wake, I slowly adjusted to the trauma of living away from home, and actually turned out to be good boarding school material. I perked up and calmed down. I caught up in schoolwork and joined the choir. I became accustomed to the indignities intrinsic to communal life. I resigned myself to playing lacrosse and rounders and cricket in the rain and snow and sleet. I loved the gray, stodgy food; chronic hunger meant that everything was delicious. I even acquired the surgical skills of boning a kipper and decapitating a soft-boiled egg.

In fact, as far as I soon became concerned, life was fine.

Thalia Oldham completed our Heathfield triad, and was another of my bridesmaids. She had a wide animated smile and an inborn spirituality that portended an unworldly future. But she did marry—a clergyman, interestingly—and has two grown children. She was enormous fun and down-to-earth, and it intrigued me to see in someone my own age such maturity and depth of religious conviction.

England was still suffering all manner of wartime hardship, including stringent food rationing. And having never wanted for anything material myself, I was spellbound to hear of Commander Oldham's bringing to his family three naval oranges and a hand of green bananas while on leave during World War II. *Oranges and bananas in short supply?* I'd never imagined such a thing.

Thalia also told of a trip up to London with her mother one weekend to do some window-shopping. Jackson's of Piccadilly— the epicurean's shop to end them all—displayed a single giant purple Spanish onion, brilliantly floodlit in the middle of the window. No blush-pink mango or toothsome pastry or pungent cheese; only the humble onion—alone, cheap, and raw. And the silent understatement seared its way deep into my little world of thoughtless abundance.

As was tradition in 1954, when we left Heathfield, our names and those of all our classmates were carved for posterity on the back of chapel pews. I expect they've run out of pew space by now, but "Jane Fairey," "Lane Middleton," and "Thalia Oldham" appear side-by-side, in bas relief, in the front row of the choir section where Thalia and I sat in the alto section. Jane didn't sing—Jane *couldn't* sing—but even so, the powers-that-be decided the three of us should be memorialized together.

Thalia and I gradually lost touch but met up again at last two months ago, at the funeral of Jane's husband Vivien. Thalia has aged well, with nary a wrinkle or a gray hair that I could see.

"And her clothes still fit like loose covers," Jane added, with her rich throaty chuckle. "Some things never change, do they?"

Dinah MacFadden, an American, was my third bridesmaid. Her father Bob, a saturnine, uncommunicative man, worked with the London branch of the Manufacturer's Hanover Trust Company, and was my parents' banker. According to Daddy—in a moment of rare non-charity—Dinah's mother Emily was "shamble-footed." Like her mother, Dinah was pigeon-toed and very tall, but she was fairly presentable in a cardboard sort of way, except first thing in the morning.

Hoarse and sneezing, eyes still mostly shut, barefoot and clad only in her Marks & Spencer shorty nightdress—which exposed long unshapely legs always covered with mysterious bruises—she would make her unsteady way downstairs to the kitchen for a cup of coffee. Each of her prematurely hammertoes was wrapped carefully around with lamb's wool. Jumbo curlers were anchored under a stretchy net tied in a lopsided bow on top of her head. A crooked cigarette drooped from dry livid lips. And endless wads of damp Kleenex left a Hansel and Gretel trail all over the house—evidence of rampant year-round allergies.

Dinah was a thoughtful friend, and her generosity to my children was way above and far beyond. But she was blind and deaf to social innuendo—as was borne out, for example, by the very peculiar behaviour she adopted while briefly employed by Revlon. She began wearing a faddish meat-coloured lipstick and painted each of her 10 fingernails a different shade of varnish. When I asked her why she did this strange thing, she said she considered it her professional responsibility to advertise, on her person, as many of her company's products as possible, all at the same time.

Her idea of sexy simpering while on a date was to discuss the latest edition of London's *Financial Times*. I even once overheard her asking her dinner partner to explain to her the Sherman Antitrust Laws. The man did attempt to clarify the nuances of that abstruse legislation but became so engaged with his own pontification that he never noticed when she disappeared to the ladies' room. He was still talking animatedly to himself when she came back 20 minutes later and sat down.

By way of casual greeting, she would often slap strong men on the back, causing their knees to buckle. And at dances, usually without warning or invitation, she would drag her escort of the evening onto the floor, where she'd make him do the Twist or the Charleston till he dropped. I could go on and on. But what we all enjoyed most about Dinah was the way she frequently mixed her metaphors to truly hilarious effect.

"I *refuse* to put all my eggs on one horse!" she declared passionately at supper one evening, thumping the table so furiously that our wine glasses jumped and spilled. I don't remember the culprit issue—probably real estate or the stock market or something equally unpredictable—but her mangled indignation brought the house down, and I'm sure our raucous reaction could be heard in the next county.

Early one spring, one of our mother cats was delivered of four variegated kittens. Dinah, who happened to be spending the weekend, adopted the one female of the litter and named her Mole. Several weeks later—after the kittens were weaned—Dinah came back to Essex to collect Mole, and they returned to London on the Monday morning commuter train, Mole in her shiny new blue cat carrier.

Late that Sunday night, as usual just before locking up, I tossed all the cats out onto the terrace, shut the kitchen door behind them, and turned off the stoop light. There instantly erupted a loud accusing yowl. I quickly switched the light back on and peered anxiously after them as they trotted off in all directions. Everyone seemed fine, though, so I continued on up to bed. A few days later, the telephone rang.

"Lane, I just wanted to let you know," Dinah's basso profundo voice announced sourly at the other end with no preamble, "that while Mole and I were watching the television just now, she got up during the commercial break to go have a snack. And left her tail behind. Right here. On the sofa next to me."

I laughed shamelessly. Dinah hung up.

Assuming that Mole now looked like a Manx, I was perplexed the next time they came to visit to see that her tail appeared still to be of quite ordinary length. I didn't tell Dinah I thought she'd been making a storm in a teacup over Mole's tail of woe. But I did conclude that when I put the cats out that night several Sundays before, the back door must have caught Mole's tail at a vertebra near the tip, which subsequently atrophied and then fell neatly away. Onto Dinah's sofa. Mole was a long-haired tortoiseshell, whose luxuriant fur completely concealed the slightly foreshortened appendage. So unless you actually stroked her tail—with the customary sweep that anticipates a smoothly tapered end—you didn't notice anything was amiss. Or, I should say, missing.

There is no accounting for what becomes stored in permanent memory. With utmost clarity, I can still "feel" my hand resting lightly on Daddy's arm as we walked with measured step up the aisle of the Grosvenor Chapel on the day of my wedding. Wanting to acknowledge this symbolic moment of separation, I smiled through my veil a pledge of eternal devotion and was shocked to see that he was fighting back tears. Too callow to fathom their source, I did sense they were unrelated to a father's ordinary sentimentality over his baby girl's growing up, and a melancholy presence accompanied us to the altar.

Years later, after I was divorced, Daddy attempted to explain the unhappiness he'd been feeling as he led me to my groom. "Francis was certainly a nice enough sort," he began, "but I also thought he was, well, fey. And aimless and ungrounded."

And he admitted he was worried about me, too. As much as he loved me, he couldn't deny I was still very immature and prone to angry impatience, and he doubted Francis and I would learn to tolerate our differences before hurling slings and arrows of elemental animosity at each other.

My parents believed in dealing with personal problems quietly in private, and I expect Barbara and Jack Kinsman subscribed to the same general philosophy. Totsy even claimed to have been the model parent.

"I've always done my best, and the angels could do no more," she stated with challenging finality. She wasn't bragging. She was merely going on record that she had met her own goals.

So having never witnessed anything but a sort of staged harmony between our respective parents, much less any real acrimony, Francis and I entered our own marriage trusting we'd follow suit. And I'm sure he felt just as disillusioned as I did when the insidious bickering that finally disabled our relationship got off to a portentous start the very morning after our wedding.

We were standing outside the Hyde Park Hotel, where we spent our week's honeymoon. And whatever the bone of contention, it has long since fled my mind. But what I do remember is that as our quarreling grew barbed and bitter, the haze of recent celebrations was rudely replaced with the stark stare of reality. And as we glared and fumed at each other about what must surely have been a relatively trifling matter, I could see in Francis' eyes the same visceral misgivings that I knew must be reflected in mine.

Was it the finality of the wedding itself that exposed the perilous odds against us? I think we'd both convinced ourselves that our well-suited senses of humour would defend us against life's little trials. But there on the sidewalk of Park Lane that beautiful Sunday morning, midnight struck and the fairy tale was over. Yesterday's vows shrilled in my ears—*for better or for worse*—deafening me with a despair that made me feel ill. I was angry and frightened and bewildered. Neither of us had given much thought to the future—*so long as you both shall live*—and we were certainly not equipped to make promises that included eternity.

How could "worse" be happening already? Doesn't being in love mean feeling giddy with excitement? I like him a lot, and he's so sweet and so smart. But I don't feel over the moon about anything at all. And I don't think he does, either. He just thinks I'm funny, and he likes the idea of having an American wife. How could we have been so stupid? Why did we pretend it would be enough if we liked the same jokes? Spoke the same language? Knew the same people? Oh, God, what have we got ourselves into? We haven't a clue what we're doing. This is all wrong. This is all so terrifyingly wrong.

As my rose-coloured spectacles crashed to the pavement, I squinted past the sunlight into Francis' face as I looked at him—*really* looked at him—for the first time. Of course, I recognised his features but not what lay beyond. And in spite of having never been permitted even the narrowest view of the uncertain reality that develops between two people who try to spend their lives together, I knew my own resources weren't equal to that vast no-man's land.

Very few couples of our generation came together with any real life experience—in those days, people seldom tested the waters by living together before being married—but most managed eventually to build enduring partnerships. The strife between Francis and me, on the other hand, was far more complicated and fundamental than the emotional bumbling of two well-meaning innocents. And while there's no point in cataloging how and where we went wrong, suffice it to say that the tension of ordinary give-and-take finally grew into insurmountable aversion.

Looking back, I'm surprised we managed to hang on as long as we did. I was 21 and Francis nearly 25 that mild August morning in 1959—mere babes in the woods. And we were already well on our way to trampling each other's dreams while we waited to grow up.

Our first address was 14 Laxford House, Ebury Street, London, SW1 *[part of the Duke of Westminster's estate]*, and I'm sure Daddy pulled a string or two. It was a flat not much larger than a doll's house, and the monthly rent was £8. In those days, I was still reflexively converting pounds to dollars and, at $2.80 to the pound, I was staggered to find that our monthly rent was an extortionate $22.40. Talk about babes in the woods.

My parents sent for most of the furniture they'd left in storage when they moved to England and turned it over to us. They had also, since our arrival in 1950, been accumulating for me an old-fashioned dowry: crystal stemware and two sets of English bone china from Thomas Goode on South Audley Street; hand-embroidered and monogrammed Irish table linen from the White House on Bond Street; monogrammed sheets and pink bowknot towels from Fortnum & Mason in Piccadilly; and heavy sterling flatware by Walter Willson of King Street, St. James. Totsy confessed to having made a "significant personal sacrifice" by not trading with me her own American Pointed Antique for the infinitely superior Charles II Trefid. And since the thought actually crossed her mind, it's still a mystery to me that she didn't "persuade" me to swap.

Barbara and Jack Kinsman gave us a bed and a pair of blankets.

Only a handful of my parents' American friends made the trip to England for the wedding, but others sent cheques. These were channeled, with Totsy's artful nudging, toward the purchase of a few very pretty inessentials, most of which we bought from Hofsass Antiques on the Brompton Road. At our first visit, we pounced on a mahogany cheese coaster on revolving casters; a satinwood tea caddy with its own crystal mixing bowl; and a knife box with its original innards and an inlaid ivory rosette on the lid. A week or so later, Mr. Hofsass called to say he thought we should drop by and have a look at a new shipment. Again allowing no grass to grow under our feet, we bought a bow-front dressing table with an oval shaving mirror and a round piano stool bench; two chests-of-drawers; and a bergère library chair with dark green velvet cushions.

Somewhere on his wanderings along the King's Road, Daddy found a painted Italian console table that he thought would be ideal for our narrow entrance hall. And the last of the wedding present money was put toward an Adam-style gilt mirror and matching sconces, to be made for us by Mr. Thomas of East London, the "Chippendale of the '50s."

We were well set up, with more "mod cons" than anyone else we knew—anyone else our age, that is. The already-cramped bathroom at Laxford House came equipped with a Calor gas contraption that produced miserly amounts of hot water, but we managed to squeeze a Hotpoint clothes washer into the corner at the end of the tub. In 1950s England, automatic washing machines were as scarce as television sets. As a freshman housewife, I knew no better at first than to wash a load of Francis' socks and shorts along with my pillarbox-red Van Raalte nylon pyjamas. The black socks remained blackish, but Francis wore flamingo-coloured undershorts for years.

We even had a refrigerator. It was barely 30" high, to be sure, but this was when most English households still stored perishable food in larders; marble slab shelves and screen domes helped keep things cool and free from flying insects. Food was eaten before it could spoil. Nothing, absolutely nothing, was wasted.

⁓

When I became pregnant with Blake in the early spring if 1960, I availed myself of the then excellent services of the now questionable

English National Health Service, and when I became due, I was admitted to a seven-bed maternity ward at The Westminster Hospital in London. It was England's largest teaching hospital, and my obstetrician, Mr. Briant Evans, held a position on the Queen's own panel of physicians. Interestingly, in England, when a doctor attains the superior rank of surgeon, his title reverts, paradoxically, to Mister.

In those days, the NHS permitted the inexperienced new mother to stay in hospital with her baby for 10 days, compliments of the state—certainly an indulgence compared with today's out-after-24-hours routine. It provided the perfect opportunity for the hospital staff to help mother and child become acquainted and to give lessons in bathing, changing, and feeding.

Trite to say but true, these supposedly inherent skills do not necessarily come readily to the first-time mother. But by the third day, I felt I was beginning to get the hang of things. At lunchtime as usual, the babies were brought to us from the nursery in their bassinets-on-wheels—pink or blue, depending—and we all sprang from our beds to gather up our progeny, impatient to practice changing their nappies and to nurse them as best we could.

Blake was asleep. It seemed such a pity to disturb him, but I longed to hold him. First I turned him carefully onto his back and tucked his shawl more securely around him. Then I twirled a lock of his hair—lots of straight, vigourous Middleton hair that didn't want to lie down smoothly. Finally, I picked him up and arranged him close against me. As I said, I'd already found this part to be surprisingly tricky, but suddenly we both seemed to know exactly what we were doing. Completely hypnotized, I watched as the power of instinct engaged at last.

Continuing to study him as I would a rare jewel, I was thrilled to see that the faint pressure mark between his eyebrows had already faded. At his birth, the midwife assured me that the minor imperfection would disappear in about six weeks, so this was stupendous progress. I always knew my baby would be precocious. And then there were his ears. They were beyond adorable, neat and shell-like and soft as peach fuzz. It vaguely occurred to me they were perhaps not quite as close to his head as I remembered from earlier that morning at breakfast, but then I concluded that the nature of ears was probably to extend a bit after their owner emerged from the cocoon he'd been living in for nine months.

Blake looked at me steadily—out of focus, of course, only I didn't know that at the time—and he treated me to the newborn's mirthless smile. I smiled back, with lots of mirth. I held him against my shoulder and patted him softly. He obliged with a hiccup. I shifted him into the cradle of my other arm and carefully drew a tiny hand from inside the shawl. I kissed his alabaster fingers. He was my own and my heart spoke to me. I murmured my love and put him back in his cot.

Then, with great ceremony, one of the nurses' aides handed me Blake.

"Wha'? The *wrong* baby?" I shouted. It took me a moment to absorb what she was saying. "What do you *mean* I've nursed the wrong baby?"

I looked down sharply at the new infant now squirming in my lap. This one was fretful and restless. This one was definitely hungry. *Hungry? How could this child possibly be hungry?* My brain was turning over very slowly. But there between his brows was the same old pressure mark. And these ears were positively streamlined. By God, I *had* nursed the wrong baby!

With that, there exploded among my fellow "guests" much undignified glee. My head swam with the undertones of what was fast becoming a farce, and the staff rushed around trying to determine what had gone wrong. The precautionary measure of footprinting babies before they left the delivery room was not yet in place in England, and thus still wide open was the potential for changelings to become new branches of old family trees.

Meanwhile, the matron-in-charge attempted to subdue the uproar by explaining to us that the first little lad's mother was off somewhere in a room by herself, wrestling with severe postpartum depression. There was apparently real concern that if the unfortunate woman got wind of the fact that someone else—an *alien*, no less—had fed her son and heir, she'd go round the bend completely, possibly never to return.

Nothing daunted, I proceeded to give Blakie a generous luncheon. And on the strength of that not inconsiderable accomplishment, I was cordially invited to join the hospital milk bank. For six shillings a pint.

Only moments after Blake's birth, the midwife reappeared at my side, holding a small tray.

"Do you fancy a nice cup of tea, Mrs. Kinsman?" she inquired, pushing my hair away from my face with her free hand. "Or perhaps you'd prefer a Guinness?"

My expression must have reflected a certain inner conflict— *Jeepers! That sounds divine! But why would they be offering me a beer at a time like this?*—for the woman smiled broadly.

"Oh, it's quite all right, mum," she hastened to explain. "You see, Guinness is chock full of Vitamin B and is ever so wholesome for the lactating mother."

Of course, I chose the Guinness, and slurped down the heavenly lukewarm, honey-coloured foam rising over the rim of the tankard. A real pewter tankard. In a *hospital*.

Only in England.

Book X
East, West? Home's Best!

If anybody had ever suggested to Daddy that 42 Society Street might one day fetch $334,000, he would have rolled his eyes heavenward and summarily dismissed the idea. "Tsk, pshaw," he would have said. "That's absurd!"

In fact, it *did* bring that handsome amount when Totsy sold it in 1987, the year after he died. And if he'd still been with us only three years ago—when the property again went on the market and promptly sold for a cool $1.5 million—I suspect he'd have fainted dead away. In 1961, he bought it for the then-outrageous sum of $35,000.

Fanny recently told me of the following contemporaneous events, to which I've added a few bits of relevant historical background:

The eastern half of the lower peninsula, originally the walled city of the 1600s, has always been regarded as Charleston's prime real estate. So Totsy had naturally assumed that when they retired, she and Daddy would be looking for something in that area—at any rate, somewhere south of Broad Street, which was the northern boundary of Charles Town in the 17th century. To that end, they'd even made a trip back home in the mid-1950s, when two fine properties on Meeting Street—Russell House and Geer House—came on the market. But somehow neither managed to be exactly what Totsy had in mind.

When they finally returned for good, their temporary base while house-hunting downtown, was Bill and Sarah Prioleau's beach house on the Isle of Palms. One afternoon, Daddy drove into Charleston to visit the offices of Historic Charleston Foundation—a recently formed eleemosynary organisation whose enlightened mission was to rehabilitate degraded areas of the city by means of a revolutionary concept known as a revolving fund. He met with his old friend Frances Edmunds, founder and director of the Foundation, and asked about the organisation's becoming primary custodian of the city's internationally acclaimed architectural heritage.

Though one would reasonably assume that Totsy was equally interested in this avant garde but laudable business, she actually stayed at home that day—for reasons unknown—and then had to live with the life-changing consequences of letting Daddy go off like that without a chaperone.

Anyway, in businesslike and apparently irresistible terms, Mrs. Edmunds outlined the principle of the revolving fund. Using private donations, she explained, the Foundation would acquire a rundown property and undertake its basic restoration. The property would then be offered to any qualified buyer who agreed to the restrictive covenants imposed by the Board of Architectural Review. The proceeds would in turn be directed toward the acquisition of another property in that same borough—or village, as some of the areas are designated—and thus, in the fullness of time, entire districts would be "brought back."

Mrs. Edmunds managed skillfully to steer the conversation toward the matter of Ansonborough—the oldest residential area of Charleston, and the first project to be tackled by the Foundation. Ansonborough had indeed become a slum, she allowed, but if Daddy and Totsy took up residence there, her implied guarantee was that lots of their friends would follow. All that was needed, Frances said, for the once smart palmetto-lined streets to achieve renewed prestige was for someone—"a Middleton, say"—to take the first entrepreneurial step. Such a person's being willing actually to *live* in Ansonborough, she promised, was bound to attract a great deal of favourable attention.

Frances Edmunds was already famous for being "able to pluck money for [her] foundation out of thin air," and by the end of her meeting with Daddy, she had bamboozled him into buying an altogether unexceptional "single" house—one with two main rooms on each of three floors—at 42 Society Street. Softened up by all the flattery, he made the impulsive decision to help spearhead the local chapter of this nascent national enterprise. And without a single moment's consultation with Totsy beforehand, he signed on the dotted line. Right then and there. His decision would soon come to be seen as a gesture of fundamental consequence to the Foundation. But the unilateral nature of that decision also carried with it some fairly serious domestic consequence.

"In Totsy's opinion," Fanny told me years later, "there was nothing—repeat *nothing!*—in Ansonborough that could *possibly* suit her. Do you remember those two wonderful houses on Meeting Street? The ones she wasn't willing to even think about? Well, you can imagine there was a good deal of tension in the air while she digested the fact that Blake really had actually *bought* that awful little property way up there in *Ansonborough!* Lord have mercy!"

In time, Totsy pulled herself together and did a complete volte face. She realised her best defense against being perceived as living on the wrong side of the tracks was to become a champion of historic preservation. So she adopted the old if-you-can't-beat-'em-join-'em tactic and, before long, her newly stoked enthusiasm furthered the Foundation's cause even more than had Daddy's initial grand salute.

She joined the Board of Trustees. She organized a sale of furniture and bric-à-brac. People everywhere were attracted by the flurry of activity on behalf of their cherished dilapidated City, and many of them eagerly contributed long-forgotten treasures foraged from attics and closets. The sale was a great success, fetching sufficient funds to buy outright from the Metropolitan Museum of Art an enchanting small portrait of Alicia Russell by Edward Savage.

And Totsy persuaded Daddy to allow the best of their own 18th century English furniture to be copied by the Historic Charleston Reproductions Program, a branch of the Foundation which was to become an extremely lucrative source of revenue.

In short, Totsy threw herself energetically into every aspect of this cause célèbre, becoming in the process one of the Foundation's most vocal and productive proponents and benefactors. But she never forgot the former blow to her pride. And 25 years later—within a year of Daddy's death in 1986—she sold 42 Society Street and moved to 5 Legaré Street, into one of four newly converted condominiums overlooking Charleston Harbour.

Legaré is south of Broad. But I expect you've already figured that out.

The portrait of Alicia Russell—the one the Foundation bought from the Metropolitan with the proceeds of Totsy's rummage sale—now hangs in the music room of Russell House, formerly the headquarters of the Historic Charleston Foundation.

Alicia was the elder daughter of Nathaniel Russell, Charleston's "Merchant Prince." Prodigiously rich from the shipping trade, Russell hired European craftsmen and artisans to build the Federal-style house at 51 Meeting Street, which he furnished with 18th century English masterpieces. The beautiful house was completed in 1800, and is best known today for its breathtaking, free-flying elliptical staircase.

The following little graph illustrates my father's descent from Arthur Middleton, the Signer and his brother Thomas Middleton. Daddy retired when he was 60 years old, and he delighted in telling

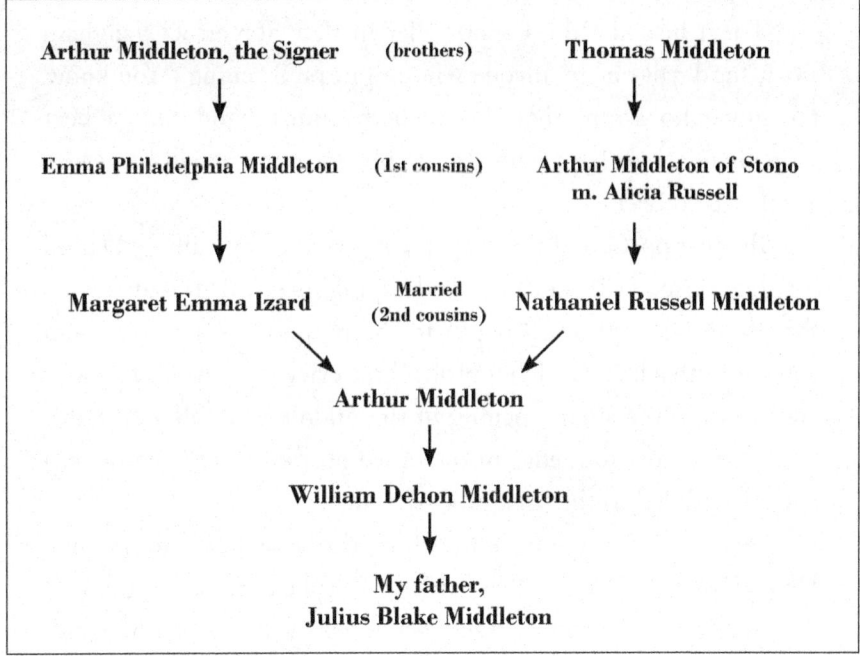

people that he was "now in the springtime of [his] senility." As things turned out, though, he really shouldn't have stopped working at such an early age. He had assumed his next-younger brother, Will, would fold up his tent soon, too, and that the pair of them would live out their days on the boat, fishing. But my Uncle Will didn't stop putting in a daily appearance at his office until he was almost 90. So, bereft of a playmate, Daddy's natural inclination to solitude entrenched.

He fanatically cosseted his small round lawn. Like a vigilante, he hunted down impudent weeds and killed them swiftly. And I can visualise him still, when the heat index was well over 100°, laboriously pushing the temperamental old hand-mower in ever-decreasing circles over the thick, cushiony Charleston grass. He'd sweat profusely, and after an hour or so of pure drudgery, he'd start cussing under his breath.

"I feel just like the Comptroller in that Somerset Maugham story," he'd call out to anyone who might be listening. "You know, the guy who swore that if somebody didn't hand him a beer immediately, he'd have a fit." Invariably, someone would hand him a can of cold beer.

The rear portion of the property was artificially built up behind a 3'-high brick wall—a clever landscaping mechanism that created the illusion of additional depth to the property as a whole—and covered with a layer of rich topsoil. Three brick steps from the lower lawn led up to a small opening in the middle of a tall yew hedge that grew at the front edge of the raised portion. And from there, a narrow path led to the back property line.

Thus, discreetly out of sight behind the hedge, this area became Daddy's perfect little kitchen garden where he spent a great deal of time tending a few choice vegetables as well as the ginger lilies and pale pink shrub roses that Totsy used in her flower arrangements. He always picked the courgettes and tomatoes and French beans while they were still young and tender. And to his most favoured lady-friends, he would occasionally present two or three prize bib lettuces—with damp earth still attached to the roots—usually at around lunchtime, when the cook had already cleaned up the kitchen and was about to go home.

If it was too hot to stay outside for any length of time, Daddy would hibernate in his sitting room on the third floor—his "country" he called it—where he chain-smoked unfiltered Marlboro cigarettes and devoured the love poems of John Donne. Otherwise, you'd probably find him on the downstairs piazza, drinking coffee and working crossword puzzles by the score and watching squirrels run back and forth along the telephone wires. It fascinated him that pigeons sitting in the squirrels' path would lift off the wire just long enough to let the varmints scurry underneath them and then drop back down again until the next lot began their tightrope aerobatics.

My father's one true hobby at this point was working macramé fishing nets and belts and watch straps for friends and grandchildren. Totsy was appalled when she went up to take him his coffee one morning to discover that he'd driven dozens of small nails into the top of his Edwardian kneehole desk.

"But I have to tether the string like that," was his simple explanation. "It's the only way I can yank on it hard enough to make sure the knots are good and tight."

For Totsy and Betty Bonner, he tied those elaborate knots into slim, envelope-shaped evening purses—barely big enough to hold a house key, a handkerchief, and a pair of folding reading glasses. The two little bags were works of art. And their owners showed them off and talked about the "brilliant man who made them" until he blushed.

"Tsk, pshaw."

<hr />

Betty Bonner is a widow from Missouri and a very good friend of my parents. My mother particularly admired the way Betty would tantalise the local gossips by hinting at having had several husbands before moving to Charleston but never revealing just how many.

"It's simply amazing," Totsy would exclaim, "that Betty's managed all these years to keep her private life private!"

She must have been a knockout as a young woman—she actually confided to Totsy that she'd been a Chesterfield Girl in the 1920s—because even today, though she's well into her 90s, you find yourself wanting to stare at her. Remarkably, too, her hair is still mostly a natural auburn. If you can get near enough to look closely without being too obvious about it, you can spot silver strands flecked through the Titian-red chignon and the flat curls arranged in little swirls over her forehead.

"But that just proves it's natural," Totsy would patiently inform you. "You see, it's like a good mink coat. If there are still a few white hairs scattered throughout the pelts, you know it's never been dyed."

Betty is also an accomplished amateur sculptress and has often said her best work is a bust of my father. It's an almost heart-wrenching likeness; you sense strongly that it was shaped and molded by someone who knew him well and loved him. After its completion in 1978, it was cast in bronze in the kiln at the College of Charleston. And now, from the top of Ma's writing desk in front of a window in my drawing room, Daddy's pleasantly aging face looks on whenever anyone comes to call.

Of course, the bust is alive only in my heart, but I often feel smiled upon. And I love the way the shaggy metal brow still shades the eyes that were once so blue.

I remarked earlier that 42 Society Street was unexceptional, by which I meant that the house was built no earlier than 1840, that it has no notable ironwork, and that the fireplaces and crown moulding are plain and unadorned. So frankly, aside from its museum quality interior furnishings, the only feature worth mentioning was the garden. It was one of the many Charleston gardens designed by Loutrel Briggs, the renowned New York landscape architect of the 1950s and '60s.

At his direction, there emerged from a rabbit warren of scrub and neglect at 42 Society a lush but formal little oasis that could be glimpsed from the sidewalk through wide, wrought-iron gates.

Immediately on entering, you'd feel at least 10° cooler; the shrubbery was a dense green all year round and seemed somehow to mitigate the brutal summer heat. And depending on the season, there'd be the unmistakable scent in the air of ginger lilies or jasmine or tea olive.

The only other flowers Briggs permitted were lacy crêpe myrtles and banks of big, floppy white azaleas. And should you dare question such sweeping restrictions to your own property, his dismissive explanation—arrogantly challenging your personal taste—instantly silenced you.

"I agree they're fragrant, but magnolias are too messy. They shed constantly. And gardenias aren't dependable, either. They smell like heaven on earth, but they turn brown too easily and then they look awful. Anyway, flowers don't count. Form is all that matters."

The drive and terrace were paved with English brick *[in this context English defines dimension, not origin]*, and separating 42 Society from the property nextdoor was a shoulder-high openwork brick wall. A tall espalier of cherry laurel was trimmed neat and flat against the wall, and beyond the drive was Briggs' hallmark circular lawn, manicured to the nth degree and edged with chamfered dwarf boxwood.

The Board of Architectural Review gave permission for the house to be painted the palest of pale lavender and the shutters the ubiquitous "Charleston green"—a dark shade produced by mixing black with just enough green to prevent its looking like pitch. Lightweight, charcoal-gray aluminium garden furniture formed convivial groups along the piazza, and broad steps lined with potted cherry laurels led down to the terrace. When the air wasn't too humid and buzzing alive with mosquitoes, this was where my parents held their candlelit summer cocktail parties.

At the end of one such evening in 1969, Daddy waved goodbye to the last guests pulling out of the driveway and closed and locked the heavy gates. Together he and I walked back up the steps to the piazza. And leaning side-by-side against the railing, I watched out of the corner of my eye as he lit a cigarette and looked over the trees and rooftops, out into the star-filled night sky. Inhaling deeply, he held his breath for a moment and then blew an impressive series of rings at the full moon.

"I really do know those guys went up there," he mused aloud, shaking his head slightly and blinking past the smoke rings at the great yellow orb, "but I don't believe it." He flicked cigarette ash onto the grass below. "Dammit, I just don't believe it."

Smiling at me, he turned to open the screen door and followed me into the house. The man in the moon smiled back.

⁂

Of the myriad family photographs now in my possession, one of my mother deserves honourable mention. I have also inherited a provocatively unconventional watercolour portrait of her. Taken together, you wonder, as you squint first at one and then at the other, *Surely that's not the same person? Can't be.*

The black-and-white photograph is, in fact, of both my parents fishing in 1946, on Lake Charles, Louisiana. In her early 40s at the time, Totsy is standing in the mud holding a sporty string of fish in one hand and a spool of fishing line in the other. She's wearing ungainly boots, a disreputable ill-fitting jacket, a faded hat with a crooked brim, and an all-American smile. Among the first to benefit from modern orthodontics, she'd gone to New York in 1921, to live with her maternal grandmother while her teeth were being straightened.

The sloppy fishing togs, incidentally, weren't at all characteristic. With an unerring eye for what best became her, my mother had crafted her own "look" at an early age—learning deftly to tie a scarf, drape a stole, pinch a curl, tweak a French beret—and she gained the lifelong reputation, wherever she was, of best-dressed and most soignée woman in town.

The watercolour is by a sardonic Scot named Harry Moore Gordon, who was lured several times to Charleston during the 1980s by numerous natives who liked to think of themselves as the local élite. The best way I know to describe this eccentric artist's typical work is as skillful caricatures. He was a gifted student of human nature, his insight usually being revealed none-too-subtly in gorgeously grotesque parodies of his subjects.

His portrait of my mother in no way resembles the unkempt young woman photographed in a Louisiana bayou with mud on her shoes and curly hair flattened by a shapeless cloth hat. Here instead is the socialite extraordinaire—still the coquette, but now a fully realised, shamefully pampered woman—surrounded by the paraphernalia of a chic existence she considers her birthright.

Lounging on a cream-coloured damask sofa, Totsy is drawing through her fingers a jewel-tone diaphanous silk scarf, allowing it to cascade onto the long skirt of her apple-green gauzy gown. Her hair—her glory of short, silver-white ringlets—frames her face in an oval halo, and her embroidered golden shoes and ivory-and-gold jewelry are represented in the most faithful detail.

Then, by strangely uncomfortable contrast, the painter decides to give us a minimalist backdrop—depicting as few as possible of the exquisite furnishings actually surrounding her—so that nothing detracts from the dramatic, slightly sinister perfection of the seductress on the sofa.

Sometime in 1955, while my parents were still living in London, Daddy began toying with the notion of having Totsy sit for Pietro

Annigoni. Then a little-known Italian portraitist, Annigoni's style was reminiscent of his Renaissance predecessors', the subject generally dominating a ground of quiet landscape and classical architectural elements. But before Daddy could make up his mind, Annigoni's beautiful oil portrait of Queen Elizabeth II was unveiled. It had been commissioned a year earlier by the Worshipful Company of Fishmongers, a group of uninspiring reputation who were now—amidst great fanfare and fêting—suddenly the astonished owners of one of the world's most famous works of art.

The portrait literally transfixes one's gaze. Instead of the downs of the Westcountry, the life-sized masterpiece places the new English queen alone among bare trees under a wintry Italian sky. Standing small within a blue velvet cloak that hangs heavy from her narrow shoulders—and armed only with the Regalia of the Order of the Garter—she looks calmly into the face of her ancient destiny. You pray God will grant her faith and fortitude against whatever may lie ahead. You want to wish this second Young Elizabeth well, with all your heart.

Now the undisputed Court painter, around whom the international art world was turning somersaults, Annigoni became overnight well beyond the reach of the general public. This meant that Daddy's dithering cost him the chance to have Totsy tactfully immortalized by a great modern master. And the consolation prize, which turned out to be anything but consoling, was Moore Gordon's disturbing watercolour. Unlike his Italian counterpart, the dour Scot did not indulge in flattery. He crafted a ruthless vérité that put one in mind of Oscar Wilde's *Picture of Dorian Gray*.

Book XI
The Sun Never Sets on the British Empire

Francis and I lived at Laxford House for three-and-a-half years, until April of 1963. Then quite out of the blue—when Blake was just over two and Emmeline barely a year old—a cousin of my father asked Francis if he'd be interested in managing a jute mill in East Pakistan *[now Bangladesh]*.

Moving to South Asia wasn't exactly on Francis' projected career path, but with barely a second thought, we began making plans for what became a memorable but short-lived adventure. Life in the primitive Bengali village of Narayanganj proved more of a challenge than we coddled westerners were prepared for, and we returned to England three weeks after John was born in September of the following year.

While we were abroad, most of our London friends had moved their expanding families to East Anglia, within reasonable commuting distance of Liverpool Street Station. With three children of our own now in tow, we decided to join the trend. Furthermore, instead of going back to Lloyds, Francis joined a Middle Eastern commodities conglomerate, with a branch in the City. So everything about this new beginning was indeed brand new.

But before I get too far ahead of myself, I must fill you in with a little background information. Daddy's first cousin Buck Brown and his wife Ethelind were from Belton, South Carolina. Buck was born with only one arm, but mustering the ingenuity so often possessed by the handicapped, he was almost totally self-sufficient. The only personal skill that remained forever beyond his reach—so to speak—was how to make a Windsor knot in his necktie, but for this Mr. Speights, his black manservant, came to the rescue whenever necessary.

It was Speights, too, who kept Buck's deluxe mahogany yacht *Sea Hawk* shipshape, and who cooked for the lavish cruises the Browns hosted for the Middleton brothers and their wives; Buck was a gourmet of the first order, and Speights an able apprentice. Captain and first mate have both long since gone to their great reward, but *Sea Hawk* today rests somewhere deep in the bowels of *U.S.S. Yorktown*, where it is being preserved as an outstanding example of its now obsolete class. *[The World War II aircraft carrier is itself anchored at Patriot's Point on the Cooper River in Charleston Harbour, and serves both as a memorial to American naval aviation and home to the United States Medal of Honor Museum.]*

Buck's company, Pakistan Fabric International, was one of numerous jute mills in East Pakistan that produced bagging for the American cotton industry. Traditionally overseen by Scots, the manufacture of jute was at its height during the British Raj, when the Empire was at its most global and glorious. But after Partition in 1947, and the end of British rule, the mills were no longer all managed exclusively from Dundee.

Buck's nephew, Carroll Hart, had been his lieutenant in Narayanganj for several years, but Carroll and his wife Jimsie were now expecting their second baby, and were soon to return to the South Carolina headquarters. Buck planned to retire at that point, but he wanted to establish another family member in the foreign end of the business before relinquishing upper management to Carroll; hence his unexpected offer to Francis. I don't specifically remember Francis' reaction, but I was wholeheartedly in favour of our becoming latterday colonials, and envisioned myself "doing good works and making a difference."

Easily tempted away, we gave up our London flat in April of 1963, and set out in opposite directions—Francis to Narayangang, to take over from the Harts and to settle himself before we joined him; and Blake and Emmeline and I to Charleston, where we spent the next two months in an apartment across the street from my parents.

We left America at the end of June. The children slept through most of our journey of more than 9,000 miles over nearly 36 hours, but even so, I was as worn out when we arrived as if we'd circumnavigated the globe. Francis met us at the airport outside Dacca *[the capital of East Pakistan]*, and drove us in a decrepit automobile that coughed and backfired for 16 miles down a narrow, bumpy road that dead-ended at the edge of a muddy river.

There we boarded what Francis laughingly referred to as the "company launch." Indescribably dirty and dull and chipped and unpainted, it reminded me of the *African Queen*. I settled Emmeline and her blue teddy bear on my lap, pulled Blake over close to us, and sniffed a derisive sniff.

Slowly the boat putt-putted half a mile across the sluggish water to the other side. I picked up my little daughter, and held her tightly in one arm as I climbed out onto the sagging boardwalk leading to the mill property. Francis swung Blake out of the boat, and then hoisted himself up and set off toward the house, a suitcase in each hand. Blake stood uncertainly, looking back at the river and then at me. I shifted Emmeline onto my other hip and followed Blake's solemn gaze.

Oh Lord, this can't be it! My spirits sagged. *This can't be Narayanganj!* The air was dense and still and dank. *This is even hotter than Charleston! I didn't think any place in the world was hotter than*

Charleston! My forehead and neck were clammy. *I've got to get my hair up off my neck and away from my face. I can't stand this. I'm going to have to grow it into a pony tail. How long will that take?* My shirt stuck to my back. *What are we going to wear every day? What are we going to do? This is impossible! This is just plain unbelievable!*

Our new home was a disastrously poor village that lay on a bend in the Sitalakhya River, a tributary of the sacred Brahmaputra. The boardwalk stopped at a pebble-lined path, at the end of which was a low iron gate—swinging nearly off its hinges—into our private compound. On top of each of the gate's supporting columns crouched a straggly gray vulture, noisily flapping gigantic scrofulous wings, and leering evilly down at us. These hideous scavengers had been eyeing their luncheon—carrion and decaying vegetation in noxious piles all over the ground—and they seemed sorely vexed by the interruption.

With this disgusting welcome, my grandiose fantasies of becoming Lady Bountiful faded out of sight, and overwhelming doubts assailed me as to the wisdom of this little foray into the unknown. Buck had never lived on the Indian subcontinent as pater familias, nor himself fallen victim to any of the indigenous diseases whenever he traveled there. So he couldn't be blamed for not forewarning us. But we'd obviously bitten off much more than we could have been expected to chew. Only the most limited of medical facilities were available. There were frequent and dangerous riots. There was more than a reasonable quota of deadly snakes. And most significant of all, Blake was fast approaching kindergarten age, and there wasn't a school of any kind, anywhere, for over 100 miles.

As I picked my way through the noisome garbage littered about at my feet, I lodged an indelible mental note that we would be hightailing it back to England the very minute our two-year contract expired.

Buck did, in fact, go to considerable lengths to do right by us. Aside from those factors over which he had no control, he saw to it that everything we really needed was "found," so Francis managed to salt away most of his salary. We were even offered air-conditioning, but we declined. It was carefully explained to us that such a system would be effective only if the house were hermetically sealed, which meant we would suffocate any time the newfangled electricity went on the blink. Which turned out to be every couple of days.

The summer heat was stupefying, especially—inexplicably—after dark. During a power failure, the huge punkah ceiling fans would creak to a halt and, within minutes, the bed linen would become drenched with sweat. In desperation, I often whiled the night away in a cool bath, looking out into the heavy black-velvet night until the fans started whirring again. Gecko lizards were always pacing about upside down on the ceiling—they had handy little suction-pad feet—and we couldn't figure out how they managed—when they dropped—never to fall among the fans' blades.

With Buck's carte blanche, Totsy and I had bought a lot of household equipment—mainly from the old Kerrison store on King Street in Charleston—to be shipped to us at PakFab. Totsy also chose several garden party hats for me, "against invitations to the Governor's Mansion." She assumed our overseas jaunt would be an updated version of the early days, in Sumatra, of their own marriage, when they "frequently went to important parties," and she wanted me to be suitably garbed for such formal occasions.

But she needn't have bothered; the Governor's Mansion was nowhere near Narayanganj. I kept one of the hats anyway, for auld lang syne. I even wore it to a wedding later in England, but people stared at me as if I were in fancy dress and it's been hidden away ever since. If my children ever happen upon it—with its wide, moss-green velvet brim strewn with limp, peach-coloured organza roses—they'll think I stole it from the Queen Mother.

At Buck's suggestion, we also sent ourselves a General Electric freezer. He said he wanted me to have proper storage for the copious amounts of ice cream I'd be making to refresh us "on those enervating sultry afternoons," and he suggested I use ripe mangoes and buffalo milk as the basics. I knew Buck was a connoisseur of good food, but *buffalo milk?* This struck me as grasping at very short culinary straws.

The freezer arrived several months in advance of our other belongings, and the mill's head electrician—a tall, bearded man named Jalal Addin—installed it in an enclosed portion of the back veranda. The advent of electricity was only quite recent in the forgotten villages of East Bengal, and the multi-coloured wires were themselves considered objects of great beauty. So rather than follow the established western practice of chasing them into the wall, they were left in full view to be admired by all as they traced their way from ceiling to outlet to switch to appliance.

I was summoned when the electrical work was done and duly presented myself. Jalal Ad-din greeted me and inclined his head politely toward the double switchplate next to the door where I stood. Aside from the freezer, the room was empty. I flipped the switch nearest me, and the freezer's engine came to life with a quiet hum.

"Thank you, Jalal Addin," I said, "this is really wonderful. But what's the other switch for?"

Beaming, Jalal Ad-din glanced over at his rainbow spaghetti of electrical wires, and respectfully placed his palms together beneath his chin.

"For show, Mem Sahib," he said, bowing low and smiling modestly. "For show."

The company also paid for our furnishings to be shipped from England, but the gesture backfired. The cumbersome plywood crates eventually arrived after several weeks' wait on an open dock in Chittagong during the rainy season. With mounting excitement, we watched from our jetty as they were punted across the river— each precariously straddling a kisti, the local flat-bottom boat—and I can still remember the rancid odour that stung my nostrils as the tops were prised off, exposing the contents to the air.

Our anticipation turned to abject dismay. Everything we owned was ruined, soaked beyond repair. Loose covers disintegrated at folds and seams. Veneer peeled away from sodden furniture like the skin off a banana. Books were reduced to puffs of dust. I cried for hours. Surprisingly unmoved by the parlous state of affairs, Francis pointed out that I was mourning "things." I kept blubbing.

Our large one-storey house faced the river and presented a striking approach from a boat. In sharp contrast with its squalid makeshift surroundings, the building stood plain and handsome, with thick walls, spacious rooms, and high ceilings. But from a distance, it was the full-length screened veranda, accentuated by five wide arches, that caught the eye. Simplicity of design emphasised its imposing dimensions, and the bleached stucco shone white in the blistering sun. Off the veranda—which housed huge tubs of pastel hibiscus, as well as wicker garden furniture and a double-wide Pawley's Island rope hammock—were the five large main rooms, each about 20' by 20'. Along the back of the house were the bathrooms, the storage rooms, and a portion of unscreened porch, with steps that led down to the lawn.

In that climate, all the vegetation seemed to grow while you sat back and watched. Soon after we arrived, I had the malis *[gardeners]* plant along the waterfront a row of 6"-high seedlings, 18" apart. I don't know their botanical origin, but they had small shiny leaves, and white velvety blossoms with a nosegay fragrance. And in less than a year, they had become a hedge so tall and profuse that I couldn't see over it or through it.

Separating us from the mill property on one side was a high wall hidden by tangled bougainvillaea. Another sweet-smelling flowering hedge provided privacy on the opposite boundary. The children's bedroom was shaded by a giant Bombay mango tree that shared a symbiotic relationship with wild cypripedium orchids. They say there are as many varieties of mango as there are apple— the Bombay usually ranking number one—and the neighbouring coolie children usually made off with most of ours the minute the fruit was ripe. Once, when we did manage to beat them to it, I tried making Buck's ice cream with a hand churn that was among my supplies from Kerrison's. But as I suspected, the combined textures of buffalo milk and mango pulp coated the inside of your mouth with a layer of what felt like puréed chalk.

As usual in those parts, the cookhouse was separate from the living quarters—at the back of the property—and could only be described as a dark, fearsome shack, hopelessly infested with God-knows-what vermin. So I ordered a new kitchen—one that I could more or less keep my eye on—to be built in one of the empty rooms at the back of the main house. The result was rudimentary at best, but at least rats and cockroaches the size of Volkswagens didn't race for cover when you turned on the light in the middle of the night.

Francis and I took our meals on the riverside veranda and, at lunchtime, Blake and Emmeline ate at individual child-size wicker tables set opposite matching chairs on the path at the foot of the veranda steps. The universally accepted practice was never to sit in the shade of a tree lest a snake drop from the branches into your lap. The only cobra we ever saw belonged to one of the mill workers, who kept it in a basket and occasionally played to it on his atonal pipe; the snake would puff up obligingly and sway about as they are expected to do.

But the Krait variety of reptile was an undeniably real and extremely present danger. The Pakistanis called it the "one-step" snake. In the 1960s, there was no known antivenin, and if bitten, you would succumb, permanently, in frighteningly short order. Worse yet—being short, thin, and brown—the Krait was treacherously inconspicuous. And in a never-ending attempt to prevent such trespassers' moving about unnoticed, the malis kept the grass around the house clipped as close as a putting green and the shrubbery branches trimmed bare for at least 12" up from the ground.

To this day, I wonder why we didn't keep a mongoose. I've always heard mongooses give snakes a really good run for their money.

<hr/>

In her exquisite partially autobiographical work, *Two Under the Indian Sun*, author Rumer Godden wrote of life in India at the turn of the 20th century, as if through the eyes of an English child. Her father worked for the Inland Navigation Company, and in early 1911, he and his wife took their two small daughters to northeast India. The area became known as East Pakistan after Partition in 1947, and eventually as Bangladesh in 1971.

The girls were sent back to England the following year to live with their grandmother and four maiden aunts, who presumably would see to their proper education. But with rumblings in the distance of what would become the Great War, the children were soon returned to India, where Rumer lived on and off for the rest of her life.

The Godden's house was directly across the Sitalakhya River from ours, whose distinctive Moorish architecture she describes in *Two*. The river was about a half-mile wide at that point in its meanderings and evidently occupied a prominent place among Godden's childhood memories. It was fascinating to compare photographs taken after we arrived in 1963 of the same stretch of water that had come alive under her pen decades earlier. As if time had stood stock still, the images from 1915 were nearly identical, the latter showing no sign of influence—or "progress"—from the outside world for nearly 50 years.

⁓✴︎⁓

One unexpected luxury during our time in Narayangang was having our beds made twice a day—in the morning and again after the midday nap—each time with two freshly laundered sheets. I've never experienced such domestic extravagance anywhere else, before or since. Shuffling groggily onto the veranda after one such afternoon repose, I noticed that the usual clutch of coolies at the river's edge seemed especially engrossed in the goings on up at "Sahib's house." Mouths agape, they were staring at the screen door at the top of the steps leading from the lawn up to the veranda.

I continued along, yawning and trying to wake up, until I reached the door. There outside on the top step, flicking his glistening black tongue at me, stood a 5'-long iridescent iguana. His countenance was friendly—he appeared even to be smiling—but I shrieked all the same and fled back into the house. The commotion alerted the malis, who gave furious chase to the hapless animal, who in turn probably fed most of the village that evening. East Indians consider iguana a great delicacy.

As the resident English family, we never went hungry, but our meals would have been lamentably uninspired were it not for Josef, my Hindu-cum-Christian cook. Before joining PakFab, he had worked for a Greek river-steamer family upstream from us, from whom he learnt to make, among other things, the wonderful ethnic lemon-rice soup and a hot lemon soufflé that fell on the tongue like a cloud of citrus zest.

Josef's proud specialty were fresh spices, which he would painstakingly grind and present for my approval—arranged artistically in bright little heaps on a platter—before adding them to a sauce. His tastiest supper dish was poached bechti—a flaky, white river fish resembling Atlantic cod—and he could do wonders with rangy chickens the size of Cornish hens.

We often had delicious fluffy omelets made with eggs hardly bigger than marbles, and there was that one unforgettable evening when Josef served us curried goat. Or rather, more accurately, *stringy* curried goat. As far as I was concerned, no amount of curry could camouflage the gamey aftertaste, and though Josef assured us he'd properly pounded and marinaded the meat, I felt I was chewing on old boot laces.

It was prudent to soak fresh produce from the market in potassium permanganate; untreated, it would almost certainly make us ill. But the purple hue was repulsive, so we ate only vegetables grown in our own garden. The available fruit—mangoes, pomegranates, and dwarf pineapples—was heavenly. Breakfast always consisted of coffee and toast, and a whole mini-pineapple each, pared spiral-fashion to remove the eyes, sliced crosswise and sprinkled with honey and lime, and re-assembled with its spiky leaves adorning the top.

Remarkably imaginative and creative, Josef consistently made the best of minimal resources, and I remember him with tremendous respect and admiration.

Further complicating an already-fraught set of circumstances was the fact that our household included Hindu, Muslim, *and* Christian faithfuls—the Christian element being converts from the Hindu. Coexistence was dodgy at best, but during the religious squabbles which were constantly fomenting, the Muslims would automatically regard any Christian as being still Hindu, and therefore as still their age-old enemy.

Partition, the goriest of these insurrections, was in 1947, when it was said that the Ganges ran red with the blood of the massacred. This historic upheaval resulted in the withdrawal of longtime British rule, as well as in secession by the predominantly Muslim eastern and western regions of the Indian subcontinent, from the countless central Hindu population. For a generation thereafter, the two new far-flung nations of East Pakistan and West Pakistan, separated by nearly 1,500 miles, savaged each other in a no-holds-barred struggle for autonomy. And at last, in 1971, the new state of Bangladesh emerged from the ravaged battlefield of East Pakistan.

One phase of this restless political evolution flared while we were there, in early 1964. It seemed that a relic hair of some minor prophet had been misplaced. And though such carelessness seems hardly to justify fullscale war, simple logic is seldom a primary factor in mass decision-making. As a disincentive to their mutual annihilation, we housed our multi-denominational staff in our guest quarters, and for several anxious weeks, everyone expected the house and mill property to be stormed at any moment. More than once a bloated corpse on its way downstream became snagged against our dock, and Francis or David Gamble *[the mill overseer]* would have to stomach the horror of prodding it off to continue on its watery way. We were ourselves in great peril, a fact which became even more apparent in retrospect. But I think anyone would agree we acquitted ourselves with an adequate showing of the requisite British phlegm.

Traditionally, European newcomers could expect to inherit from their predecessors a corps of servants—cook, vegetable scraper, gardeners, boatmen, bearer, nursemaid, sweeper and laundress—all of whom they would promptly dispatch to the local English doctor to be vetted for parasites. And for anything else that might represent a threat to their number of days on Earth.

What we didn't know in trying to follow this custom was that the average Pakistani dreaded a parasite purge far more than an actual bout of infestation. So, to avoid the temporary indisposition, they would attempt to acquire bacteria-free samples—boldly so-advertised in select sidewalk shops, at black market prices—to be submitted to the doctor for analysis. This way they could return to work with satisfactory reports and no odious regimen to follow. And continue to be silently contagious to everyone else in the house.

But sometimes such preemptive substitutes would be either unavailable or too expensive and, once at the doctor's office, the patient would have no alternative but to produce a sample of his own. And more often than not in such cases, the bloodwork would reveal serious or even life-threatening maladies for which the fatalistic victim would flatly refuse treatment.

It was this version that presented itself when we were there. Those so afflicted with amoebic dysentery, tuberculosis, syphilis, or leprosy were therefore let go without appeal, but not, alas, before I managed to contract amoebic dysentery, probably from the ayah *[nursemaid]*. When we later returned to England, I was informed by the Hospital for Tropical Diseases in London that the amoeba is too wily ever to be isolated and permanently expelled from its ill-fated host. So, to reduce the likelihood of future flare-ups, they advised me to avoid living in a tropical climate again. Of course, South Carolina isn't considered the tropics per se, but the heat and humidity here are certainly on a par with India's, and my old nemesis still occasionally rears its hateful head.

Needless to say we all survived, but chaos infused every crisis. Francis fell ill at one point, with severe and unrelenting stomach ache, and tells of his hair-raising trip into Dacca to visit Dr. James Bassett, the local English medical practitioner. We had wondered a bit about Bassett. There was no question he was competent, but there was a "dark horse" air about him. We concluded he'd decided to work where he could avoid scrutiny by the British Medical Registry yet still pursue, to his heart's content, his passionate interest in tropical medicine and skin diseases. For this, East Pakistan had no equal.

But I digress. Halfway into town, Francis was horrified to find himself in the midst of a student riot, a favourite national pastime. And he was certain that but for his manifest extremis, his car would have been tipped into the river, leaving him either quickly to drown or be strangled by water weeds. On finally arriving at Dacca Mission Hospital—bent double with pain and hardly able to crawl up the steps—he offered himself to the mercy of the Almighty when the Emergency Room technicians correctly diagnosed kidney stones, and then briskly ordered X rays—of his leg.

As luck would have it, at about the time Francis was scrabbling up those hospital steps, I was winging my way to Charleston; our contract with PakFab entitled us to two weeks' leave every six months. My flight on Pakistan International Airways went well, with no untoward delays anywhere—Tehran, Hamburg, Paris, London, Shannon, Gander, or the usual dreary milk-run down the eastern seaboard.

Totsy and Daddy met me, and we drove straight to 42 Society Street. Pregnant with John and wilted from the heat, I was relieved to be back on terra firma. All I wanted was a short word with Jackson—my parents' yellow tabby cat—and a long nap. First, though, as Daddy unloaded the car, I retrieved the stack of mail from the letterbasket hanging on the inside of the piazza street door. On top was a telegram addressed to me.

How can that be? I wondered, my heart starting to thump. *I've only just arrived.* With trembling fingers I tore it open, and scanned its incomprehensible contents:

DETAINED DACCA MISSION HOSPITAL STOP
SUSPECTED KIDNEY STONES STOP
DON'T WORRY STOP FRANCIS STOP

I read it again, this time more slowly. Still unable to take it in, I handed it to Daddy. Without a word, he picked up my bags and put them back into the car. I swallowed a Coke while he called the airlines and booked me on the next plane, and the three of us drove in shocked silence back to the airport.

In spite of Francis' saying I needn't worry, it never entered my mind to stay the remainder of my leave in Charleston, and Totsy and Daddy concurred entirely. We had heard far too many accounts of Pakistani servants' doping their young charges with opium when the parents were away. And with Francis in hospital indefinitely and unable to monitor activities on the homefront, I had visions of Blake and Emmeline as angelic little zombies with dilated pupils tottering irrevocably toward the perdition of addiction.

I felt like a zombie myself when I stepped onto our jetty late the next day. But the children were in good fettle, and about an hour later, Francis arrived in a taxi—tired and gray but holding his own.

I should clarify that the principle behind drugging toddlers was not to corrupt them but to keep everything on an even keel. Generally speaking, the average Pakistani is an indulgent, patient parent and caregiver, including—or joining—their offspring in almost every activity. And, as if children themselves, our own employees played with Blake and Emmeline at the least excuse.

I can still see Blake at not quite four years old sitting next to Faisel *[one of the malis]* on the steps off the back porch. Each was hunched over a colouring book, Faisel every bit as intent as Blake, who watched with approval as his friend drew stubby crayons over the page.

"Try and keep inside the lines," Blake advised tactfully. "Like this. See?" Faisel spoke only Urdu but he understood Blake perfectly.

As the insufferable heat bore in on us after the new year, I often sought relief in the hammock that swung in the shadows on the riverside veranda. I'd lie there for hours on end, often dozing to the drone of the heavy monsoon rain. I was expecting John in September and my increasingly unwieldy frame was eased by the air suspended around me.

Or I might work on a piece of needlepoint to cover the little ebony Victorian nursing chair that Totsy had given me just before my wedding. One of her more brilliant finds at the Caledonian Market, it was still set on its original ivory casters, and the ormolu bead trim had remained securely tacked along the low-contoured outer scroll frame. These small chairs were designed with ergonomics in mind. Seated barely six inches from the ground, a person automatically acquires a deep lap in which comfortably to cradle a nursing baby. The rusty-rose velvet upholstering was now cobweb-thin, however, and about to fall apart, and Totsy had suggested I might enjoy making a needlepoint replacement for it one day.

So, before leaving for East Pakistan, I took the chair to the Royal School of Needlework, where I pored over dozens of designs and finally settled on a repeat pattern of minuscule yellow-and-white roses on a terra cotta ground, each spray within its own stylized, black fleur-de-lys. After selecting the necessary palette of single-ply wool, I asked if someone there at the Royal School could complete one cluster for me before I started so that I might be confident of having an accurate sample to follow.

The soothing, rather monotonous project occupied most of my pregnancy, and when at last, I initialed and dated the finished canvas, I commemorated the new person that my own person was quietly assembling inside itself. Each creation—the baby and the needlework—took nine months to complete. I was thrilled with both.

John was born on September 28, 1964, at the Roman Catholic Mission Hospital in Dacca. At nearly 10 pounds, he was a fine figure of a baby. And when he was just three weeks old, we packed up and left for England. The rest of us had often been ill during our time away, and I was determined that no unwashed Pakistani hand should touch my new baby and compromise his sturdy constitution. Compared with his little comrades in the hospital nursery, he looked like Hercules.

Ben and Bridget Fisher *[Blake's godparents]* met us at Heathrow—which was, as usual, under a lovely cold wet drizzle—and drove us into London, where we stayed for several days with them at their flat in Eccleston Square. I'd forgotten how beautiful the gray English sky is. I'd forgotten that English rain is the softest rain in the world.

My mother's well-developed haggling instinct was in its element at the Caledonian Market, and she soundly beat the vendor at his own game the day she found the nursing chair. Walking away with her new treasure, she congratulated herself for having parted with the princely sum of only £5.

Daddy came home from work that afternoon as usual at about six o'clock. Totsy put down her book when she heard his key turn in the lock, and got up to greet him with a kiss and a Scotch and soda. Returning her kiss, Daddy suddenly spied over her shoulder the decorative little chair that had been placed just inside the front door.

"Good Lord, Tot, are you trying to tell me something?" he asked as he stepped back abruptly, his eyes wide in feigned alarm. Totsy blushed prettily, and they both laughed. It was the sweetest moment.

Book XII
Jerusalem

In April of 1965, about six months after returning to England, we bought a small house on not quite an acre of land in Great Maplestead, in Essex. Home to barely 50 souls, the unspoilt East Anglia hamlet provided all the essentials to life in an English village: a pub, a 14th century flint church, a one-room schoolhouse, and a country store with a countertop that doubled as a Post Office. And some of the most beautiful countryside on Earth.

Known in ancient times as Much Maplestead, the village is still intersected by only two thoroughfares—Lucking and Church streets—which even today are traveled scarcely more than when they were narrow earthen paths. Great Maplestead is in the heart of Constable country, so called after John Constable, whose 18th century pastoral landscapes are characterized by the slow hills and small fields of the Essex-Suffolk border. By drystone walls and cut-and-laid hedgerows. By England's green and pleasant land.

Little Maplestead, an even smaller village—up the hill and past a stream—is famous for its round Norman church. The unorthodox ecclesiastical design was an architectural phenomenon conceived by the Knights Templar and is found elsewhere in Britain only in Cambridge, Edinburgh and London.

The Knights were a religious military order that emerged from the First Crusade, and in deference to the revolutionary concept of democracy, they sat in a circle as they worshiped. Claiming the

Church as their authority, they skirted the anti-usury laws with impunity, amassing untold wealth which they distributed solely among themselves, and are generally credited with establishing the basis of the modern banking system. Their corporate purpose was ostensibly to offer protection to pilgrims en route from Europe to Jerusalem but, following the unscrupulous example of their Crusader predecessors, these warrior clerics in fact committed abominable crimes in their pursuit of money and power—all, of course, in the name of God.

The Mossings was the name given centuries ago to our circa-1540 house. Picturesque and very old—even by English standards—it had low ceilings and exposed beams, and lath-and-plaster outer walls that had been faced with brick sometime in the late 17th century. Now worn to a soft salmon colour, the brick exactly matches the Elizabeth of Glamis standard roses—named after the Queen Mother—that grow inside the low street wall. Punctuating the roofline are dormer windows with simple pargeting under the eaves. And the overall trim is white, except for the front door, which I painted the famous Charleston green.

We conjectured that The Mossings started life as a row of four contiguous labourers' cottages—each "one-up-one-down"—that had served the village squire's house nextdoor. George and Evelyn Newton were the latterday squire and his wife. And their house—an unlovely Victorian structure on the original site from the Middle Ages—was in the midst of a great tract of agricultural and dairy farmland, which George and his sons and their forebears had worked for countless generations.

I stocked up every week on their free range eggs with brown shells and orange double yolks—and Jersey cream so dense that you had to dig it from the carton with a spoon. I am more proud of my "Newton" ice cream than anything else that has ever come out of my kitchen.

A year or so after we moved to Great Maplestead, Evelyn Newton decided it was time to modernize her kitchen. Soon, with no drawings or blueprints as guidelines, her husband and three sons began ripping up the floor, under which they found a well-preserved Roman mosaic of a playing fountain. The American in me was totally nonplussed; the occupying Roman army left Britain around 400 A.D. But Roman artifacts are constantly turning up all over East Anglia—the oldest recorded part of Britain—and the locals were typically blasé.

A few such objects find their way to the museum in Colchester, but more often, remains of historic interest are "scheduled." That is, while left undisturbed, the precise location of such a site is recorded for future reference. I already knew Colchester was the first Roman capital of Britain, but I was interested to learn through this extraordinary experience that the word *Colchester* means "Cole's Castle"—*chester* being the Roman word for *castle*—and is a reference to Old King Cole of the Merry Old Soul nursery rhyme.

The Newton's kitchen floor was relegated to the "scheduled" category. "It's survived fifteen hundred years," the authorities told them, "so if you cover it up again properly, there's no reason to think it won't do nicely another fifteen hundred."

Mrs. Newton chose smart black-and-white Marley tiles to replace the old floorboards, and I expect she's forgotten all about the Roman art under her Aga cooker as she moves about her bright new kitchen, baking her sponge cakes and sorting those wonderful eggs.

The Aga cooker originated in Sweden. Made of enameled cast iron that never chips, these stoves now come in bold modern colours. Each of the several ovens and hotplates maintains its own specific, constant heat. And being connected through the wall to the central duct system, the system produces hot water and warmth for the whole house, whether cottage or mansion.

You sometimes see Agas advertised, for small fortunes, in culinary catalogues. They've been the mainstay of English households for generations; my friend Jane in Hampshire has one that's been going strong since 1936. But, in spite of being the most multipurpose, failsafe and dependable appliance of its kind anywhere, the Aga has never really caught on in the United States. Probably because they never wear out. The American consumer likes consuming things that are new.

⁂

My son Blake is buried at St. Giles Church in Great Maplestead, his grave high on a hill crowned with Lombardi poplars. He can look down from that hill and see The Mossings, and the "fallen-down" apple tree that bloomed and fruited heavily every year, even after a storm blew it over one winter. The tree's bowers formed a flowery, umbrella-like cave where he and Emmeline and John loved to play with our cats, three of whom were Jewish.

This bit of whimsy—affecting a Hebrew lineage for them—evolved after we named the first one Mazaltov. I'll never know how I could have got it so wrong, but I was somehow under the impression that there was a furrier in New York named Mr. Mazaltov. And that he was Jewish. Our kitten was ermine-white from nose to tail, and before the fur-salesman mix-up was ever sorted out, the Kinsman Jewish cat syndrome had taken on a life of its own.

Mazaltov spent most of her life sitting Sphinx-like on the fence alongside our nextdoor farmer's pit across the street, endlessly waiting for a mouse to venture out. Evidently hope sprang eternal that if she remained perfectly immobile—notwithstanding her vibrantly Persil-white coat—the mice wouldn't notice her and would amble in droves across her path, just waiting to be caught. We doubted she had much success in this pursuit, however, for we never noticed any Rodentia remains anywhere. But she did manage to bag the occasional pheasant and ferret—creatures at least twice her size—whose intact carcasses she always left tidily in the middle of the mat outside the kitchen door.

She redeemed herself from her mousing inadequacies with prolific motherhood. Pregnant more often than not, her issue became permanently over-subscribed. Whenever she was known to be in kitten, there always formed a list of clamouring takers long before her due date. And like fawns whose spots disappear after infancy, all her kittens—invariably white, regardless of sire—were born with dark smudges on their heads, like tiny yarmulkes, that would fade away by the time they were fully grown.

Mazaltov somehow seemed more Emmeline's cat than anyone else's. And it's still irresistible, more than 30 years later, to tease Emmeline that this cat of hers was really rather dim. Even now, she'll rush to Mazaltov's defense the minute you recall how the nubile little flirt would stretch out attractively on the kitchen stoop, as if trying to figure out why all the local farm cats kept yodeling at her at the top of their lungs. Becoming even more ruffled when you remind her that Mazaltov's best mouse attack tactic was to remain absolutely motionless, Emmeline protests that you're missing the point.

"Such self-discipline," she argues strenuously, "surely implies a considerable intellect."

Jaffa was the next to join us. Because of his orange stripes, we named him after the exceptionally delicious eponymous citrus fruit that grows in the region around the ancient Israeli town. Blake rescued him from the vicar's coal shed one cold November 5th. Standing around the obligatory Guy Fawkes bonfire in the field next to the vicarage garden, the whole village heard plaintive meows coming from somewhere beyond the crowd, and Blake followed the scratchy little sound through the dark grounds until it led him to the shed. Huddled inside was the young vagrant—trembling and famished and covered with coal dust—who meekly allowed himself to be scooped up and tucked inside Blake's warm parka.

Jaffa proved to be a hippie sort of cat, grooming himself with never more than a lick and a promise, but an otherwise worthy father figure and rôle model. In time, he assumed the avuncular responsibility of corralling Mazaltov's kittens when they would wander off and restoring them to the bosom of their litter. He managed also to maintain a detached demeanour in spite of being surrounded by the rest of our menagerie—the motley occupants of the fish tank, the bird cage, and the gerbil palace—who were all housed in tantalising view but frustratingly beyond the itch of his magnificent predatory claws.

Then there came Moggie, a kingly gray tabby with dainty feet and a mezzo-soprano meow. In Cockney lingo, a *moggie* is a cat, so in the interests of uniformity, we decided there were probably lots of Jewish Cockneys. Moggie contracted feline enteritis one winter. The disease is almost always fatal, but on the vet's instructions I held him in my lap all night—while sitting on a cushion on the kitchen floor next to the boiler—and dosed him every hour or so with a mixture of warm milk, egg yolk and a few drops of Scotch whiskey. This I administered, amidst a lot of feeble spitting and flailing around, by forcing a nose dropper between his tiny little clenched teeth and rapidly squirting in some of the hot toddy. When the protests gathered strength, I gathered hope.

Our wonderful big cat rallied and lived to be 18. The Mossings' new owners, the Haylocks, have told us they loved him dearly—like a fixture, he conveyed with the house at the time of purchase—and that when he finally gave up the ghost, they buried him with all due solemnity at the orchard end of the garden wall. Mr. Haylock added that he was "so undone by the tragic turn of events," he couldn't make it to work that day.

Moggie personified feline laziness—he seemed to consider himself entitled to room service 24 hours a day, seven days a week— and though he was a mere mog with no pedigree, his extraordinary leonine beauty could have won him every blue ribbon at the show.

Possum was another in our herd of cats, though he never converted. He was solid black and glossy as glass. One afternoon, I took him to the vet for his annual checkup and inoculations. The vet, whose name I'm afraid I've forgotten, asked me to hold Possum's front end firmly while he aimed for the flank. I was glad to oblige but, as the needle reached its mark, the frightened animal bit me in the hand in the soft flesh at the base of the thumb, all the way through to the bone. Pandemonium reigned briefly, as blood spurted and fur flew everywhere. Possum hadn't really meant to bite me—he was just caught off guard, you might say—and in clear apology, he leant against me, burying his head in my arm.

The vet mopped up both of us and, after a good look at the gash in my hand, he said I should see my own doctor right away— something about "tetanus setting in" if I didn't get a booster. Feeling none too steady on my pins at this point, I gratefully accepted his offer to drive us down the hill to our GP's surgery, where he left us at the door to fend for ourselves. Clutching to my shoulder with my good hand the bristling, growling ball of fur and claws that was Possum—and struggling at the same time to keep in place the towel the vet had wrapped around my bleeding hand—I fought my way loudly into the waiting room. But before the receptionist had a chance to take my name, Dr. Peter Train appeared in the doorway. I imagine he wanted to see for himself what was causing all the kerfuffle.

"Well, Lane, what's all this? Aha! Hoist by your own petard, eh?" he laughed, correctly interpreting the scene before him. Completely ignoring my unlikely explanation, and without showing even the most token interest in *my* plight, he painstakingly unhooked the clinging Possum from my sweater.

"Poor old cat," he crooned softly. "Whatever have they been doing to you, my poor old boy?" Stroking him, he gently handed Possum to the startled woman behind the desk.

Dr. Train's sympathy for my cat obviously outweighed his concern over my own impending lockjaw. Still muttering about the hazards encountered by innocent animals at the hands of their heartless owners, he ushered me into an examining room and barely glanced at my wound as he shot Novocain into it. Then he pushed up my sleeve, rubbed my arm with alcohol, and jabbed it with anti-tetanus. Threading an exceedingly fine needle, he commanded me to hold still. Minutes later, all I had to show for the morning's misadventures were five neat stitches under a modest little bandage.

Finally—and endearingly beyond the call of professional duty—Dr. Train himself ferried Possum and me back up the hill to the vet's office where my car was parked, and was still slapping his thigh and cackling when he let us out and drove off.

Aside from trying to avoid squashing Possum, who flattened himself almost enough to fit under the accelerator, driving home was a breeze. No one really appreciated the nicer points of my story, though. As a matter of fact, I'm not even sure anyone believed me at all. But there is still a thin pale scar on the pad of my right thumb. And I still think Possum's vet and Peter Train are the ultimate in country doctors.

Book XIII
Two Nations Separated by a Common Language

Francis and I started divorce proceedings in August of 1976, and I returned to America. I'd lived in England since 1950, when I was 12 years old. Now 38 and single, with no marketable skills nor professional qualifications to my name, I was a dinosaur, and I needed to reinvent myself as quickly as possible. Rural Essex was impossibly distant from the mainstream so, thinking my parents' contacts might come in handy, I decided to try finding new bearings in Charleston.

For a long time after coming back, I was convinced I'd made the worst possible mistake. England had been my home for most of my life, and I now felt disenfranchised and dispossessed—and profoundly unsettled by the cultural differences I now encountered. George Bernard Shaw wasn't joking when he said we were two nations separated by a common language. I pined for my children and old friends with an ache that bordered on despair.

After several years of working first as hostess at the faculty-alumni club at the College of Charleston, then as docent *["unpaid teacher," according to Webster's Dictionary]* with Historic Charleston Foundation, and finally as salesgirl at an antiques store, a friend suggested I sign up as a "mature student" at the local technical college. It seemed not a bad idea—certainly I had nothing to lose—and I began brushing up on my typing and trying to learn my way around a computer. I'd been warned it wasn't easy to go back to school and was greatly relieved, after one semester, to be hired at entry level by the Legal Department of the Charleston County Government. There was a tremendous amount for me to learn. I'd never before had what I was now calling a "proper job"—and God knows I knew nothing about government, let alone the legal profession—but I was given generous leeway as I felt my way forward.

That was January of 1985, about 13 years ago. At last, in 1994, those elusive Charleston bearings hove into view, and my morale reached for the skies as I clung to the handful of women who helped me reenter a world I'd turned my back on since Blake's death. Nancy Bloodgood, Cookie Emery and Gayle Bustraan were then, respectively, Deputy County Attorney, Administrative Assistant, and Receptionist, all located in the suite comprising the County Administrator's Office and the Legal Department. They offered me a camaraderie that has enriched my life, and restored an equilibrium I'd forgotten I ever had.

When Nancy joined the department in 1991 and became my boss, her circumstances were not unlike my own of 15 years earlier, except that she was handling the tribulations of a collapsed marriage with more grace and fortitude than I had done. Cookie is one of the world's securest underpinnings. And Gayle comes from a big family that sings and plays poker together, and her natural good looks never fail to turn heads. I love them.

⬥

As I mentioned earlier, I was a docent for several years at the two museum houses then operated by Historic Charleston Foundation: Edmondston-Alston House on East Battery and Nathaniel Russell House on Meeting Street. I also trained briefly to be a Charleston City Guide, during which time I managed to make a complete fool of myself on more than one occasion.

The most memorable of these occurred late on a stifling August morning. As I was easing my tour bus away from the curb at the Visitor's Center, I reached for the microphone. Filled to capacity, this particular bus was bigger than any I'd driven before, and I prepared to give these nice folks "from off" a treat they wouldn't soon forget.

"A very good morning to you all," I said warmly into the microphone, turning to smile at everyone. "I'm so pleased to welcome you to Charleston." Dead silence. *Where's the ... what's happened to the sound?* I wondered.

"Testing, testing?" I tapped the top of the microphone as I spoke. Still nothing.

I tapped again, this time rather more firmly, and instinctively looked around again at the people sitting in the first row. Anticipating a well-informed tour of the historic peninsula, they were watching me politely, but each face also bore an expression of guarded amusement. Now thoroughly puzzled, I looked directly at the object clutched so firmly in my hand. My heart sank like a stone. I had been greeting my guests—in my most confident and authoritative manner—through the cordless cigarette lighter on the dashboard.

Another such incident took place at Russell House one year, during the annual Gala Evening sponsored by Historic Charleston Foundation. Those elegant, romantic parties were extremely well-attended. Guests arrived in evening dress. Candles were the only form of lighting throughout the house, lending soft drama. Fragrant, seasonal flowers were everywhere you turned. And the dining table beckoned with champagne and hor's d'oeuvres.

There were four docents on duty, strategically positioned throughout the house, each fluently conversant on local history, as well as the architecture of the house itself and the provenance of its exquisite furnishings. My specialty was the circular staircase and its supporting cantilever physics that gave the illusion of floating on air. I had researched the conundrum—how the stairs could be safe when there were no visible means of support—and knew how to explain it in simple terms.

My station, therefore, was the stairwell, which was central to the entrance hall, the study, and the dining room. When half a dozen or so people had gathered there, I welcomed them, encouraged a bit of small talk, and finally began my little lecture. With my hand on the newel post, I leant backward slightly in order to gesture upwards towards the third floor, and almost immediately became aware of a thick, strong, unfamiliar smell. At that instant, the two men in front of me reached to grab me and began beating at my head. My hair was on fire! When leaning backward a few seconds before—in the dimly lit room—I hadn't noticed a torchère floor lamp standing immediately behind the newel post I was holding. My hair had fallen on the small flame.

A few seconds later, it was all over. My back hair was fuzzy, my face was red, and my hands were shaking. But to all intents and purposes, I was fine. The real punchline came the next morning. I wasn't present, but I am told that when Frances Edmunds, Director of Historic Charleston Foundation, heard about the previous evening's little drama, she gasped in horror. "Oh, thank God the house is all right! Are we properly insured?"

The tour guide industry in the United States is generally taken very seriously, and such personnel are expected to provide information with flair if possible, but with accuracy at all costs. Yet, I have frequently been flabbergasted by the latitude some of the guides allow themselves—the following example being the undisputed champion.

Edmondston-Alston House handsomely illustrates American Greek Revival architecture. But even more than for its design, I would recommend visiting the house for the stunning view from the second-floor piazza of Charleston Harbor. On a clear day, you can see for miles, well beyond the confines of the various islands and old forts.

One afternoon, I paused with my group for a few minutes at the French doors leading onto that piazza. The previous docent was out there with her own guests, winding up her little Civil War history lesson, and we couldn't help overhearing her unforgettable pitch as she gestured out toward the middle of the harbour.

"Y'all see that island way out there?" she trilled. "Well, that's Fort Sumter. Y'all have heard of Fort Sumter, right? Well, anyway, it was Citadel cadets hangin' out there on the Fort that fired the first shots of The War of Northern Aggression at one of them Union ships tryin' to get into the Harbour."

Then, with a flourish, she pointed to Castle Pinckney, a smaller island closer to the Peninsula, where Federal prisoners of war had been incarcerated during The War. "And if y'all will come over here a little closer, you'll see that little island over yonder. That's Castle Pickaninny," she stated, with mind-boggling creativity. Several mouths fell open. "That's where we locked up them Yankee boys once we caught 'em."

I stared at her in disbelief as she sent her confounded guests on their way. "Well, so long," she said, smiling. "Hope y'all had a good time. Enjoy your stay in Charleston, y'hear? And hey, come on back and visit us again sometime, okay? The azaleas are real pretty in March and April."

Several years ago in October, my office girlfriends prevailed on me to go with them to the Coastal Carolina Fair in Ladson. I'd never before been attracted by the idea. Turnips and cows on steroids? But this was going to be different. There were going to be eight white Bengal tigers doing tricks, they told me. So, of course, I agreed to go.

It was a cool sunny day. There were hundreds of people, all wearing the most jaw-dropping clothes and tattoos and hairdos, all milling around and buying useless odds and ends. And like most of them, I ate enough pastries and barbequed ribs to sink the Bismarck.

We clambered onto the rickety bleachers around the tiger enclosure just in time for the last performance of the day, and in trotted the dazzling creatures, nuzzling their trainer's face and neck, and yawning. Visibly bored at being made to do anything more complicated than drop to the ground and roll onto their backs, they behaved like souped-up versions of their domestic cousins—only lazier.

The equally casual trainer managed to persuade three or four of them to climb onto absurdly small stools and then to walk around the ring, following each other like elephants at a circus. But all I could focus on were the muted stripes under the pale, buff-coloured coats, and their languidly blinking blue-green eyes. The tiger is surely one of nature's greatest inspirations. I've read somewhere that the Chinese character for the word *emperor* is taken from the pattern of stripes on the great cat's forehead.

When the show was over, the tigers padded back into their sizeable individual cages, hooked together like the cars of a train. Most of them promptly flopped down and tucked their enormous front paws under their chests, obviously expecting to be admired and cooed over. The safety barrier between the animals and the public was barely arm's length, and I found myself baby-talking to one fine fellow who particularly took my fancy. He looked back steadily at me, with what I interpreted as friendly curiosity.

"Wuz a sweet boy," I babbled, my eyes watering in wonder. I was almost nose to nose with this superb animal. "Wuz *such* a lovely boy … wiz zuh sweet face an' zuh beautiful blue eyes. An' zose stripes! An' I *love* zuh boy's pink nose! Wuz such a sweet, *lovely* boy!"

With that, he slowly unfolded his majestic self and stood up. He stretched. He stretched so hard, he quivered. Still looking at me, he seemed to sense the adoration behind my asinine driveling. Drowning in the blue-green sea of his completely expressionless eyes, I almost reached through the bars to touch him.

He then turned slowly away, I thought to settle down again. But he stopped—now facing away from me—and raised his tail. AND SPRAYED ME. All over. From head to toe. Lots of it. *Lots* of it. This was a huge tiger, you understand. And he reached his mark with the precision of a sharpshooter. I didn't move. My sunglasses were dripping. My shoes were squelching. There was a puddle in the gusset of my good leather handbag. And my friends were blotting me down with wads of paper napkins, laughing wildly.

"Hey, Lanie girl, you're his woman now!" Gayle yelled at me through the confusion. I felt myself grinning idiotically. *Oh boy, that cat really likes me!* I stood there, rooted to the spot, patting my damp jacket with smug satisfaction.

"Honestly, Mom," Emmeline's voice was pensive, and laden with envy when I telephoned her the next morning to tell her about my trip to the Fair. "You're terribly privileged. You're certainly the only person *I* know who's been pee'd on by a tiger. Did he say anything? Did he purr?"

Book XIV
The Stars Stopped Sparkling

The Holy Bible talks about immortality with persuasive simplicity but when Blake died all those years ago, the distilled message of the Scripture became fanciful and empty. He was my firstborn, and his short life seems, in retrospect, to have been a series of grim dress rehearsals for his premature death.

They began in late autumn 1966. We had returned to England two years earlier, when Blake was almost four years old. Standing one Saturday afternoon between his father and me on the High Street in Halstead, he was holding our hands and daydreaming as we waited for a break in the traffic before crossing over to the green grocer opposite. As I reconstruct the nightmare, I can only assume that something interrupted his reverie, because he suddenly broke loose from us and ran headlong into the path of a car coming down the hill. Car and child collided and Blake was thrown backward hard onto the street.

Staring at his motionless little form, I felt nothing. Unable to move—unable even to walk over to him—my mind locked instead around a hypothetical telegram to my parents. I phrased it and re-phrased it, focusing only on the pulse of the words drumming in my ears, knowing that whatever words I used—however I expressed it—they wouldn't, *couldn't*, believe that the child who was "too good to be true" had just been killed. My mother's own words of love and wonder were roiling in my brain, ecstatic words that seemed all at once to have become a curse.

"Puddin', I've never seen such a baby. Not even you or your brother!" she had said, as she gently lifted Blake out of my arms the first time they met.

He was 13 months old, and I'd brought him to Charleston to visit his grandparents. Totsy kissed him—she seemed to breathe him in as she stroked the back of his head, her nose buried in his silky hair—and then held him away from her to look at him again. He stretched his arms around her neck and kissed her chin.

"Oh, Darling," she smiled over at me, her eyes brimming, "he's perfectly beautiful. Doesn't he ever cry? This can't possibly last, you know. He's simply too good to be true!"

Now in Halstead, sitting on the curb with my feet in the street, I was wondering whether there were such things as children's coffins. Everyone around me appeared to be moving in slow motion, dragging. Sounds and voices echoed thin and surreal, as if I were in a vault. Perhaps I was dreaming. *Yes, that's it! I must be dreaming!*

Then Blake stirred and tried to get up and our rejoicing knew no bounds.

And that was the beginning of the end.

꧁꧂

In the summer of 1971, when Blake was 10 years old, he nearly drowned in a neighbor's swimming pool. He would indeed have drowned if I hadn't decided, exactly when I did, to get up from my lawn chair and stroll over to speak to John, who was paddling around in his water wings and asking when tea was going to be ready. I was about to jump in next to him when something farther away caught my eye and then gripped my attention. Blake was lying on his side at the bottom of the pool.

At first, I thought he was playing one of his underwater games, garbling as much of the alphabet as he could, for instance, before running out of breath. Then the hair on my neck rose as brain and skin fused in the science-fiction sensation that time had become compressed. Viscerally, I registered the incomprehensible facts that my child's eyes were closed, that his thick blonde hair was waving before him like seaweed, that his face was grayish-blue. All these ghastly, telltale details were crystal clear through nearly nine feet of water. Water that was almost as smooth as glass.

Oh, my God, my heart screamed, *how long has he been down there?* My thoughts scattered, incoherent, in all directions, and then jammed. With a sickening jolt, I realised Blake might already be dead. My ears rang as fear washed over me. *Oh, God—please! Please no! Help! Please somebody help, for God's sake!*

Blake's father and his godmother Dinah MacFadden were also in the pool. Although unable to see him from where they were treading water, they both plunged down in the general direction of my hysterical pointing. Dinah was nearly as tall as Francis and just as fit, yet every ounce of their combined strength was needed to bring Blake's dead weight to the surface. He'd stopped breathing. It was John Russell, our host, who saved his life with quick thinking and artificial respiration.

After the blessed cough that brought him back to us, Blake was himself completely untroubled by what had just happened, with no memory of having been in any kind of danger. I lay down next to him on the grass beside the pool, my arms around him, trying to warm him.

"What happened, Blakie? Can you remember what happened?" I asked over and over.

"I think I fell off my horse," he answered at last, his eyes still closed.

His horse? Blake didn't own a horse. He'd never even been astride a horse. But who cared that he was confused. He was alive!

⁂

At the time of the automobile accident in Halstead, Dr. Train said Blake had only a mild concussion, and it was all but forgotten—even when he nearly drowned in the Russell's pool—until the end of the 1973 Summer Term. By then he was 12 and had one more year at Maidwell Hall—a boys' preparatory school in Northamptonshire—before going on to Eton.

In England, boys who go to prep school usually leave home at about seven years old. But as Blake approached that still-heartbreakingly tender age, I became convinced he needed to stay in the nest a little longer, and I began protesting the anachronistic custom with every ploy known to motherhood.

No one would give me the time of day. England is a proudly patriarchal society, and I was invariably dismissed as having no standing where the education of an English child was under discussion. Even if that English child was mine.

"And after all, Lane, you're only the boy's mother," was the astounding rebuff used to silence me whenever I broached the subject. Then, in case I still didn't grasp the full extent of my irrelevance in these ritualistic matters, they would add that my being American automatically disqualified any opinion I might have in the area of childrearing.

"But don't worry. Coming from across the pond, you really can't expect to understand our system. It'll prevail, though. It always has," was the specious assurance they trotted out, as if surviving the English public school system were more essential to a little boy's future than being allowed a sane childhood.

Nothing was off limits, apparently, when it came to preserving this status symbol of upper-class privilege and expectation. But far from prevailing, the iniquitous system failed Blake utterly.

"You cannot drive a square peg into a round hole!" I would snarl at Francis, as together we watched our son falter and retreat further into himself.

"Oh, he'll get used to it. It'll give him character. You'll see," was his retort.

Blake did not get used to it and the schism between Francis and me soon became pernicious. By the time I grasped the futility of my quest for equal rights where our children were concerned, Blake was permanently damaged, and Francis and I were beyond the point of no return.

Even now, my memory of that summer of 1973 twists itself in a wide suffocating band around my chest. I drove up to Maidwell at the end of May for Sports Day. But before loading the car and heading home with Blake for the holidays, Headmaster Alec Porch gently took my arm and led me to a bench under a giant sequoia, where he had me sit next to him. Distracted by the unexpected gesture, I found myself concentrating on how incongruous it was to find primaeval North American redwoods in an English arboretum.

Unconsciously steeling myself, I turned to look at Alec. His eyes were unfathomably sad and seemed to be telling me I must find courage. Instantly afraid, I tried nevertheless to smile, to make it easier for him to say whatever was distressing him so terribly. I began to grow cold. Blake was a pleasant, friendly boy, and an average student. Whatever the problem, I knew it couldn't be about discipline or studies.

Alec swallowed. In words whose harsh reality jabbed at the air between us—words that seemed to be coming from somewhere in the distance—he described how several times lately, during games, Blake had fainted, with external symptoms ominously like those of epilepsy.

What? What did he say? I kept looking at Alec, wondering why it was suddenly so hard to breathe. *I feel ill. Nothing hurts, but I feel ill. What's happening? What's he talking about? Time's slowing down again ... the way it did that other time. What other time? I don't understand. I should find Blake and go home now.*

"I didn't call you and Francis before," Alec continued quietly, reaching for my hand as I tried to get to my feet, "because the term was already so nearly over, and we thought there'd be no harm in waiting till now…"—I could hear the unspoken end of his sentence—"so I could tell you in person."

As the summer wore on, our uneasy attempts to get to the root of this forbidding situation were for naught. We unearthed no family history of what we were told was usually an hereditary predisposition—nothing which might explain its being visited on a new generation. But preliminary X-rays showed old scar tissue at the back of Blake's brain and medical sleuthing included a review of the 1966 automobile accident in Halstead. With no other evidence or data available, the radiologists concluded that the scar was probably the result of that long-ago trauma and that the subsequent near-drowning in the Russell's pool was the onset of the vicious attacks that were to menace the rest of his life.

Dormant until Blake's early adolescence, the scar had now become the active site of what is known as focal epilepsy—a form of the disease that is harder to treat than most—and the grand mal seizures became increasingly incapacitating. Invariably exhausted after each episode, he would prattle gibberish for a few minutes, and then, following a long deep sleep, remember nothing.

By the time the conventional medication Dilantin became ineffective, its common side-effect had already added cruelly to his misery by thickening his gums and ruining his classical regular features. Blake's whole life became distorted, although I never once heard him question the hopeless hand he'd been dealt.

I returned to live in America in August of 1976, soon after Francis and I were divorced. Blake was now attending Oakham School for Boys in Leicestershire. He'd started at Eton two years earlier, for no other reason than it was written in stone that any son of ours would go to that bastion of English superiority.

In fact, on the off-chance he did turn out to be a boy, we put him down for Charles Impey's house several months before he was even born. An old school chum of Francis's, Charles was now a housemaster there, and although Blake wouldn't be needing a place for another 13 years, Francis didn't want to risk Impey's not being able to take him.

But the sedative effect of the epilepsy medication made it difficult for Blake to keep to any kind of schedule, much less the brutal pace expected of new boys at Eton. And on top of that, in an attempt to shield himself from the stigma of seizures, he was becoming reclusive. So after two painfully fraught terms, we transferred him to Oakham, a school purported to be less Dickensian than Eton—and even Francis reluctantly agreed it was time for a change.

Emmeline joined me in Charleston the next summer. At 16, she had successfully sat School Certificate Ordinary Levels in five subjects at St. George's School for Girls in Ascot, thus completing the approximate equivalent to American high school. This accomplishment, however, contained an intrinsic dilemma. I felt she was much too young to start college. Life on an American campus was a far cry from that of the traditional English boarding school, but I was afraid she'd think she was being penalised if she were made to go back to high school until her grade conformed with her age.

While I fretted about how to compromise, the resounding consensus among friends and family was that Emmeline should, indeed, repeat herself and enter the junior class at Ashley Hall— Charleston's celebrated all-girls day-school.

"There's really no alternative," was the refrain. "She can't just take a sabbatical! And remember, Lane, even your mother went to Ashley Hall. Oh, and yes! So did Barbara Bush! You can't possibly go wrong. It's a fine old establishment. Excellent traditions. As much like Em's school in England as anything you'll find here. And her Middleton cousins are there, too. Why, they'll all get along like a house on fire."

Unable to counter with anything more persuasive, I gave in. It was easy to cut through the usual red tape. Just as Mrs. McComb—a lifetime before—had informed Heathfield when they were to expect me, so a local friend of my parents now told the Ashley Hall Board of Governors that Emmeline Kinsman would be gracing their halls at the beginning of the next semester. And sally forth Emmeline did.

But for all their enthusiasm, nobody mentioned that the prevailing code of behaviour for her American peers was that "anything goes." The staff at St. George's would have been scandalised by the laissez-faire atmosphere, and the girls would have died of envy. Ashley Hall couldn't have been *less* "like Em's school in England." Helpless to turn the inexorable tide, I reluctantly bade farewell to the Victorian rites and discipline that had sheltered my English daughter until now, and together we confronted the extraordinary complexities of living in the land of milk and honey. Of opportunity. Of the free.

John was 12 when I left England. He had just left Maidwell Hall—which he has since said, bitterly, was "trial by torture"—and was starting at Eton the next term, naturally following his brother's path. He performed there exactly as was expected of him and came down after five years with a good academic showing. Vehemently eschewing The Establishment—and therefore Cambridge, where his father and grandfather had both taken their degree—he had been pleased to be offered a place at Bristol University. Geography was John's chosen field, and Bristol boasted an exceptional geography department.

"But I'd quite like a year off first," he said, to our surprise. "I'm thinking of traveling across America. Starting in Charleston."

"Well, sure. By all means," we agreed, though we hadn't the slightest idea how he was going to manage such an odyssey. "You've worked hard since you were four years old. You've never malingered. Go ahead. Take a break and live it up."

So John and Emmeline and I were in America in November of 1983 when it was decided that Blake must undergo surgery. He was now a student at the University of London. A tumour had developed on the fateful scar tissue, and the almost daily seizures interfered with his studies. He was reading biochemistry and microbiology and the pressure of such scholastic ambition was taking its unmerciful toll.

I didn't go to London to be with him at this harrowing time. Francis had warned me in no uncertain terms that he'd do his best to undermine Blake's chances of recovery if I "set foot on English soil" during the ordeal. Deranged though his threat was, I knew Francis was entirely serious, and I didn't risk calling his bluff. Instead I asked friends, and even strangers on the street, to pray for us. And I waited in an agony of suspense and morbid speculation.

Blake survived what turned out to be only an exploratory procedure. His doctors determined that the tumour was too near the motor section of his brain to excise, so they simply sewed him back up again. Their conclusion was tantamount to a death sentence, with no effective date. But the night before Blake was due to be discharged, a seizure felled him while he was in the shower, and he drowned. It was November 17, 1983, at the Westminster Hospital—the same hospital, in a wrenching twist of fate, where he was born. His 23rd birthday would have been on December 10, not quite three weeks later.

In spite of its violence, I've tried to comfort myself that the drowning was a caress of God. Blake knew his cancer was unstoppable—that he was going to die—but during the fatal seizure, he would have been unconscious and therefore unafraid. If his death was inevitable, and if drowning would spare him even a single moment's dark dread, then I welcomed it for him with all my heart.

I died then, too, in a way. I needed *not* to be told to "be strong." I needed to be allowed to weep and to be held and stroked and rocked. I needed to be allowed to talk endlessly about my dear child and to berate myself for whatever I perceived had been my maternal failings. I needed to be told I *had* been a good mother, and that, of course, Blake knew how much I loved him. I needed to be told he forgave me for not being with him at the end. I needed help to eat and sleep and breathe. Most of all, I needed my mother.

But she didn't come to see me. Nor did she sit with me at Blake's memorial service a week later at St. Michael's Episcopal Church in Charleston. I never heard from my brother, either. He didn't come to see me. He didn't write. He didn't call.

Did my family abandon me because they couldn't face me? Were they afraid I would fall apart and shame them? Or was it because *they* were ashamed? Nothing like this—a child's dying of an unmentionable medieval disease—"had ever happened in our family."

Whatever the reason, it wasn't good enough.

At the time, Emmeline and John and I had few financial resources of our own, but when we asked Totsy to stake us to a trip to England for Blake's funeral, she decided that to dispense such largesse would be discriminatory.

"I can't possibly afford to give equal amounts of money to your brother and each of his children, Puddin'. That would be absolutely out of the question," she said unequivocally. "Whatever the circumstances, I can't risk their feeling I've treated them unfairly. I'm sure you understand."

What in God's name does she mean, "whatever the circumstances"?

Actually, as things turned out, it didn't matter what she meant. Francis forbade John and Emmeline to go to their brother's funeral. He regarded putting Blake to rest as a performance of sorts and was unwilling to share the stage, or reviews, with anyone else. "I have to do this on my own," he told them, as if his were the only pain that mattered. And it never occurred to them to ignore his highhanded dictum.

Some 14 years on, I was intrigued—and unnerved—to come across a tape recording of a memorial service held for Blake at St. James's Piccadilly in London, soon after his funeral in Essex.

Francis must have sent the tape to Totsy—who never mentioned it to me—and it eventually surfaced when I was sorting through her desk before moving her to a retirement community. Reading the label on the tape somehow made me feel as if I were spying or eavesdropping. I wanted to throw it away right then, but I decided to listen to it in my car before going home from work the next day. Whether it was out of base curiosity or a legitimate sense of duty, I still don't know.

A little worm of fear gnawed at me as I turned on the player. But instead of becoming salt in the wounds of memory, the recorded service infuriated me. It wasn't a thanksgiving for Blake's life. It was a contrived exhibition of theatrical grief. Francis' long and maudlin eulogy was patently designed to rouse sympathy for himself alone. It made not the barest mention of Emmeline and John—nor, of course, of me. Even Blake seemed almost incidental to the theme.

Disgusted, I threw the tape into one of those drum trash cans you always find in public parking lots.

Perhaps Francis had enlisted Totsy's support in keeping us away from England. Such an agreement between them would explain her refusal—under the guise of inequity to my brother and his children—to provide the means for us, too, to bury our child and brother. Only Francis knows the hard facts here. But in the case of a toss-up between us, it was Francis who could always be sure of my mother's vote.

Book XV
Heredity and Identity

John became oppressed at an early age by the vagaries of war. Usually chatty and easygoing, he was noticeably down-at-the-mouth one afternoon when I picked him up from Miss Blyth's Little School in the neighboring Essex village of Sible Hedingham. He was only five years old, but he trudged toward me with the dejection of a hopeless old man. I gave him a kiss, which he returned apathetically. Unsmiling, he took my hand as we walked over the gravel to the car. I doubted I could drive away his doldrums, whatever they were, but I thought I'd try.

"Hello, Darling. Have you had a nice day?"

"No," he said, so quietly I could hardly hear him.

"Oh, gosh. Why? What's wrong?"

"We keep losing," he mumbled. "Last week, we learnt about the American Revolution. We lost." As a British subject, he was obviously chagrined to find that the jewels in England's crown began dropping out so long ago. Sighing from his very depths, he looked up at me with respectful resentment.

"Then today we learnt about the American Civil War," he continued drearily, kicking a bit of gravel with the toe of his shoe. "We lost again."

This last was, of course, an allusion to his Confederate connections, and he was now consigning himself to a state of ignominy by default for the rest of his life. Hardly more than a toddler, the link he made between these two conflicts and his own complex heritage was extraordinarily shrewd. His staunch loyalties in both cases were impugned, and his sense of justice stung by the high price of freedom so often associated with the birth pangs of a new nation. How could such a very little boy have grasped such multi-layered subtlety?

I was at a loss. John was so unhappy, and my first instinct was to change the subject. But he deserved better than that, and I bent to the task of trying to explain the long-term results of the two conflicts and to assure him that his kin and countrymen were heroes, regardless of on whose side lay their allegiance.

He would not be mollified. It was the disgrace of surrender that was humiliating—not the death of a cause that had proved unworthy—and he sat on the terrace steps after we got home until it was time for supper, looking sorrowfully at his knees.

John's "year off," after coming down from Eton in 1982, evolved into eight, and by the time he was ready to pursue his undergraduate degree, he had forfeited his place at Bristol. In 1990, he applied to Exeter University and was accepted. His activities in the interim were varied and enterprising; he didn't footle away a single moment of his extended sabbatical.

First he came to Charleston, and within days applied for jobs at Another Restaurant and Lounge—a bar on Folly Road—and at the McDonald's a few blocks away. McDonald's said they'd hire him if he'd cut his hair. Those were John's afro days. He had inherited thick hair from me and curls from his father, with a result so vibrant that his own grew directly against gravity. He agreed to have it trimmed—at least enough to fit inside the little white cap required by the Health Department to be worn by people in food service. Another Restaurant and Lounge hired him, too.

He and Emmeline and their second cousin, Mary Ann Middleton, lived together in an apartment on Camp Road on James Island. John cycled everywhere. At daybreak, he would arrive at the bar, which he would tidy up from the revelry of the night before. Then he'd get back on his bike and peddle down the road to McDonald's, where he would don his cap and take up his post behind the grill for the afternoon shift.

"The bar was owned by two rather seedy brothers called Don and Sonny Sottile," John told me. "Don was the one with the brains and the money and the gun, but Sonny had the winning personality. He would normally fall into the bar sometime between 10 and 11 in the morning, by which time I would have almost finished the cleaning. 'Get me a goddam beer,' would invariably be his first amiable comment of the day to me, 'and get one for yourself!' By the time I left around noon to go and flip burgers at McDonald's, he'd have reestablished his blood-alcohol ratio at a cosily stratospheric level."

In 1983, John set out for Weaverville, an agricultural town in northern California, where he stayed for a year with a family who owned a natural food store called Mountain Marketplace. Working in that store afforded John bed and board, and his time there must have had something of considerable value at its core, because he describes it as a "major turning point" in his life.

Totsy managed to involve herself in his Weaverville experience. She had heard about the project through a friend of hers—whose nephew owned the food store—and she later paid for both John and Emmeline to study at the Rudolf Steiner College in Sacramento. I resisted my children's wish to attend this rarefied institution, but it appealed to Totsy that its reputation was known primarily to those in academe, that it seemed more exclusive than the conventional institutions of higher learning. And naturally her pocketbook trumped my parental authority.

Born in Austria in 1861, Steiner believed that "the capacity for conscious spiritual perception within each of us can be awakened through disciplined inner activity." This discipline has become known as Anthroposophy and is central to the Waldorf system of education, founded by Steiner in 1919, which has grown to over 650 schools throughout the world, most of them in the United States and Canada.

Steiner described Anthroposophy as "a science of the spirit, a path of knowledge that can lead the spiritual in the human being to the spiritual in the universe," and his Waldorf schools strive "to educate the whole child, hand and heart as well as mind, while cultivating imagination and creativity alongside a sense of responsibility for the earth and its inhabitants." Graduates of the Steiner College are not recognized as university graduates within the accepted American or British scholastic criteria, but they are qualified to teach in all Waldorf schools, worldwide.

John was 18 when he fell in love with a fellow student at the college, Janine Beauséjour, who was an engaging French-Canadian single mother with a nine-year-old son. I was fascinated to hear that she was paying for her tuition in kind, by cooking for the entire school. I met her during a brief visit to Sacramento and could easily understand John's attraction. As well as obviously adoring him and hanging on his every word, she seemed a sweet, good young woman, who John says was his first real love. Certainly her impact on his life has been valuable and long-term.

Once equipped with his Steiner credentials, John came back east to Harlemville, in New York state, where he taught for a year in a Waldorf dairy farm school for underprivileged inner-city children. He says he was very much at home there. He's always had an unaccountable affinity with cows—as well as an innate knack with small children.

⁂

In 1987, under the auspices of Peggy Watson, John began the sort of traveling that would mark his life. Peggy was an old friend of ours from Essex. Long a divorcée with three grown sons, she was now living in the village of Ruwa, roughly 30 kilometers east of Harare, Zimbabwe *[formerly Rhodesia]*. She and her partner, Sandy Katz, had established the Steve Katz Education Foundation in memory of Sandy's son, who died in his early 20s shortly after Zimbabwe's Independence in 1980. Young Steve had been climbing in Domboshawa *["Great Red Rock" in the Shona language]* when he fell from a ledge to his death. He was an idealist who strongly supported the black liberation struggle, and the mission of the Foundation was to provide likeminded Britons and Americans an opportunity to contribute to Zimbabwe's post-Independence efforts in a way that Sandy knew his son would have endorsed.

Sandy and Peggy arranged for John to be granted a permit to work in Ruwa, and he eagerly seized the opportunity to teach again. He was made Head of History—a department comprising two teachers—and proceeded to spread himself very thin, teaching African history, early 20th century European history, the English language, basic science ... and volleyball.

John tells of a hiking trip with his friend Dan, one of the volunteers at the Foundation, to Domboshawa, the rock where Steve Katz had died:

"We arrived an hour or two before sunset, only to discover that the Red Rock was too rocky to pitch a tent on. So after our snack supper, we laid our sleeping bags on the sunwarmed stone and tried to sleep. However, some 'Apostles'—dressed all in white, praying and chanting and singing through the night—had also come to Domboshawa, albeit on the other side of this great rock, and sleep was not to be had. Around midnight, one of the Apostles ventured away from his group and stumbled upon Dan and myself: two bearded white men, lit by a full moon, wrapped in shrouds and lying on the ground. He shrieked and ran away, certain, no doubt, that he had seen—well, why not?—Jesus and John the Baptist!"

It was in Ruwa that John first encountered casualties of AIDS, the global scourge on which his career in health promotion focuses so intensely. During a visit to Charleston long after the fact, he told me a short story that illustrated his baptism into the horror now insidiously infecting the world—an uninspired account, yet heartstopping in its implications.

"I used to go with Joe Mutonono, a colleague at the school, up to Nhekairo's beer hall on Friday evenings, a couple of miles' walk through the bush. Nhekairo's was not exactly a five-star affair: Somebody had scrawled 'uyo mughodi' on the wall at the back, which means 'don't piss here.' There would always be a small number of women in attendance, hoping to attract a man for the evening and make a few Zimbabwe dollars in the process.

"Joe had a weakness for these ladies and would occasionally disappear into the bushes, with one of them giggling nervously at his side. The security guard once came up to me while Joe was thus engaged, and harangued me for not following suit. He said he would even organise one of the women for me, and when I declined, he looked at me in shock.

"'But, Kinsman,' he exclaimed, 'what is wrong with your organ?' The man must have thought I had some sort of rash, because clearly, from his perspective, there could be no other conceivable impediment to debauchery. Joe subsequently died but not before infecting his wife and two babies. Who also died."

⁂

I kept all of John's letters of that era, as well as copies of mine to him. The combined chronicle is too voluminous to include here in its entirety, but the following excerpts of our correspondence are representative of our radically dissimilar everyday lives.

St. Vincent's Secondary School
P.O. Melfort
ZIMBABWE
September 14, 1987

Dear Mum,

Thank you so, so much for your lovely letter. The last time you typed a letter to me was the first one you sent me when I was at Maidwell and I'd asked you to type it because I couldn't read your writing then! You sound well just as when I left. Please give the poor kitty cat a really good skin pull for me!!

So here I am on the "Dark Continent." It was an epic and frightful journey over here, I must say. Across the Atlantic took *UGH* 12 hours, as we had to land in Manchester because Heathrow was fogged in. At last, I arrived. We were so late that one of my bags, having been put on the plane to Paris (!), had already come back to London! The Ethiopian flight was equally awful it was 23 hours London to Harare, mainly because of a hopeless delay in Addis, in which I had a first taste of the lacadasical (sp?) attitude Africans have to time! At last, totally exhausted, I arrived at Harare at about 6 p.m. on Tuesday, September 1, just as the sun was setting.

Peggy picked me up without any trouble and we went to her place in Harare. (Peggy Watson was our old friend from Maplestead who married a Zimbabwean in the late '70s.) I stayed there till Saturday, going out to St. Vincent's and fixing up my room, which desperately needed a paint job. (Hitchhiking here is as simple as falling off a log; it's the way most people travel, and people are very obliging about picking people up especially white hitchhikers.)

Peggy is very well and is amazing about everything. She wants to be sure that I have everything I need. We went on a little shopping expedition so I'm fully equipped. (You'll be relieved to hear that they bought a new bed for this room no bed bugs!!)

I was surprised to find that my room has an electric light. It doesn't always work, but I have been extremely grateful for it. It's dark by 6:30 so the light is a big plus. There's no other electricity though, and the water situation is more or less as I imagined it to be, except that there are fewer people per tap only about 25. The only people who live here at the school are teachers; I was wrong in thinking that farm workers also live here. But I am the only white person, and I felt so incredibly conspicuous for the first days that I was rather uncomfortable about going out. People, mainly children, would simply stop whatever they were doing and stare unabashedly at me as if they'd never before seen anything that remotely resembled me. They don't do that so much now, but I do feel very conspicuous whenever I go out!

The people are very warm and hospitable, although I think they sometimes look at me (in their minds) as rather an oddity, because of my attitudes towards various things. As soon as I arrived, people jumped on me to find out my political views. People are incredibly politically aware, but they have a very narrow viewpoint, and this is a Marxist nation. (People often refer to others as Comrade Whoever.) But they sometimes had a hard time understanding my not really being either Capitalist or Socialist. They assumed, I guess, that as an American (they can't understand that I'm actually British!), I must be wildly capitalist. One boy asked me how much he might have to pay for a wife in America; I didn't really understand what he meant so he explained that here, in rural areas, a young man would have to give a "lobola" to the bride's father, a gift of maybe 12 cattle and a new suit. I tried not to look too astonished.

The school itself is a good place, very primitive facilities but good people working there. I discovered very soon that the secondary school headmaster is also white, a South African who left that country shortly after independence here, because of South Africa's policies. He is a wonderful man, very open-minded. I was a little hesitant to tell him of my Steiner teacher training for fear of his laughing at me, but, amazingly, he knew about Steiner and had once visited the Steiner school in Cape Town. He actually suggested that I start a Waldorf school here in Harare!! He has two beautiful horses and owns a lovely piece of land, with his wife and two young ones, across the valley.

Right now, it's very dry. There has been a virtual drought for the last couple of years, and people are hoping that this year there will be a good wet season. It begins soon so the whole landscape will suddenly change from a parched dry sandy one to lush and huge green growth. I'm very much looking forward to it and also the storms. They must be tremendous, because quite a few people are really quite scared of them.

The politics of this whole area are really something. At Danhiko, where I spent last weekend, there are many people who fought in the independence war here and also who are refugees from Namibia and Angola. What has become apparent to me is that the foreign policy of South Africa is in reality infinitely more disruptive than its domestic policy of apartheid. South Africa supports the MNR, the Mozambique guerrillas, who are nothing but butchers trying to destroy the nation and guerrilla groups in Namibia and Angola. The South African government is rather embarrassed by the relative success of the present Zimbabwean government; it would love to prove once and for all that a black-run nation just can't work, so in subtle but definite ways, it attempts to undermine this government. I have gathered this from European volunteers who definitely have their heads screwed on, as well as Africans, so it's not just Socialist propaganda of which there is a lot.

When I first came out to the school, I had a strong sense of loneliness and of being separated from "my" world. I had anticipated and expected this but, in a way, I was surprised at just how different and how separate it all is. I thought of family and friends a lot, and longed to see someone I knew. Last Thursday, I had my first real contact with Mac McGuire, the headmaster, and found such joy in communicating with someone culturally similar; although in England or America, our cultural similarities would appear very small! I had supper with him and his wife that night and stayed over at their place, and since then have begun to feel far more at home and settled.

I can see that this year is going to be absolutely incredible. Just looking at the combined experiences of the last two weeks, I realize how huge they are. But it won't always be easy by any means. There are so many things that are just a pain; things are unreliable electricity, etc. Bathing is almost impossible except for sponge baths. Cooking on a one-burner paraffin stove makes gourmet meals a problem. The problems of communicating with the Shona people are complicated; they often say Yes when they mean No (e.g., "Don't you have your books with you?" "Yes," meaning "No!"). And difficulties in understanding their English as their accent is as thick as frozen honey, etc., etc., etc. But, for all these funny and ridiculous aspects, there is something of a romantic dream come true in the living of this life. As I see it now, a year out here will be plenty, but Oh, the riches that will be gathered in that time!

Well, I could write to you forever it seems there is so much to talk about! By the way, I don't expect to send you a copy of a "general friend letter" to be distributed for a while. I think for the time being, I'll use aerograms which are quite short but just more personal. Maybe I'll ask you to do something like that for me around Christmastime, but not just now. Thanks anyway. But, of course, please share any of this with anyone you would like to Totsy and Em especially.

If you hear from Em, by the way, please let her know that the package she said she'd sent has not yet arrived. I only hope it's not lost or stolen. But I won't write to her for a while in case it does come, and then I'll reply to her later.

I'm writing to lots of people so please don't worry if it's a while between correspondence; I'll split my notes to you and Totsy, so you'll hear from me alternately. It's so funny not being easily accessible by phone, isn't it?

My paper runneth out, my cup runneth over!

I love you, Mum.

John

St. Vincent's Secondary School
P.O. Melfort
ZIMBABWE
January 25, 1988

Dear Friends,

I was delighted, when I returned from a 4week trip to South Africa, to find over 30 letters (!) waiting for me, all anxious to be read and replied to. In order to keep my memories fresh and alive, I decided to write a "form letter" as a response, so please forgive this less personal approach.

Being so close to a place such as South Africa, which the whole world is watching with such interest, I felt I had to visit the country and see for myself a little bit of what's going on there. So many views about South Africa have been expressed to me here in Zimbabwe, covering all shades of the political spectrum.

Hitchhiking is, without any question, the best way to meet the people of a country, and this is how I traveled the 6,200 kilometers of my journey. I spent five days in Johannesburg, a bit longer than I'd have liked. It's quite a dreary city, despite the great riches there. It's a place of great contrast, as, indeed, is the whole country incredible wealth and indescribable poverty. I was fortunate to have a man who has lived and worked in Soweto for 30 years show me around some of this township of over one million people. Indeed, some of the houses are fine places; well-cared for, relatively expensive. But the average house there appeared inferior to the average township house here in Zimbabwe; overcrowding is a terrible problem. In some of areas, small squatters' shacks are piled next to each other, with alleyways between the shacks just wide enough to squeeze between them. The stench is appalling and these places must be utterly disease-ridden; a strong sense of unhappiness and despair fills the air.

But on to better things . . . In Natal, close to Durban, I had the great privilege of being one of two white men to witness a Zulu witchdoctor dance, surrounded by over 200 other highly enthusiastic Zulus. This was an incredible experience, very powerful; their traditional dress is all very symbolic. They wear hats onto which are stuck the gall bladders of all the animals they have killed in their various ceremonies (rather smelly) and they have beads, beads, beads, all different colours, beautifully woven together.

I made a quick stopover in Durban it's very touristy, especially over Christmas and then headed south into Transkei, one of these so-called "independent" states within South Africa. I got a ride with a fat Austrian fellow who makes bricks in Johannesburg, and we actually ended up traveling together for about six days; he ended up taking me all the way to Cape Town. In the Transkei, on the "Wild Coast," I thought I had found heaven on earth. The Wild Coast is wild, and we traveled for several bumpy hours on a very rough road to get there, but it was worth the trip.

For four days, we hiked along beaches, over rocks, on top of cliffs some of the best hikes I've ever done. There aren't a lot of white people there, and although the local blacks live in great poverty, I feel they actually have a very beautiful life; they eat lots of fish (it's very good fish, too!), and the beaches are all surrounded by great groves of banana trees. Pineapples and mangoes were in season I've never tasted such good fruit. God must have been in a wonderful mood when he created the mango. The beaches are totally unspoiled and often totally empty. Swimming in the great blue Indian Ocean gave me so much joy, as did building sand castles and having children one by one approach me, asking with their eyes (as they often don't speak English) if they could help. I once had a crew of eight working in complete contentment, the only noise being the crashing of the waves as the tide gradually approached our shortlived but beautiful creation. Tearing ourselves away, my fat friend and I continued down towards the Cape. I spent Christmas a little north of Cape Town itself, at a camphill community. From behind the cow barn at the camphill, I could see Table Mountain beckoning to me, and I could hardly wait to get there.

Cape Town is, by South African standards, a liberal city, and I felt very strongly the goodwill that exists there, especially among the English South Africans, as opposed to the Afrikaaners, or Boers. There genuinely seemed to be a "mass will" amongst many in this group to create harmony in the country, and a healthy transition to majority rule. Almost everyone seems to realize that majority rule is inevitable, and I found the attitude of the English South Africans so encouraging. I think it's true to say that the media presents quite a one-sided picture of the situation; I know that I was certainly not aware of the positive side of South Africa before I came here.

My trip has put the problems in a human light. Instead of seeing South Africa just as a terrible fascist monster, I now also see many people (white as well as black) struggling bravely against an uncompromising and immensely strong government and army. Positive transition can only come through goodwill, and although I spoke to many hard-line right wingers, I spoke also to a large number of liberal people who love and care deeply for their country, and who won't allow it to be destroyed by the violence that so many people wish on the country.

Standing on Table Mountain, I had a great sense of the beauty and importance of South Africa. Looking northeast, you can see both the Indian and Atlantic Oceans without moving your head; before you is the vast expanse of Africa, leading all the way to Israel and Arabia; behind you, water, all the way to Argentina and Antarctica. Down to the left is Cape Town itself, in many ways reminiscent of San Francisco; it's even got its own Alcatraz, Robben Island, where Nelson Mandela spent so many years. I looked out to the Atlantic and imagined sailors 300 years ago who had braved the South Atlantic waves, who had traveled for weeks and weeks in the same direction: South. Then finally they saw Table Mountain way up ahead of them, then the Cape of Good Hope (not named that for nothing there are the remains of an ill-fated ship wrapped around rocks, thick steel girders bent as if they were little sticks), and they triumphantly changed direction, sailing now into the rising sun.

I stayed in Cape Town until my money almost ran out. With 30 Rand in my pocket, I reluctantly left the beautiful city, wondering when and if I might return to it, and if I do, how it might have changed. I imagined my 2,600 kilometer trip back to Harare would take four days, but I was lucky to get a ride with an Afrikaans man who was going all the way to Pretoria. We were both practically broke, but scraping our money together, we got about halfway there. It was not a very comfortable ride; the window on my side was broken (my companion's right hand bore the stitches that told the story of the fight that had broken the window), so the chilly night desert air whipped down my neck all through the fully moonlit night. We picked up a couple more hitchhikers who put a bit more money in the tank, but by 9 o'clock the next morning, we were still five kilometers south of Johannesburg, all flat broke and with a now empty tank. The enterprising chap went to a pawn shop and tried to pawn his (bald) spare tyre; of course, they wouldn't even look at it, so he offered them his headlights for 10 Rand. We unscrewed the lights, cut the wires and received the money, enough to take us to Pretoria.

The evening of the next day, I arrived back in Harare, less than two and a half days after I left Cape Town. I felt I had just completed one of the most incredible and eyeopening holidays of my life.

Lots to think about, lots to digest, lots to remember.

John

63 Rutledge Avenue, Apt. 21
Charleston, SC 29401
October 2, 1989

John Darling John:

I wonder if you've heard or seen any news of Hurricane Hugo which slammed into our coast last Thursday night, September 21st? It has been described as one of the most destructive storm ever to strike the eastern seaboard. It ripped through Puerto Rico the previous weekend, and by Monday, September 18th, people here were beginning to take it seriously, getting out their hurricane checklists and watching the news carefully. On Tuesday evening I decided it was time to go to K-Mart to buy some battery-operated lamps. Over the years, the Lowcountry has been the target of practically every natural hazard imaginable (except avalanche, of course), so theoretically we're fully aware of the possibilities. Everyone has also been fed endless advice by the Emergency Preparedness Division of County Government as to how to protect life and property. But even so, with no real personal experience at all to draw from, one mentally walks around in unconstructive circles when actually facing an approaching cataclysm. I, for one, shall be much better organized next time.

I got to Harris Teeter Wednesday morning just as the doors opened, to buy bottled water and general survival items: batteries, cheese and crackers, salad makings and fruit, tinned soup, hand-operated can opener (!), etc. By the time I left the store, barely 20 minutes later, there wasn't a single loaf of bread or bottle of water left. Strangers everywhere were talking to each other, comparing notes, wishing good luck and embracing.

Midday at work, we all began securing our own offices, taping the windows, putting anything possible on top of tables and desks, and draping everything with heavy sheets of plastic. When I got home at 6:00 that evening, various friends were congregated in the halls, all discussing the pros and cons of staying in the building during the storm—which was now certain to reach us—or evacuating to somewhere. Totsy had already left earlier that afternoon for Summerville to stay with our cousin Peggy Walker, and I planned to follow the next morning after getting my apartment secured.

Several friends were opposed to my leaving, saying that our building was one of the most massively built structures in the City, and they worried about my traveling on I26 when everyone else would be trying to do the same thing. But I had to go on to Summerville, if only because Totsy would be nervous if I wasn't right there with her. By now, all news channels were giving minute-by-minute instructions to the local citizens; all the barrier islands had been issued mandatory evacuation orders, and everyone in Charleston County living in a one-storey house was told to leave at once. A gigantic tidal surge was expected.

I spent the night getting the apartment as ready as I possibly could. Hard to believe, but there are approximately 140 window panes in my small flat and I taped up every one of them; not just regular crosses, but neat little Union Jack diagonals as well. I moved as much furniture as possible away from the windows, took down all the pictures, piled rugs on the kitchen table, put lamps and breakables in drawers and closets, did a final load of laundry, had a bath and washed my hair, filled the bath and all large saucepans and plastic milk containers with water, checked my overnight case, packed up all valuable correspondence (from you three, your schools, etc.), put ice and perishable food in the cooler and got together all the other food I'd prepared to take to Peggy's, took out the garbage, loaded the car, and waited for dawn.

I was too pent up to sleep, and finally it was time to get up and dress. I finished putting things in the car, including poor Totsy Cat in her basket, and we left at about 9:30 a.m. The city was ominously empty but about five miles onto the Interstate, the traffic was so clogged it was almost at a standstill. It took five hours to drive the 25 miles to Summerville. Totsy Cat meowed constantly. I was thankful she was too preoccupied to remember that she might need to go to the loo.

Peggy lives in a heavily wooded copse containing one old Lowcountry house and three or four very comfortable, scaled-down new ones, one of which is hers. She met me outside and cheerfully glanced around, saying, Well, Lane dear, let's find a place for your car where a tree won't fall on it. I looked up at the hundreds of tall pine trees and left the car right where it was, on the concrete apron outside her garage. If trees really did start coming down, it would be a miracle if my car escaped. Peggy and Totsy had been having a happy time, reminiscing and getting lunch together, after which we all began watching the television.

Peggy is eight or nine years younger than Totsy, and never stops bustling around. The most generous and conscientious hostess, she offered her own bedroom to Totsy and put me upstairs in her son Eddie's bedroom. She herself stayed in the spare room, and it was under that bed that Totsy Cat huddled miserably the whole time we were there. Unfortunate little cat, she was bewildered and fiercely put out, and I don't think she ate a bite for two whole days.

We spent the rest of the afternoon and early evening glued to the box. Mayor Joe Riley and the Chairman of County Council, Linda Lombard, were no longer giving evacuation orders; they were saying it was now too late and too dangerous to move, and that people should stay where they were and prepare themselves as best they could. And they offered prayers that God be with us all.

Blake and Joan rang (from Minneapolis) at one point during the evening, and then Emmeline managed to get through (from England); the telephone worked only intermittently. At 10:00 p.m., the wind was steady at 125 mph. Peggy's house is well-insulated, so despite the wild turmoil outside, we had a curious sense of security. I stepped outside onto the porch a couple of times and looked through the green-black darkness into the driving rain and howling wind, and quickly returned to the muffled sanctuary inside. Because of having been up all the previous night, I was exhausted by 10:30, and decided to go up to bed. Totsy and Peggy were still chipper and chatting while half-tuned-in to the continuous newscast.

I prepared for bed, climbed in and fell heavily asleep. I'd done all I could to protect everything in my flat before leaving town, so now there was nothing left but to try to dream my way through the chaos and hope for the best.

Some time later, my numb subconscious wrestled against an insistent, unfamiliar noise. I finally woke up in time to get out of bed just as a 120' pine tree ground its way through the eaves of the dormer window at the head of my bed and came to rest on the roof outside, about three feet away from my pillow. In the days that have followed, I have felt an overwhelming conviction that Blakie was with us that dreadful night; that he leaned on that tree just enough to stop it actually smashing through the wall onto me while I was asleep. Emmeline told me several days later on the telephone that you, too, had been certain, a few years ago, that Blake was climbing along with you in Yosemite National Park, and caught you up when you missed your footing and almost fell to oblivion.

Very interesting thought, isn't it?

Totsy and Peggy were rushing up the stairs as I started down, all of us with flashlights in our hands, and though it was obvious from the flooding from the battered roof over the bathroom and closet that a large tree must have crashed onto the house, it was too dark—the inkiest, blackest night I've ever seen—to have any real idea of the extent of the damage. No electricity, of course, so we resorted to the battery radio I'd brought (the television stations had long since been forced off the air) which warned that the eye of the storm was now passing over us; the wind had completely stopped. The fury started up again about an hour later, and the storm finally moved on about 5:00 Friday morning.

The new day broke clear and calm and balmy. I crept downstairs again sometime after 7 o'clock, and we all hugged and kissed each other. I couldn't quite interpret the extravagant spontaneous gestures at first; I guess they were merely expressions of feeling at one with the world now that we'd weathered the storm. We walked about outside, aimlessly, speechlessly, surveying the tree through the roof, the whole property wrenched up and hurled back down, transformed from flower beds and paths and mature stately trees into a dense tangled, splintered jungle. I thought of films of the Viet Nam war.

The exit onto the main road was completely blocked by a

fallen giant live oak. Hundreds of pine trees were snapped off almost uniformly about 20' above the ground; we later learnt that there had been thousands of tornadoes. Every house in sight was damaged; more than a few destroyed. Windows had exploded from the record-low barometric pressure; broken glass was everywhere. Every vehicle left parked outside was crumpled and flattened ... except mine, which looked as if it had just been through the in-and-out car wash, with a few pine needles sticking out from the window frames and door hinges. I couldn't speak.

Dear sweet Peggy. When Totsy and I wandered back into the house, Peggy had already made our beds and straightened up the disarray from the darkness of the night before. She calmly handed us each of magical cup of hot coffee (no hot water or electricity, so I can't imagine how she achieved such a thing), and then carried on arranging a lovely shrimp salad luncheon for us, taking care that silver salt cellars and linen napkins were on the table. In the midst of so much confusion and personal inconvenience and loss, her unfailing cheerfulness kept reminding me of some of the happiest times of my childhood, spent there in Summerville with Ma and Pa, when routine and good spirits were always the order of the day.

On Saturday morning Totsy and I agreed we should try to get back to Charleston, so we loaded our cars—I finally persuaded Totsy Cat to come out from under Peggy's bed—and kissed Peggy goodbye. We both drove home slowly, I'm sure for the same reason—not because the roads were still impassable or because the traffic was backed up, neither of which was the case. It was just very hard to concentrate on driving at all. The spectacle of our butchered countryside was totally distracting; it was as if a giant sickle had wantonly, viciously lopped off the tops of hundreds of thousands of acres of pine forest in a single swipe. I feel sure that for the rest of my life, the sharp fresh smell of sap and kindling and Christmas trees will instantly recall these recent days. And the hundreds of maimed and ruined houses and buildings, roofs off or caved in, exposed, sodden, vulnerable, forever changed ...

Martial law was in force, primarily against looting, and the National Guard were stationed all over the City, M16s loaded and at the ready. Help had already started arriving from all over the country, from basic disaster relief, to individuals in pickup trucks with chainsaws and tarpaulins, to mammoth Georgia Power utility trucks on whose sidepanels was written WHERE HUGO, WE GO!

Otherwise, there was almost no one else in sight as we drove into the city, silent and deserted. The highway had been relatively clear, but Charleston itself was a maze of détours and fallen trees. Lethally sharp tin roofs were rolled up like tumbleweed, all over the streets; bricks, masonry, shingles, nails, glass, all hazards to car tyres. There had been a storm surge of over 9' on the lower peninsula, and although the water had receded the day before, you could see the telltale muddy line high on buildings everywhere.

We couldn't get down Legaré Street from Broad, so we approached via East Bay, Water Street, Lamboll Street and then across Legaré into Totsy's drive, which was 3" deep in thick greasy, black pluff mud. Muddy water had filled the Peterson's apartment (ground floor of Totsy's building) to above my shoulder, and from the dried mud splashes on the 12-foot ceiling, it was clear that the flood occurred so fast that it created roiling waves, inside the house. The unfortunate Petersens had retired to Charleston from Boston, having moved in only five days before the storm. Their real estate agent had apparently forgotten to tell them that No. 5 Legaré Street was at one of the lowest points on the entire peninsula.

The building appeared structurally sound, and after carefully negotiating the mud in the driveway to the front door, we anxiously made our way up the now mud-encrusted blue carpeted stairs (obviously the lift wasn't working), really dreading what we might find upstairs. Unbelievably, everything was fine. A heavy rain several days later showed there had, in fact, been some minor roof damage, but, basically, everything at Totsy's had been spared. Thank God. Although why everybody keeps thanking God, I simply have no idea.

After settling Totsy, I set out for Berkeley Court, many blocks off my usual route because of the trees ripped up by the roots lying across nearly every street in the City, and major live power lines draped all over the place. South Battery was almost unrecognizable, but Murray Boulevard was the most pitiful of any street in that general vicinity; brick walls crushed by trees, wrought iron fences mangled like macaroni; whole sides of houses blown in or off; underpinnings and foundations washed away leaving the houses teetering on frail, loosened joists.

And everywhere people were out in the sunshine, standing around in the mud, sweeping and hosing down doorsteps and plants, emptying their houses of soaking mattresses, carpets, appliances ruined by the salt water, greeting and waving to each other, starting somewhere, anywhere, to restore order.

I drove by the Bridges' on Tradd Street. Jim had been called to the Emergency Operations Center and Judy had already hired somebody to clear out the worst of the mud in their house. They hadn't yet been to McClellanville (among the most severely affected rural areas in the Lowcountry, submerged by a 20' tidal surge) to check the fate of their weekend house there. I passed Burbage's Grocery on Broad Street, and both Mr. B and Al were sweeping mud and decaying food out the front door.

Finally home to Colonial Lake. Most of the palmetto trees were still standing; they are usually flexible and resilient. A narrow path around the lake had been carved through other fallen trees and demolished automobiles. Great holes gaped through the windows and roofs of almost every other house. The entrance to my parking space at the back of Berkeley Court was blocked, so I left the car on Beaufain Street and carried Totsy Cat upstairs.

Another miracle. All was well. I couldn't believe my eyes. We hadn't lost a single window pane or shingle off the roof. The palmetto tree outside my bedroom window was down and the basement had filled with the same black foul muddy water, but even the first-floor apartments were all safe and dry. Since the building had proved so strong, it was ironic that only a half-dozen people had decided to stay there.

I unloaded the car and visited briefly with a couple of my neighbours. They had apparently migrated around the building to each others' apartments as the hurricane wore on, camping in Frances Cantwell's, on the ground floor facing Beaufain Street, when the winds had sounded most ferocious, roaring down Rutledge Avenue. I had plenty of water stored from the Wednesday night, but I got back in the car to go in search of food; eventually, everything out of cans all begins to taste the same. Saffron's on East Bay was open, and was giving away large supplies of cheese, orange juice and boned chicken. I hadn't the least idea how I was going to cook the chicken.

It was about 3:30 in the afternoon by now, and with nothing to do but read (no electricity, no running water, no telephone, no nothing, and I felt altogether disinclined to set about putting the apartment to rights), I made myself comfortable on the bed with Totsy Cat and a pile of magazines beside me. After flipping through a few pages, I nodded off and slept like the dead.

A day or so later, I picked my way through White Point Gardens, and engaged in silent communion with a squirrel who was wandering back and forth along a huge oak limb, which was now on the ground. Instead of peering down at me as he normally would, I was instead looking down at him. The squirrel would take a few tiny steps, stop and gaze up at me, perplexed. I stood very still. Of course, the little animal was disoriented; his natural domain had been turned completely upside down. Farther on, a Regency chair sat upright amidst the Spanish moss and shattered tree limbs; very Salvador Dali. Presumably sucked through the window of some smart dining room on South Battery, the chair had, improbably, survived intact, its yellow striped silk like new.

One of the really upbeat stories that came out of all this involved a family in McClellanville. They evacuated, as ordered, but as the shelters allowed no animals, they left their two bird dogs in the house and a couple of downstairs windows open. When they returned 48 hours later, there was no evidence of their having ever lived at that spot. No house, no dock, no boat, no foundation, no dogs. They kicked their way through the rubble into the woods a short way, and suddenly heard a joyous yipping. Ahead and 20' up, in the crotch of a pine tree, was their boat, and the two dogs looking down at them, barking their heads off. Apparently, as the water rose in the house, the very smart hunting dogs jumped out an open window, swam to the boat which was now loose from its mooring, scrambled in, and hung on while the boat rose with the water until it settled snugly into the embrace of the tree. Boat and dogs stayed put, of course, as the water finally receded, and then waited until their owners found them. You can just picture it, can't you?

Undoubtedly, all of us who went through this storm will talk of little else for months. It will surely have changed our lives, even those of us who suffered almost no hardship. A friend from work mentioned that when she was in first or second grade, in the early 1940s, her black nurse—who had lived through the Great Earthquake of 1886—was still talking about it, some 60 years later.

Jane Bellamy telephoned and told me about a headline in the London Times last week: CHARLESTON GONE WITH THE WIND.

I'll write again soon, Darling.

Devotedly,
Mummy

At my request, John recently emailed me his perspective of the Zimbabwean liberation struggle—a savage affair which he describes with sober and scholarly insight.

"It effectively started in 1965, when the Prime Minister of Southern Rhodesia, Ian Smith, made a Unilateral Declaration of Independence from England. Britain was rapidly relinquishing her African colonies during the early and mid-1960s, but no agreement had yet been reached between the Crown and the extremely diverse interest groups (white and black) in Southern Rhodesia over power sharing. The white Rhodesians controlled everything and were unwilling to give up anything, and naturally the blacks—who saw their brothers and sisters to the north taking control of their own destinies—wanted to follow suit. These goals were, of course, mutually exclusive, and since no agreement was even remotely close, Ian Smith decided that since Britain obviously had no intention of giving Southern Rhodesia its independence, the Rhodesians were going to damn well take it for themselves.

"The new 'Rhodesia' was an illegal and largely unrecognised state and instantly became an international pariah, vilified as racist and reactionary, flying counter to the progressive Winds of Change. *[The "Winds of Change" refers to British Prime Minister Harold MacMillan's famous 1960 speech in Capetown, in which he acknowledged the inevitability of African independence.]* It was several years before the war between the Rhodesian government and the two main black guerrilla armies really got going, but by 1975, the guerrillas had enlisted the enthusiastic support of the USSR, China and many of the newly independent

African states. Rhodesia was backed by South Africa—and a handful of English right-wing extremists.

"All sides committed grisly atrocities, but many white men in their 30s and 40s who picked me up during my extensive hitchhiking journeys around the country would tell me—perhaps as a way of exorcising the ghosts of their grim past—of 'ops' they had been involved in, villages they had torched, babies they had drowned in buckets of water in order to make a grandfather tell them when the 'terrorists' had passed by and where they had gone, and of young men they had thrown out of helicopters from 5,000 feet. It was a war of attrition, and, of course, it was the rural peasants who suffered most. There is a highly relevant Shona saying: 'When two elephants fight, the grass gets squashed.'

"Finally, in 1980, peace talks at Lancaster House in London brought about a ceasefire, a transitional puppet government, and then elections which were won by Comrade Robert Mugabe. At last, Rhodesia was legally independent from Britain, and Zimbabwe was born. The amazing thing to me was that in spite of the intense vitriol that was whipped up by the politicians on both sides during the war, I never once—not even once—was on the receiving end of any racism during my 2½ years in Zimbabwe. Yet now, once again, Mugabe is on the warpath, preaching hatred of whites, bombing opposition newspaper headquarters, intimidating anyone who so much as whimpers about his autocratic rule, and bringing his once-thriving country to the brink of complete collapse. It's heartbreaking. And it also stings the soul when the likes of former Prime Minister Ian Smith—who still lives on his farm in Zimbabwe—stands up and says 'I told you so.'"

John's constant companion in Ruwa was Nam'pa Shivolo. Her home was a village in the far north of Namibia, and she was living in Zimbabwe in exile. The story of Namibia's fight for independence is as savage as that of Zimbabwe, and Nam'pa's mettle and personal commitment captured John's deepest respect.

"Originally German South West Africa, this vast land of desert dunes, diamonds and uranium, was given to South Africa at the Treaty of Versailles, as part of Germany's World War I reparations in 1919. South Africa dropped the 'German' from the name, although there are still quite a few German speakers there, including one who famously raises his Swastika flag every April 21—Hitler's birthday. South West Africa gradually became ever more consumed in the apartheid furnace, and sometime in the mid1970s, SWAPO (South West Africa People's Organisation) pitted its own offensive against what the official media called the 'Racist Republic'—that is, South Africa.

"Nam'pa and I met late in 1988. I walked past her one evening in Harare, at a school for ex-fighters and refugees from South Africa and Namibia, and asked a mutual friend to introduce us. She had witnessed her own father's murder in 1977 by Koevoet soldiers (South African-trained thugs) who accused him of harbouring SWAPO 'terrorists,' and although only 20 years old, she then joined SWAPO herself. She wanted to become a soldier, but since—in Namibia— any association with that liberation group meant almost certain death, she had to get to Angola where SWAPO had training camps. This involved traveling by foot across the desert at night. An experienced SWAPO guide who took her and two other recruits between safe houses all the way up to the border, and they crossed over to Angola without incident.

"She survived the most notorious massacre of SWAPO soldiers in 1979, at a place called Kassinga, when 900 of her friends and comrades died at the hands of the South African army and air force. She and her comrades were lined up for the morning parade at dawn when they heard approaching tanks, and then the sudden scream of jets overhead, followed by exploding bombs. She said she still remembered she was wearing her red dress that morning, and that she fled into a ditch where she hid all day, only reappearing after dark when the bombing and shooting had subsided. The depth of her trauma really came home to me when we went to see a James Bond film in Harare in 1989—10 years after this event. At the climax of the film, with explosions and gunfire galore on the screen, she clung to me, shivering, and scarcely spoke for the rest of the evening.

"She was less lucky in 1981. She was riding in a large truck with her boss, a senior political commissar, when they ran over a landmine that had been laid by UNITA: Angola's rebel group which, in those days, worked hand in hand with the apartheid régime in South Africa. There were 21 people in the truck and she was one of only three survivors. Her right hip and left foot were badly injured, and she was sent by the SWAPO Party to Sarajevo in Yugoslavia for reconstructive surgery and rehabilitation, a process that spread over the next seven years. Her gratitude to General Tito and the people of Yugoslavia for their support of her country's struggle remains profound.

"She and I were together for the last few months of her exile, when the war in Namibia was clearly drawing to a close and everyone knew that SWAPO was about to clinch power. I made the trip across the Kalahari over Christmas and New Year 1988 to see the country she had not be able to visit for 11 years, and to report back to her. I found a place full of hostility and suspicion. Finally, after endless delays and an emotional roller coaster ride for all concerned, the United Nation Transitional Assistance Group declared at last in August 1989 that is was safe for SWAPO refugees to return, so Nam'pa flew home and was placed in a United Nations returnee camp. A few weeks later, she was allowed to leave, and found her way to the home of one of her brothers in Katutura, the main black township for the capital, Windhoek.

"Nam'pa means 'the only girl.' She had many brothers, but she alone joined the fight and was prepared to give her life for what she knew was right. The brother she stayed with was a successful businessman who smuggled illegal ivory from the north of Namibia to the lucrative market of South Africa; I was horrified on the first night of my visit there later that year to discover two huge tusks under our bed. Nonetheless there was euphoria in the air—after all, SWAPO had won the war—and we attended the rally at Katutura stadium where SWAPO's president claimed victory over the Boers (South Africans).

"We spent our last night together in a miserable hotel in Ondangwa—the hottest and most desolate place I have ever visited—and the next day we hitched out across the desert to a track off the main road south, which she would follow back to her village. It wasn't safe for me to visit her home because there were still Koevoet units terrorising the area, who would relish the prospect of slaughtering a symbol of Namibia's inevitably multi-ethnic future: two people who loved each other, one black and one white. We waited silently under the scorching sun, and finally a car appeared through the mirage on the horizon—dust trailing—signalled left, and stopped a few yards from where we stood. It was Nam'pa's lift.

" 'See you,' she said, and smiled at me.

" 'Maybe,' I replied, a lump in my throat.

"She picked up her bags, got in the car, and was gone."

Book XVI
The Beginning of Wisdom

My brother says he defected to the Midwest as a young man because he "couldn't stand what Charleston represents." By that, I believe he was referring to the pretensions of a culture based solely on money—old *or* new—and family connections. But by leaving the South behind, he also ensured the preservation of his immaculate reputation there, because nothing he did—or didn't do—could become grist for the Charleston tattle-mill. Once in a while, he would grace the Holy City with the briefest of visits, confident of the advantage always accorded him on those seldom occasions. His looks and manner happily reminded everyone of our father, and since he was smart enough to keep his mouth shut most of the time, he managed not to wreck his own saintly image.

I, on the other hand, have spent the last 20 years or so as Totsy's faithful sidekick. She has exerted upon me a constant pressure to become an acceptable player in the local social scene—a person deserving of a position somewhere in the farthest reaches of her shadow. But to suit my mother without losing myself was not possible. She saw me as intense and undisciplined; I saw her as shallow and manipulative. She wanted me to sit on volunteer boards and attend black tie functions; I was grateful to have an actual job and to be solvent and self-sufficient. She found my spontaneity unladylike; I considered her a poseur. She berated me for "losing [my] well-born English consort;" I struggled to rise from the ashes of my former existence. She perpetrated the myth that stress would give her a heart attack; to accommodate this fable, I kowtowed my self-respect right into the ground.

Then one day I stopped trying to mix oil with water and sought solace in one of my father's favourite bon mots: "The beginning of wisdom is to see things as they [really] are."

Totsy's bogus political correctness left her innate racism stark naked. The first time I was forced to contend with it head-on was when Emmeline played the title rôle in Mary Poppins at Ashley Hall—Totsy's own alma mater, and "the only school in Charleston good enough for [her] granddaughter." With her well-pitched English voice, Emmeline was the logical choice for the lead, a challenge she met with considerable aplomb.

In order to augment the audience, the cast was urged to invite friends as well as family, and Emmeline asked Saundra Greene *[my coworker at the College of Charleston]* to join Totsy and me. Saundra was a comely black woman whom Totsy had previously met and claimed to admire.

"She's quite striking, Puddin'," Totsy had said at the time, "particularly those green eyes. How do you suppose that came about?" How, indeed.

Saundra and I arranged to take the afternoon off and drove in tandem to Ashley Hall. After parking on Rutledge Avenue, we made our way across the campus to the auditorium, and installed ourselves first-row center. Just as the curtain rose, Totsy appeared and stiffly seated herself next to me—or rather, as far away from me as the narrow seats permitted. I smiled an automatic welcome and was met with a stony stare over a squared chin. With no time to analyze what this might mean, I turned my attention to the stage and tried to ignore the fraught atmosphere seething beside me.

The play was a success. The ingénues excelled. And the applause was loud and long at the last curtain. As Saundra and I got up and moved toward the aisle, I turned to speak to Totsy, but she wasn't there. She'd vanished without a word to anyone. She hadn't even waited to congratulate Emmeline, the star in whose light she would normally have expected to shine. I was mystified. But after casting a furtive glance down at myself to see if perhaps I'd forgotten to wear some vital piece of clothing, I decided to let the matter go and exchanged goodbyes with Saundra.

Thinking Daddy might like to know his granddaughter was the future Vivien Leigh, I drove over to 42 Society on my way home. Daddy was his usual genial self. Totsy was even more tight-lipped and grim than she'd been during the play. And I was mystified all over again.

Finally, after several more days of being given the cold shoulder as only Totsy could give it, I resolved to get to the bottom of things and went back over to 42 before work the next morning. After letting myself in through the kitchen door, I went up to Totsy's bedroom and stood in the doorway. Thelma, her maid of many years, had just brought up the breakfast tray and was drawing back the curtains; I noticed vaguely that an early camellia was on the tray next to the coffee pot.

As Thelma and I bid each other a good morning, she smiled at me in a way that could only be described as tentative. *How odd*, I thought as I patted her shoulder, and smiled back. Totsy was buffing her nails and looked up in silence without greeting me. *How odd*, I thought again, and took a deep breath.

"Mommie, I hope I'm not too early," I began, as Thelma quietly withdrew, "but I decided to come and ask what's wrong. I mean it's obvious you've been angry with me these past few days, but I can't think why. Of course, if I'm mistaken, then never mind. But otherwise, I really wish you'd tell me what's going on."

While I was falling thus all over myself, Totsy's face set hard and ugly.

"Yes, I'll tell you what's wrong!" she spat. "How dare you expect me to sit next to a black woman at a social occasion! For Emmeline's sake, I realised I had to stay. But when I came into the auditorium at Ashley Hall the other day and saw you sitting next to that woman who works in your office ... well, I almost walked back out! What's the *matter* with you? I've never been so humiliated in my life. Did I teach you nothing? Have you no respect for me? For the rest of your family? For your *daughter?* To give your own daughter such an example! How dare you!"

She was shaking and ashen gray, gripping the edge of her tray. The coffee cup chinked in its saucer. The tendons in her neck stood out like ropes; I could see them throbbing. Fury boiled in me as I stared back at my mother and wondered what was happening.

"I dared because it didn't occur to me to do anything else!" an unfamiliar voice raged through my clenched teeth—although I wasn't quite sure what I was so strenuously defending. "I had nothing to do with who was invited to that play! Saundra was Emmeline's guest, not mine! And anyway, didn't you notice that several *other* members of the cast were black? Didn't you see the *parents* of those black kids? They were sitting in the audience, right there behind you! Have you honestly forgotten, Mother? Integration is now the law in this country! Even here in the *South!* Even Ashley *Hall* is integrated! Your old school now takes *black* girls! But even if it *didn't*, I dared because it was the right thing to do! And I'll go *on* daring as long as I live! And *I'm* humiliated that *you're* such a bigot!"

I was shaking now, too, and probably equally ashen. I still didn't know what it was I had "dared" to do, but I felt a surge of power as I tore downstairs and out into the new day. What had possessed me? For the first time in my life, and without pausing to count the cost, I had taken on my invincible mother—and won hands down. At least I *felt* I had won, such was my indifference to the possible repercussions of my outburst. I knew I was right, so help me! And surprisingly, there never were any repercussions. Maybe my mother actually heard something of what I said. At any rate, we never again tried to cross that particular minefield together.

Years later, I noticed that when Totsy made her annual visit to the County Office Building on Meeting Street to pay her property taxes, she would never come up to the fourth floor, where I work in the Legal Department, to say hello. But, of course, God forbid she be obliged to pass the time of day on equal terms with Gayle Bustraan, our receptionist—a beautiful black woman who Totsy had been acutely embarrassed to learn was one of my best friends.

Gayle has a strong mezzo-soprano voice, by the by, and she has agreed to sing Schubert's *Ave Maria* at Totsy's funeral on Saturday. And Big Tony, her brother-in-law, will lead us in *The Battle Hymn of the Republic*—the great American hymn that never failed to reduce Totsy to tears. Of joy. Of pride. Of collective national remorse. Of whatever display of dramatic emotion would seem to her most relevant to the occasion.

Book XVII
Take Joy

M y mother enjoyed discussing the trappings of her own swan song, and greeted me late one afternoon with the shining eyes of someone who has just stumbled upon the elixir of life.

"Come in, Dear, and let me show you what I've decided to be buried in."

Carefully laid out on her bed were her emerald-green Chinese banker's coat; a camisole that exactly matched the coat's powder-pink silk lining; little gold shoes embroidered with flowers; and carved ivory earrings from Sumatra. I realised the exotic ensemble was a tribute to my parents' early years in Indonesia, but Totsy's effervescence over the thought of her own burial had startled me into silence, and she interpreted this rare occurrence as my doubting her choice of shroud.

"Do you think I should try to find something more becoming?" she asked, clearly disappointed by my lacklustre expression, and turned to look through her closet again.

"No, no, really, it's perfect. You'll look gorgeous in that outfit." I managed a strangled sort of laugh.

Totsy had already revealed her philosophical approach to such matters during one of my earlier visits to Charleston while I was still living in England. On our way home from the airport, she had made a détour from the more direct route and slowed down outside St. Philip's Episcopal Church.

"Let's go look at the plots your Daddy and I recently bought," she said gaily, pulling over to the curb. She might just as well have been asking if I'd like to go to the movies.

"I don't remember telling you about them, have I?" she asked. "They're just over there, under that big dogwood. It's a beautiful spot."

She turned off the ignition and reached for the door handle. Then she turned to look at me. I stared back. Maybe she was joking. I couldn't make myself move.

"Well, Dear," she kept trying, "don't you think it makes more sense to organise all this now than to wait until after your Daddy and I have been made into darling angels? It'll really be much easier on you if you don't have to start from scratch. I *assure* you, it will. Come on now, Puddin', let's go look. I know you'll approve."

Oh, God, I thought, *this can't be happening.* But I managed to prise my reluctant body out of the car and trailed after Totsy around the markers and through the grass to the far side of the graveyard. She was right. It *was* a beautiful spot. The dogwood tree—the one sheltering the graves—was itself under the umbrella of an ancient live oak, whose canopy of branches would shade and fan my parents' rest for the next 1,000 years. And Totsy's advance preparation did stand me in good stead, because when the time eventually came for me to act on her behalf, most of what the media coyly refer to as "final arrangements" were already in place.

The inscriptions on their gravestones read, respectively, *Requiescat in Pace* and *Jalan Sama Tuan Allah*, Daddy's being the familiar Latin benediction, and Totsy's—not surprisingly, knowing her affection for Sumatra—the Malay for *Walk with God.*

"There!" she gave a little snort when she conceived the plan. "That'll really confuse the tourists, won't it? Uh-ha. Uh-ha."

I would like for my own marker to bear the words *"Take Joy."* They are from a mediaeval greeting of hope and solace; one that Emmeline came upon in her early reading travels. Like the eyes of a portrait that seem to follow one's own, the verse goes like a laser to the very core of human aspiration.

I SALUTE YOU!

There is nothing I can give you which you have not;
but there is much that, while I cannot give, you can take.

No Heaven can come to us
unless our hearts find rest in it today.
TAKE HEAVEN!

No Peace lies in the future
which is not hidden in this present instant.
TAKE PEACE!

The gloom of the world is but a shadow;
behind it, yet within our reach, is Joy.
TAKE JOY!

And so, at this time, I greet you with the prayer that for you,
now and forever,
the day breaks and the shadows flee away.

~Fra Giovanni c. 1513

Over many years of coping with compressed vertebrae, several cracked ribs, and a fractured ankle and elbow each, my mother had become good friends with Dr. Waddell Gilmore, a well-known local orthopedic surgeon with the somewhat misleading nickname of Bubba. He's a brilliant doctor and a very engaging person, and early in their relationship, Totsy enjoyed telling her friends what "an absolute jewel" he was.

"But you know," she would add guilelessly, "with a name like Bubba, wouldn't you think he'd be more suited to fixing a person's automobile transmission than their elbow?"

Gilmore heard about this through the grapevine. And the next time Totsy needed his professional services, he set the ground rules.

"So nice to see you again, Mrs. Middleton. But before we get started with this X-ray, please understand I'm not taking any guff about *my* nickname from someone who calls herself *Totsy!* Okay?"

She adored him for his wit and audacity. He gobbled up her saucy old-lady flirting. And their friendship deepened and endured until she died.

On returning home after a stint in hospital with a recurring back problem, Totsy was still so miserable that I decided to arrange for round-the-clock sitters. We even placed by her bedside a porta-potty onto which she could easily be lifted. It seemed that even the few steps to the bathroom were more than she could manage without falling. She had always been something of a hypochondriac, but these days life was much easier for everyone if she was automatically given the benefit of the doubt.

Stopping by after work one evening—as usual around six o'clock—I overheard Totsy call to the sitter as I was walking down the hall. "Alice? Oh, Alice! Please bring me my Scotch and soda. Thelma's left it in the ice box. It's all measured and ready. All you have to do is add a splash of soda." Her voice rose with anxiety—or petulance; I couldn't tell which. "Alice, can you *hear* me?"

Alice smiled as she sidled past me into Totsy's bedroom. She was new to the household and unfamiliar with how we did things, but her answer came with an inflexibility that belied her accommodating, earth-mother appearance.

"Well, Mrs. Middleton, I don't know 'bout dat. I don't have no written permission from the doc sayin' it's okay to mix no whiskey with yo' medication."

Stunned by the woman's gall at daring to oppose her and categorically unwilling to forgo her evening highball, Totsy threw back the covers, swung her legs over the side of the bed, and flounced out of the bedroom. Holding up the skirt of her nightdress so as not to trip over the hem, she strode across the dining room and into the kitchen, where she speedily put together her own drink.

Inevitably she spotted me on her way back to bed—I was by then standing directly in her path—but instead of remembering to hobble, she grinned wickedly and guzzled her Scotch.

"Oh, hello, Dear," she said between noisy sips, "I'm so glad you dropped by. Fix yourself something, and come join me."

Book XVIII
The Royal Birthday

In 1993, at not quite 90 years old, Totsy's elder sister Marion went to her great reward. She was an attractive, plainspoken woman, and I remember thinking how much I'd miss her goofy animal jokes and her loud exuberant laugh. As youngsters, my brother and I had envied her noisy family of four children and one very clever Springer Spaniel named Totsy. But most of all we liked the chronic hospitable Shattuck disarray. The Middleton household was always relentlessly picture-perfect.

Totsy talked for months about her sister's poetic demise—how Marion had simply slipped away one afternoon, comforted by the loving ministrations of one of her several daughters, lulled into whatever lay beyond by the hypnotic strains of Palestrina on her bedside radio.

It all sounded a most desirable way to go.

There had previously been considerable interest in planning a bang-up family reunion on Totsy's own 90th birthday, but since the two sisters presumably had similar body clocks, we now thought there was a good chance Totsy might follow her sister's example.

So the Shattuck cousins and Brother Blake and I decided to arrange a "royal" celebration sometime in the spring of her 90th year, instead of waiting until October 17, her birthday proper. We were sure she'd like the idea of borrowing from the inside realm of royal license and etiquette. While living in England, she didn't hesitate to incorporate into her own speech various local idioms and outré pronunciation. And she also became partial to the peculiarly English conceit of celebrating anniversaries of national or historic significance on royal—or convenient—dates rather than on their actual dates.

So, early in the new year following Marion's death, the four Shattucks and Blake chose a weekend in March when they and their spouses would gather in Charleston for the surprise party. They would be coming from Connecticut, Florida, Illinois, Minnesota, and the District of Columbia—literally from far and wide—to pay homage to The Great Aunt Totsy. The affectionate but decidedly tongue-in-cheek moniker had been coined by Marion's eldest daughter, Pat.

As the day approached, while I was buying filet mignon and Totts—what other?—Brut Champagne, making pâté, and decorating a fudge-nut cake with crystallized African violets, Totsy was languishing in hospital with an aching back, from which— judging by the histrionics and vapours—real recovery seemed increasingly doubtful.

I gather she even demanded to know "whether the help here is any better at the weekends." The arrogant complaint was met by her doctor's terse reminder that she was in the hands of highly professional healthcare providers, *not* at a second-rate hotel.

Hoping—oh, so hoping!—that she would soon improve, I decided not to mention her indisposition to the Shattuck contingent. And as good fortune would have it, by the time they'd settled into their beach hotel the day before the festivities, Totsy was at last sent home to recuperate. She still knew nothing of our plans and was charmed—though I imagine a trifle confused— when Blake and Joan turned up unannounced at her door late that same afternoon.

"We just decided to make a spur-of-the-moment visit to welcome you home from the hospital," was their unlikely explanation. "We'll be staying for the weekend, if that's okay?"

A spur-of-the-moment visit from *Minnesota?* Beguiled by all the attention, Totsy suspected nothing more.

I knocked myself out with the preparations. No other bash I'd ever hosted—even in my heyday in England in the 1960s and '70s—came even close, in outlay and attention to detail, to the soirée of March 12, 1994. There was cobweb-thin smoked salmon with capers and lemon and olive oil. Pink roast beef with lime dill mustard and homemade silky mayonnaise. Pots of rich liver pâté with baked buttered toast. Pagodas of trimmed skinny asparagus with hand-coaxed Hollandaise sauce. Mounds of toasted pecans and spotted Graber olives. Piles of sweet-sour "wilted" cucumber wedges and ultrashort cheese wafers. And oceans of champagne.

"For Totsy, every night is First Night!" was Cousin Pat's sardonic observation.

Indeed, the stage was set, the audience agog. Pink Perfection camellias gleamed waxy in the candlelight and the soft glow of silver and crystal flattered every face in the room. A birthday card decorated with laminated dried violets was propped next to a box of chocolate-covered candied orange peel—Totsy's favourite comfit—which lay on the table next to the chair where she would sit. And my cousins and I were just beginning to congratulate each other on pulling off such a coup when the telephone rang.

"Lane, I don't think Mother's going to be able to make it," Blake's voice croaked through a raucous silence at the other end. "She says her back still hurts too much to try getting dressed."

I could almost hear him ducking. I'm sure he thought I was going to come unglued. Instead I grabbed my glass, downed its contents in a single gulp, and held it out for a refill.

I often think about that evening. Of course, we missed Totsy—who Blake swore had tried valiantly to bestir herself—and everyone called on her the next day with thoughtful offerings and tasty treats. But I still regret that she participated only vicariously. The party was a gift of love, and I had very much hoped for her approval.

Anyway, the champagne prevented our being got down by the letdown, and we reminisced until far into the night, hoarse from proving our worth as superior raconteurs all. Totsy's skill in such matters was the acknowledged gold standard, but each of us put our fanciest foot forward, and I know she'd have been gratified by our good intentions.

Book XIX
The Springtime of Her Senility

That was just over four years ago. Two months after the Royal Birthday, Brother Blake and I made the presumptuous decision to move Totsy to a local retirement community—presumptuous because we dared wrest control from a person herself accustomed always to having the last word. In fact, she turned the tables on us by readily conceding she could no longer live alone and gave us all due credit for properly performing our filial duty.

I had been visiting her every day, sometimes twice, and couldn't fail to see that she was about to embark on that unchartered course so often traveled by the very old. Barely finding my own halting way beside her, I tried to remember how I'd handled the towering uncertainties of childrearing so many years before. In many ways, the circumstances were not dissimilar.

Totsy was still fairly spry—taking her morning constitutionals, winding the clocks, and watering her wonderful African violets—but a task requiring any degree of logic was no longer feasible. Her mouth often failed to synchronize with her brain and, being uneasily aware that her speech sometimes slurred, she became loath to talk on the telephone. Surprisingly, she didn't seem particularly bothered that her social circle was shrinking, but I knew the increased isolation would hasten the decline of her cognitive abilities.

There was also the matter of her evening meal. Before going home every afternoon, Thelma would always have an appetising, well-planned little supper prepared and ready to be heated in the microwave oven.

"But I'm deathly afraid of all that loose electricity," Totsy would bleat, "and anyway, I'd just as soon starve to death as wash a single plate. I couldn't possibly leave that sort of thing in the sink overnight for Thelma to deal with in the morning. It would attract all those awful insects. Frankly, I'd rather have a rattlesnake in the house than a cockroach. The kitchen's simply *got* to be in order before I go to bed."

Thelma Smalls—a black woman of unlimited intestinal fortitude—has been Totsy's conscientious maid and devoted companion for well over 20 years. She's roughly my age, with four children who do her proud and a hardworking husband whom she never mentions. She is serenely self-confident, and she is often favoured with visions and premonitions that would rival those of the ancient oracle.

I've long considered Thelma a valued friend, and it would never have crossed my mind to attempt this momentous transition for Totsy without Thelma's emotional and practical support. So, for several weeks, after finally settling on a well-recommended establishment in Mount Pleasant, I waited, heart in mouth, while she decided whether she could face driving over the "horrible" Cooper River Bridge every day.

At last, thank God, she gave in, and has continued to come to work every weekday, from 7:30 in the morning to whenever Totsy arranged herself on her chaise longue for a late afternoon nap. And I can truthfully say that, in addition to providing her good services to my mother, for which I am profoundly grateful, Thelma's constancy has been my own salvation lately—her eternal, and completely irrational optimism staving off panic and desperation more than once.

⁂

Steeling myself against the inevitable, I made the rounds of the local retirement facilities. I'd heard good reports of Cooper Hall in Mount Pleasant and, after reserving a little apartment there for Totsy, I drew scale diagrams to determine how best to set things up.

Brother Blake agreed to come for the weekend in May when I scheduled the move. My son John was already planning a visit to Charleston then. And Nancy's husband Bill also kindly made himself available, so I had three strong beasts of burden at my disposal, all of whom followed my instructions without demur. To wield such power, even for a day, was unexpectedly heady. And the various phases of the operation all dovetailed so seamlessly that my obliging beasts said the Allies would have been glad of my generalship at the time of the Normandy landing.

Fanny arrived at nine o'clock on the Friday morning and promised to keep Totsy busy until late afternoon. I could see Totsy didn't really understand what was happening, but she liked all the activity and greeted her "guests" with her usual poise. Then off they went—she and Fanny—and the rest of us got to work. I handed Bill the keys to the large U-Haul van I'd booked, and Blake and John rode in the back, saying later that they "felt ridiculous, sitting in wing chairs and eating Egg McMuffins in the dark." Thelma and I followed in my car.

There's no telling how many round-trips we made, but by three o'clock, all the heavy lifting and shoving was behind us—my scale drawings had paid off, and everything fit just as I'd hoped—and Blake and I told the others to call it a day. Worn out, but exceedingly pleased with ourselves, the two of us kept going. While he hung clocks and mirrors and pictures and sconces, I filled the closets and drawers, and the on-site handyman contrived to adapt the curtains that we'd brought from the corresponding rooms at Legaré Street—curtains which Marguerite Vaulk *[Charleston's former preeminent interior decorator]* had designed for 42 Society Street in 1961.

"They shore don't make 'em like this anymore, do they?" he commented appreciatively, as he gently picked and tugged at the fragile swags and jabots. "Things shore ain't what they used to be."

The final result was a triumph. Totsy's bedroom was a mini-version of the one at Legaré Street, and her new drawing room contained as much of her cherished furniture as the smaller space would accommodate. The African violets were in full flower under the torchère lamps. Totsy liked the Blue Boy and Ivory Fashion varieties best, with their long stems and large single blooms. The liquor cabinet and refrigerator were well-stocked, an extravagant bottle of bubble bath was on the ledge of the tub, and the latest editions of *Time* and the *New Yorker* were on her bedside table next to a box of candy.

My last task was to make up Pa's old mahogany sleigh bed. With utmost care, I smoothed the monogrammed sheets over the mattress and tucked them in, slid the pillows into their satiny slips, spread the lacy blanket cover on top of the raspberry-pink Merino blanket, and dropped Daddy's weightless eiderdown onto the end of the bed. Luxurious and inviting, the diminutive boudoir looked as if it were being viewed through the wrong end of a telescope.

We were gathering up our supplies and collecting the trash—and heartily congratulating each other—when Fanny and Totsy came walking down the hall toward us, arm-in-arm. They exchanged a goodbye kiss when they reached the apartment door, and Fanny winked at us and said she'd come back one day soon to visit, when we'd all recovered.

Blake and I hugged Totsy, and then stood aside, watching anxiously as she moved slowly from living room to bedroom, lightly touching things, trying to take it all in. Once or twice, she seemed at a loss, as if she wasn't quite sure she recognised an object here and there. Although Fanny had carefully explained to her the gist of the day's activities, Totsy must surely have been wondering, at some level, how she was going to adjust to such radical changes when she knew instinctively her mental reserves were almost on empty. Her relief at the familiarity of her new nest was plain to see. But while sweetly appreciative and bravely determined to remain mistress of her dignity, there was no denying she was disoriented.

We stayed for supper—which we raved about, hoping to enthuse her—and lingered afterward until she was ready for bed. As I kissed her goodnight, I found myself re-living the aching uncertainty of leaving each of my children at boarding school for the first time.

By the middle of the following week, however, I was convinced Blake and I had made the right decision. Instead of being in her nightclothes and slippers by early evening, restless and fidgeting, Totsy would now be seated at her dressing table, preening and looking forward to dinner. I sometimes caught her smiling at herself in the glass, pursing her lips in a soundless whistle as she fluffed out her hair and clasped on bracelets and touched the *Joy* perfume stopper behind her ears. She wore a hat and gloves wherever she went—even to meals—and always loads of jewelry.

After the routine check of her hemline in the full-length mirror on the back of the bedroom door, she would make her way to the main dining room, where she'd pause in the entrance just long enough to be noticed. Then with the merest nod acknowledging the other diners' stares—one almost expected the royal wave—she would approach her usual table in a quiet corner. There was no formal seating assignment, but no one ever usurped the spot she had appropriated early on for herself. Always waiting to hold out her chair would be an obsequious person in uniform, whom she referred to as the maître d', and whose primary mission she believed was to anticipate her every inconsequential need.

Farewell to agonising over whether or not to tidy up the kitchen. Welcome to orderly new days and agreeable new audiences at every turn.

The thermostat in Totsy's Cooper Hall apartment became the source of chronic unrest. Sensing that it was somehow associated with hot and cold air, she frequently fiddled with the setting and then, depending, would start looking through her wardrobe for either a short-sleeved dress or an overcoat.

"The weather in Charleston has certainly changed since my time," she'd say. "It's simply not fit for man nor beast anymore. You can't believe a word the weatherman says. So undependable."

And daily she would hunt down the staff electrician, whose patience she sorely tried. "I really must insist that you adjust my alarm clock properly! Once and for all!" she demanded of the unfortunate man every time she saw him. "As it is, I never know what to put on in the morning!"

A few of the other Cooper Hall residents attempted to make Totsy's acquaintance, but aside from the exchange of common courtesies, she shunned everyone but Hans and Ruth Kippenberg—

an elderly German couple who she had heard were "of noble birth"—and Dr. Pollack.

Bud Pollack was a retired history professor who immediately made a hit with Totsy by inviting her to look at his "early New England furniture over a glass of sherry." He proved to be awfully earnest, however, and wracked as he was with Parkinson's disease, his hand jerked so badly when handing Totsy her Bristol Cream that she was afraid to return his invitation. She couldn't risk his spilling sherry all over her own velvet sofa, now could she?

Curtailing their brief friendship gave Totsy a failsafe excuse never to go to Tuesday Happy Hour. "I feel terribly uncomfortable without an escort," she warned anybody who might think to argue, "and I wouldn't *dream* of going with any of those other unattached old dolls."

The particular old dolls Totsy had in mind were Dorothy Gibbs and May Connor—like Totsy both widows in their 90s—who were trying to welcome her into this strangely artificial environment. The three had been friends since their Ashley Hall days. Joining them now for a cup of tea one afternoon at Cooper Hall, I was vastly amused at May's recalling that the Goodwyn girls—Totsy and her sister Marion—had been famous for having the best-ironed bloomers at the school.

The delightful little story seemed to jog Totsy's own memory of that lost era. "Do you girls remember," she asked, flashing a dimpled smile, "that Ashley Hall fired me for kissing a Citadel cadet through the iron gate?"

They didn't remember, presumably because such a thing never really happened quite that way. But Totsy's spin on words was engaging and, once again, it was she who defined the moment; it was her contribution that lingered when the tea party was over. I wish, by the way, that she could have claimed Daddy as that amourous cadet, but he didn't enter the scene until a year or so later.

All her life, Totsy had loved to walk and even now, in fair weather, she made several laps every morning around the perimeter of the Cooper Hall complex. At first, she used only her ivory-handled malacca cane but then graduated to a walker with wheels, which she frequently asked me to take "to the nearest mechanic for a routine tuneup." On rainy days, she toured the indoor corridors—always hoping that someone would compliment her hat—until Thelma would round her up for either a nap or a meal.

For months, she sustained life with not much more than Hershey's chocolate bars and Mrs. Sassard's artichoke pickle. Sweet shooting sherry in the late afternoon had by now replaced the perennial Scotch and soda, and a cold split of champagne was always on her table at suppertime. She would promptly polish off the champagne and then spend the rest of the dinner hour rearranging the food on her plate.

Weekends were anathema to Totsy. Thelma wasn't available then to prepare and clean up after breakfast, and Totsy declined room service because waiting for someone to remove a breakfast tray interrupted her morning nap. And having leftovers on a tray—even for 20 minutes—was, of course, too abhorrent even to contemplate.

"So I'm forced to eat in the dining room with all those old people," she moaned. But she tremendously enjoyed Sunday vespers. The odd hymn or two would be loudly rendered out of both time and key, and, more often than not, there would be a guest speaker. "I can't remember what on earth he was preaching about," she laughed merrily as we left the assembly hall one Sunday evening just in time for supper, "but he was mighty easy on the eye, wasn't he?"

To other residents whom she had no intention of befriending, Totsy nevertheless loved giving proprietary tours of her miniature apartment, as if it were a compacted Blenheim Palace. She talked ad nauseam about the pair of fine Meissen birds; the important Hester Bateman salver; the rare padouk-wood chest-on-chest; the unequaled 18th century cartel clock; the elegant diamond-shaped legs of the demilune table. As self-appointed arbiter of taste and excellence, Totsy expected you to concede that her approval of something automatically validated it.

But she waxed most lyrical about her photographs and prints and paintings.

"This portrait of Thomas Middleton is particularly interesting. He was brother to Arthur the Signer, you know," she would continue relentlessly, whether or not her guest showed any interest. "Their grandfather—the first Arthur of the American Middletons—well, he was the first Governor of South Carolina. And as a matter of fact, he was also a president of the First Continental Congress. And you see, because of a marriage between second cousins, my husband was descended from both brothers. Incidentally, the original portrait of Thomas is at the Gibbes Art Gallery on Meeting Street. Do be sure to see it while you're in Charleston. You really shouldn't miss it. Benjamin West was the artist. But *my* portrait—this one—was painted by Thomas's own son, which I think adds greatly to its significance. A remarkably good effort for an amateur, don't you agree?"

She would then direct her guest's attention to a large print of London, bought in the 1950s from the Parker Gallery on Albemarle Street. It was a bird's-eye view—as from the top of Admiral Lord Nelson's column in Trafalgar Square—of the north and south aspects of the city in 1840.

"Of course, you recognize the great metropolis of the British Empire, don't you?" She couldn't resist recalling Britain's undisputed, albeit erstwhile glory. "My husband and I so enjoyed our 10 years there. We even thought about retiring in England—perhaps even in Scotland. We almost bought a castle there. A very small castle. But Blake really wanted to come home."

The colourful spiel always concluded with photographs of two of her favourite forebears: Priscilla Cooper Tyler, on her mother's side, and Albert Taylor Goodwyn, her paternal grandfather.

"And this lovely man was my grandfather, the last surviving three-star Confederate General. He fought in the 58th Regiment of the Alabama Infantry. I'm terribly pleased to have known him as well as I did. We were really quite good friends. And my great-grandmother Priscilla Cooper was John Tyler's second wife. You know, President John Tyler. They say she was the most beautiful woman ever to be mistress of the White House. Uhm, uhm."

Considering most of our First Ladies, Totsy's effusive accolade wasn't really saying very much, but she was always rewarded with Mrs. Tyler's sweetly elegant smile.

Totsy evidently loved her Confederate soldier-grandfather and remembered him with pride in spite of his Secessionist leanings. And out of respect for his beliefs, she declined to join Emmeline and me at a showing of *Gettysburg*, the superb cinematic depiction of the famous battle in which General Goodwyn so valiantly fought. Totsy felt that to watch a commercialized version of that horrific historic defeat would dishonour the memory of past gallantry.

Emmeline was deeply affected by Totsy's reaction to this film. She was fascinated that her remarkably enlightened grandmother remained obstinately loyal to an ancestor who had participated in a cause that so nearly destroyed our nation; a cause that silhouettes the single darkest moment in American history; a cause whose toxic fallout corrodes the South even today. And Emmeline was exhilarated to feel—even if only through the tangled ties of heredity—so near the heartbeat of change, however irregular its rhythm.

✦

My parents' tales from Indonesia were always extremely good value. Emmeline especially liked the one involving her grandmother's being arrested in Palembang for speeding. One can't help wondering what the speed limit might have been in Sumatra in 1926. And also whether those early outposts really did support road systems that would accommodate hurtling Ford V8s.

Anyway, Emmeline and I had joined Totsy for supper at Cooper Hall one evening, and were returning to her apartment as Totsy set the stage. Grinning in anticipation, Emmeline carefully seated her grandmother, and propped the walker against the sofa. I started making coffee.

"While I awaited the trial date," Totsy said mischievously, the famous dimples decorating her face, "I went around telling everyone I was just going to sweet-talk that fat old Dutch judge into finding in my favour." She sank back comfortably among the cushions.

"I really didn't think I'd have any trouble at all. But on the appointed day, when it came my turn to approach the bench, I suddenly felt the elastic at the waist of my underpants go *pop*. Suddenly ... POP! Because, of course, you realise in those days elastic didn't stretch and loosen gradually—it just gave out all at once. My pants promptly fell down and lapped around my ankles! Right there in the middle of that crowded courtroom.

"I tried to be ladylike as I stepped out of them and quickly tucked them away into my purse. And just *prayed* the Judge wouldn't notice—or at least that he'd feel sorry for me if he did.

247

But he *did* see. And he wasn't one bit amused. And he fined me anyway, drat it!"

I'd heard all this before, but it was still funny. We laughed and laughed, reveling in our unaccustomed sisterhood. Thinking to prolong the moment, Emmeline picked up from the coffee table a silver-clad Oriental opium pipe. A relic from Palembang.

"Totsy," she asked innocently, "you must surely be the only person at Cooper Hall with one of these?" I gazed with great satisfaction at my daughter. She matched her grandmother charm for charm.

"Why, yes, Dear, I'm sure you're right," Totsy agreed, without skipping a beat. "As a matter of fact, all I lack is a one-eyed Chinaman."

Emmeline stared at her, and then made an admirable effort to close her mouth.

"No, Dear, it's true," Totsy insisted. "Whenever we smoked—which was *often*—your grandfather and I were always attended by a Chinese, whose job it was to make sure we had everything we needed and weren't disturbed. His main duty was to make sure the coals in the pipe stayed hot. And he had only one eye. Uh ha! Uh ha!"

Now in full swing and tremendously enjoying herself, my mother turned to me.

"Puddin', talking about all this reminds me, have I ever mentioned Shorty Elliot to you? He was one of your father's favourite compeers in Sumatra. An inveterate storyteller. A *wonderful* storyteller. The best one ... the story I've remembered best all these years ... the one he told the most often was the one about the tiger and the bicycle. Shorty swore it really happened to him on his way to work one morning. He *swore* it was true.

"But to fill you in first a little. His habit—as with all the managerial staff at the refinery—was to get up early, usually around

248

five, and ride his bicycle through the jungle to the plant. The idea was to make sure everything had gone smoothly during the night, and then to cycle back home in time to have breakfast with his family.

"'Well, I doubt if you'll believe this,' was how he always began this yarn, 'but I was on my bike at the crack of dawn, as usual. And when I reached the clearing where I normally turn to take the old shortcut—you know the place I mean?—well, one of those tigers was sitting there. Right in the middle of the path, just sitting there. Just looking at me. You know, one of those really big fellas. And I could see there was no way on Earth I could get past him.'

"'Gad, Shorty,' your grandfather gasped, the first time he heard the story, 'weren't you scared?'

"'Sure I was scared. Scared as the Devil himself.'

"'Well, wha'd you do, for Chrissake?'

"'Goda'mity, Blake, what the hell do you *think* I did? I rang my bell!' "

———※———

Sooner than I expected, the assisted-living facilities at Cooper Hall became inadequate to meet Totsy's needs, and I moved her to the nextdoor nursing centre. And several months later to yet another wing, where the patients were a little less senile and a lot less apt to drift into her room and try to take up residence.

Totsy's transfer to the most recent of her new quarters was like a scene out of Monty Python. Nestled against her pillows, and hugging a litre of sherry to her chest, she was whizzed down the hall in her mobile bed, with the crib sides in the "up" position. She was dressed and bejeweled and waved regally at any and all onlookers as she sped by.

Her creature comforts were provided with care and kindness, but even my best efforts couldn't allay the nameless uncertainties that seemed to plague her. And there came a time when she didn't fully recognize me—in other words, she knew me, without being sure exactly *who* I was—but I could tell she enjoyed my daily visits. Still able to summon her stock-in-trade allure, she always brightened the minute I arrived and, depending on the time of day, we would walk, or pore over photograph albums, or perhaps take a meal. And we would chat endlessly, over and over, about nothing and everything, all at the same time.

"Do be sure to give Lane my love when you see her, won't you?" she would always gravely ask when she kissed me goodbye, her nose cool against my cheek. I would always gravely undertake to do so.

A variation to this droll lapse occurred late one December afternoon, during an outing to see the Christmas lights at the James Island County Park. The display was spectacular and Totsy was entranced. "Lane would *so* enjoy this if she could be with us. She *loves* this sort of thing," she said, her voice tinged with nostalgia.

"Aw, come on, Mommie. *I'm* Lane!" Sometimes I couldn't resist trying to weave a thread of reality through our fraying scraps of fantasy.

"I know that, Dear. Of course, I know that," she smiled somewhat vacantly, patting my hand.

I finally concluded that she had the "real" me fixed in her mind at about eight years old. It was good to know she thought gently of her ewe-lamb, as she sometimes called me, for I had never quite qualified for my adult rôle as "Totsy's daughter." She loved me, I know, but she could never bring herself to respect me. I'm not rich, and I'm certainly no longer thin, nor have I ever excelled at any one thing—the underlying criteria by which Totsy usually measured a person's worth. But it was my hostile renouncement, decades ago, of "society"—my mother's term for the milieu inhabited by the respectable—that had set me irretrievably beyond the pale.

As Totsy's mind shrank, day and night lost proper sequence, and she began living amidst increasingly fragmented senses and graphic hallucinations. These she would solemnly recount to anyone who would listen, quaintly indifferent to the fact that their often grisly nature made them inappropriate material for a social setting—even one such as hers.

"You know, I'm seriously thinking of canceling my reservation at this place," she solemnly advised Blake and Joan during one of their scarce visits. "I've just discovered they serve babies for supper here every so often."

She sounded more annoyed than distressed. Blake groaned and looked out the window. I managed not to laugh.

"And you see? Over there?" Totsy continued, pointing indignantly at her wheelchair, which was folded up against the chest-of-drawers. "That motorcycle crashed last week and the dead man's been in here—under my *bed*—ever since. The room service at this place is very poor. Really very poor."

I looked at Blake again. He'd been holding his breath and was getting red in the face. I wondered if he was going remember to exhale.

Sitting bolt upright, in the precise centre of her bed, Totsy was now engaged in peeling the blankets away from the sides of the bed and deftly arranging them in symmetrical linen-fold layers onto her outstretched legs. The three of us watched, fascinated.

"You see, if I don't fix them like this, they'll catch fire," she explained reasonably, apparently referring to the sheets. Then she reached for a piece of candy.

Totsy often asked news of "the war," a chronic figment unrest, apparently between ourselves and—variously—Russia, the Yankees, Yugoslavia, and other residents down the hall. It was never clear whether "we" were the Confederacy or the United States or England. But she was always hopeful for word of victory.

The pièce de résistance, about a year into her time there, was when a fellow resident fell dead into his soup plate one evening at supper. Totsy was aglow with excitement when she told me about it. "Three policemen came! They were in uniform! I suppose they were from the Coroner's Office. Oh, Puddin', they were *so* goodlooking!"

Totsy maintained her legendary elegance even after she became bedridden—ruffled lace bedjackets soon became de rigueur—and she remained garrulous and entertaining even after her conversation had degenerated into imaginative nonsense.

One of her more beyond-the-fringe gambits was leveled at John in the fall of 1996. He was visiting Charleston before starting a new job in Uganda. With a master's degree in health promotion from the London School of Hygiene and Tropical Medicine, he had accepted a job with the Medical Research Council to continue research into the AIDS pandemic. This was the latest juncture in his Africa affiliation.

Ever the attentive and dutiful grandson, John was hard-pressed to maintain his composure when, as he seated himself at Totsy's bedside one afternoon, she reached for his hand and looked at him earnestly. "I've been consulting my ceiling for several weeks now, John dear," she confided, going straight to the heart of the matter, "and I've become particularly interested in that third panel from the window. Can you find the one I mean? Take a look up there, on the right."

The ceilings at Cooper Hall were buffered with soundproof tiles that resembled styrofoam randomly sprayed with black dots. John studied the ceiling, the corners of his mouth twitching.

"I'm not yet sure who," Totsy went on, "but someone has invested a lot of time recording the details of my family history on that panel. And I've been having *such* a good time translating it all. In fact, I'll let you read it when I've finished if you'd be at all interested. Did you know, by the way, that one branch of my family is from Prospect, Tennessee? There at the bottom, see if you can find Prospect. It's only six miles from Pulaski.

"And John, now I think of it, you're probably not aware that Pulaski claims the doubtful distinction of being the birthplace of the Ku Klux Klan. No? Well, you see, Dear, this is terribly interesting, because your grandfather joined the Klan while he was still at The Citadel! Naturally I realised I'd have to take him in hand before it became too late for his redemption. So I told him, quite simply, that he had to choose between the Klan and me! Now what do you think of that?"

More dimples. John nearly fell off his chair. ·

Totsy *seemed* as lucid as always—her lilting voice was usually still clear and steady—but she was fast shedding inhibition and propriety. This was rich. John's own sense of propriety was completely blind-sided. He had no idea how to reconcile his grandmother's lifelong quest for the perfect blend of emancipated respectability with her demented jokes about his grandfather's youthful fascism. The only thing he was sure of, as he clung to the last vestige of intellectual sobriety, was that he'd best not look my way. Our mutual barely contained mirth would explode.

I'd never been sure Totsy wasn't playing to her fans whenever she told this story. But one of the letters from the posthumously discovered deed box does refer directly to that very issue.

"I still feel the Klan are the stuff," Daddy opined in his response to her inferred ultimatum, "and if you, my Sweet, were yourself more worldly, you too would see their virtue."

Worldly or not, we all know who won out. And thus my brother and I grew up in a virtual grab bag of political ethos, exposed to random and ill-conceived arguments over issues as opposed and exhausted as states' rights and the *Thoughts of Chairman Mao*. The sinister little red plastic book sat, preposterous, on my parents' coffee table for years. And with the tenets of such extremes running neck and neck, it's a wonder that both Blake and I travel the middle of the political road. I detest the chicanery of politics. But I've been working for local government for 13 years, and as long as I keep in mind the fact that most of my associates are probably no more politically benighted than are some of my favourite family members, I can even laugh.

Returning for a moment to the vile issue of the Ku Klux Klan, I don't know whether an apologia is due here. I don't know whether I should loudly protest my father's rightmindedness and human charity in spite of his sophomoric association with one of the most evil organisations the world has ever known. I will say that his liaison with the KKK was an aberration and that he soon grew to abhor all they stood for.

Most accounts of the Klan's history agree that it began as a social society, casually formed by a few young Confederate veterans in December of 1865, as a diversion from the ennui of small-town life. They were full of ideas for their new club but none was subversive at that point, nor did the members wish their organisation to have any military or political implications. Within a year, however—

enlarged with new members from nearby towns, and stoked by the ill will felt by many white southerners in the aftermath of the Civil War—it had taken on a chilling intimidation.

Before the founders realised what they'd set in motion, the group had become deadly. And then, as rapidly as it had spread, its influence faded, only to be revived once again after World War I, when the Klan claimed to stand for morality and to be the "defenders of pure womanhood." The fatuous euphemism was aimed at women's suffrage—a concept considered then to be out-and-out laughable—and one that went just as much against the grain of the chauvinistic white southern male as did the defeat of their armies in the field and the loss of their economic and social way of life.

It's hard today to understand how an organisation so opposed to the principles of justice and equality could twice in our nation's history have held such power. It's equally hard to believe that its regalia and superficial brotherhood—and claims of chivalrous protection for clinging southern vines—could have captured, even fleetingly, the imagination of so many estimable and humane young men of my father's vintage.

But it did. And by God's grace, most of them came to their senses before becoming irrevocably corrupted by its toxic dramatic lure.

The poison of the American Civil War still seeps through our national psyche, leaving yet unreconciled the turbulence of the 1960s, the parades and cross-burnings and lynchings of the 1920s, even Reconstruction and The War itself. Survival on the early American frontier produced a new aggressive form of individualism and enterprise and a rough-and-ready form of justice that often failed to rise above raw vigilante retribution.

My father did like being described as having an iron will; he often equated inflexibility of purpose with strength of character. And I imagine he would have liked to be the one to yell, "Damn the torpedoes, full speed ahead!" at the Confederate victory at Mobile Bay in 1864. Admiral David Farragut's sentiment was so completely and satisfactorily uncompromising.

But the truth about him—about my dear father—is that he believed deeply in "do unto others" and "live and let live." His tough words were bravado. His heart was soft and merciful.

Book XX
Family Legend ... Fact or Fiction?

Most families like telling stories about themselves and basking in reflected glory. But everyone has a few perfectly nice black sheep relatives, and I think a personal history would be drab if it didn't weave the rough along with the smooth. Imperfections add texture to a verbal canvas, like the slub in raw silk.

Totsy disagreed. She thought the only biography worth claiming is one that would qualify for notice in Burke's Peerage, meet the criteria for Emily Post, and survive the grueling media coverage of an American presidential candidate. Her own distinguished political-military family had roots in Alabama and Tennessee. When the time was right—and bent on becoming a modern matriarch—she targeted and wed into an equally distinguished landed South Carolina family, a family now of generally reduced circumstances but still resting—a bit defensively—on the laurels of its glittering past.

Totsy believed emphatically that personal histories should be not only preserved but sanctified, if at all possible, and she was a past master at rearranging the facts to conform with this reference—regardless of undeniable inconsistencies. For example, when Francis left me in the autumn of 1975, Totsy's flip but firm advice was for me to imply that *I'd* got rid of *him*. Since she doted on her son-in-law, this seemed a wry position for her to adopt. But then it occurred to me that since the situation appeared superficially to cast her own daughter in a less than favourable light, the "facts" had to be adjusted. At least for the time being. *[Francis admitted later that he left me because he was afraid he would kill me in a drunken rage if he didn't.]*

Years later, in 1989—without telling me, much less asking me—Totsy invited Francis to Charleston for Thanksgiving. He was to be her party trick that week.

"Why, Dear, it never occurred to me that you would mind," her tone dripping with wounded surprise when I accused her of disloyalty. "I must have forgotten to tell you he was coming. I've invited a few people for drinks on Wednesday. Perhaps you'd like to join us?"

My father disliked Francis Kinsman. The qualities in my husband that most appealed to Totsy were, predictably, those that most irritated Daddy. Totsy had invited Francis to use her pet name from the outset, but Daddy would have none of such informality, aware that it would imply a regard he neither felt, nor wished anyone to presume of him. When asked how he should be addressed after we were married, Daddy left Francis in no doubt as to his preference.

"I think 'Mr. Middleton' will do just fine," he said evenly, and went back to his book.

True to type, Totsy exaggerated my in-laws' claims to aristocracy to the extent that several American friends and family members—people unfamiliar with the subtleties of the British caste system—assumed that Francis was a peer of the realm. Naturally, Totsy preferred not to disabuse them. Francis' great-uncle Sir Malcolm Hilbery was a QC *[Queen's Counsel]*, and Totsy had exploited the fact of his knighthood whenever she could get away with it. Thanks to her creative claims and selective namedropping, one of my cousins was so certain that my children could assert hereditary title that my mother had the nerve to take issue with me when I tried to set the record straight with the cousin.

Another example of Totsy's historical editing was her serene explanation of her father's "abruptly resigning" his position on the faculty at The Citadel. "Pa simply decided he could no longer be part of an institution whose outmoded and reactionary administration he so deplored," she said grandly.

In truth, Pa was himself about as reactionary as they came, and he did not resign because of devotion to some set of highminded principles. The real issue was his hot temper, and having turned a blind eye to more than enough of his erratic behaviour, the administration finally fired him.

Today Pa would be described as a "loose cannon"—an epithet which endears him to me and would have seriously annoyed Totsy—and except for Brother Blake, the overall reaction of other members of my tribe on learning of Pa's clay feet has been one of cautious amusement.

Hence my black sheep theory. A few character flaws in one's relatives can even be charming as long as they're at the safe remove of a generation or two.

Brother Blake was visibly offended by this disclosure concerning our grandfather. Since then, whenever I'm with him and his family, he braces against the next anecdotal sensation I might either toss into the stockpot of ancestral lore—or perhaps even perpetrate myself. In contrast with Blake's almost neurotic reserve, I seldom allow niceties to get between me and a good story, and I think he's afraid I'm going to infect his children and grandchildren with a taste for unvarnished truth.

He was far more subdued by the rigours of our upbringing than I was, and he once admitted he'd spent a lot of time with his "head down, dodging the bullets." Since I was the target for all the bullets in our family, I found his comment to be of absorbing interest. He also said he'd secretly admired my having the nerve to protest when I considered myself hard done by. He even said he reproached himself for making himself scarce whenever I would become the family scapegoat.

Coming from Blake, such candid introspection stopped me in my tracks. It suggested an almost alien humility. He certainly is more of a traditionalist than I am, and he disapproves of rocking any boat for any reason. As far as I can remember, his only attempt, ever, at dispensing brotherly advice was to suggest I at least *try* to be discreet about my own indiscretions—advice that seemed to me to be far more trouble than it was worth.

Sometime in the early 1970s, Totsy took it upon herself to sift through certain Middleton family papers—deeds, receipts, letters—that had come to Daddy when his mother died. He had never shown any interest in them. He also claimed never to know the particulars even of his own salary. So, just as it fell to Totsy to husband their financial resources, she also took responsibility for the Middleton family memorabilia.

In acknowledgment of a certain custodial obligation, Daddy did turn over the most important of those early documents to Middleton Place, a National Landmark property and home of Arthur Middleton. But this was not before Totsy had them professionally copied, and the copies laminated and bound in a gold-tooled, dark-green leather album. It was her Christmas gift to Daddy that year. He smiled his thanks, placed the book beside him on the sofa, and never once opened it.

"Well, so much for that," Totsy muttered to herself. "I should have known better than to think he'd actually look at it."

She was well aware that a preoccupation with one's own pedigree bored Daddy to tears. He baited her endlessly about her slavish attention to "what people might think," and would appear for formal parties, dressed in one of his bespoke Savile Row suits, haberdashery from Turnbull and Asser, and white tube socks from K-Mart. He would then justify his roguish insolence with his personal brand of irrefutable logic.

"Now, look. When I'm away from home, nobody knows who I am. And when I'm *at* home, *everybody* knows who I am. So it really doesn't matter a damn what I wear. Right?"

Totsy wrung her hands over this little foible of his, yet her own life wound its way through a maze of contradictions even more convoluted. Unable to resist the temptation to boast about her Confederate antecedents—their rank and beauty, their wealth and position—she would also loudly condemn the very ideals for which those antecedents had presumably lived and died. For a woman whose primary raison d'être was the beautification of her own persona, it was a marvel that she never guessed how specious was her argument.

"Totsy, you are *the* most awful snob," Fanny once snapped, exasperated and embarrassed by Totsy's condescending manner toward a newcomer to Charleston. The sisters-in-law had been friendly antagonists for over 60 years.

"I know it!" Totsy snapped right back. "I simply can't help it, Frances! You should know that by now!"

Pleased with her single-minded organisation of the Middleton records, Totsy set about the absorbing task of glamourizing her own already more than adequate genealogy. She never let you forget that President John Tyler was her paternal great-grandfather.

Furthermore, she had discovered early on that to pose in the vanguard of so-called modern thinking lent her an air of intellectual independence and superiority. And claiming to be anti-secession and antiwar, yet pro-abortion and pro-integration, especially in the South, often placed her in the centre of inflamed controversy—a position she sought and occupied with scintillating skill.

"When I decided to explore my Lane family history," she told us, "I planned a little trip to Tennessee to visit my Cousin Ann McWhorter, whom I hadn't seen in years. We had mutual grandparents, and I thought she might like to join me in researching one or two even older ancestors, particularly a certain mysterious George Washington Lane. You see, as a child, I occasionally overheard adults whispering about him, but the minute they realised I was listening, they'd change the subject. My own mother's maiden name was Lane, so I assumed this Judge Lane was related to us. And since nobody would talk about him if I was within earshot, I decided he must be some sort of renegade.

"Well, anyway, Ann took me along to the local library, and together we dredged up enough information to confirm that the judge really was our maternal great-grandfather. He was born in Georgia in 1806 and died fairly young, in 1864, not long before the end of The War. His family had moved to Limestone County, Alabama in 1821 when he was a teenager, but he eventually settled in Athens, Tennessee, where he married a Miss Margaret Davis. Their son Hector, whom they named for Margaret's father, was my grandfather—Ma's father. All of which brings us more or less up to date."

She went on to say how elated she and Cousin Ann were to find that George Lane had been appointed Federal District Judge by President Lincoln, but their delving revealed also that he was the grandson of a Congressional Creek Indian chieftain named Corn Silk. It was hardly surprising—in the mid to late 1800s—that the Davis family didn't rush to claim a "brass ankle" among their kinfolk. But the real rub was that during the final days of the Civil War, Judge Lane openly housed Federal troops and flew the Union standard from his rooftop.

This flagrant betrayal of the Confederate cause was far more embarrassing to his bride's family—and has continued to be so perceived by most of his descendants—than was his dubious breeding. After all, the Creek antecedent was a chieftain, wasn't he? But Totsy could be depended upon to take the high road in a case like this. Always the maverick, she declared with possessive pride that Lane's stalwart resistance to secession glimmered of vision and sweet reason, and that she was "terribly proud to claim him."

In his official capacity as Judge, the story continues, Judge Lane stood in the doorway of the county jail one night, holding a loaded shotgun, the safety released. Within, a black man awaited trial for some petty or perhaps even trumped-up misdemeanor. And on the street outside, a drunken lynch mob prepared to take the jail.

"I can't stop all of you," Judge Lane shouted at the unruly crowd, "but be assured I *will* shoot the first man who tries to cross this threshold. I intend the prisoner shall stand trial tomorrow."

The prisoner did stand trial and was acquitted. And, of *course,* Totsy was proud.

It was extraordinarily brave and potentially exceedingly dangerous to ignore the bruised egos of the defeated post-Civil War South. The personal risks from every quarter were formidable, and Totsy was convinced that the family reputation was not only *not* tarnished by the Judge's iconoclast behaviour, but rather that it was thereby significantly ennobled.

I have a photographic copy of a portrait of this controversial forebear and, on examination, it is plainly from him that certain physical family traits still derive. A lace jabot ruffles at his throat under a riding jacket with a velveteen collar, and he holds a riding crop, which—intending to needle Totsy just a trifle—Daddy loved to refer to as "the Judge's peace pipe."

But it's the man's face, with its high cheekbones and strong aquiline nose, that reminds you first of Ma and then of Aunt Marion and her four children. They all have those cheekbones and beautiful nose, as well as very straight black hair and dark eyes.

Totsy, on the other hand, doesn't appear to have inherited a single one of those very distinctive genes. She was a blonde. And so were Brother Blake and I. Typical Middleton towheads we were.

***

The family saga continues. When John was about a year old, I developed on my right wrist a ganglion cyst that became quite a nuisance. Dr. Peter Train—of the saintly ilk of country family doctors—referred me to a Mr. Riddel, a surgeon in Colchester. Six weeks after the minor surgery, I returned to Mr. Riddel for the final inspection. He pronounced me well-healed, but I could see he was taken aback by the unsightly scar that had formed over the incision. It was covered with angry red lumpy welts.

"Look at this," I said crossly, thrusting my freakish wrist under Mr. Riddel's nose. "Can you fix it? Will these horrible nodules disappear in time?"

The doctor took my hand and squinted through his spectacles at my disfigured wrist.

"Mrs. Kinsman," he said, giving me back my hand, "I hope you don't mind my asking, but do you happen to know anything about your family background?"

He sighed loudly and suddenly looked rather tired. I had no idea what he was talking about. He couldn't have failed to notice I was American, and I couldn't imagine what else could possibly be germane.

"Yes, I do," I answered impatiently. "I know quite a lot about my family. Why?"

"Well, quite honestly, Mrs. Kinsman," he said slowly, "these 'nodules,' as you describe them, are actually known as keloid formation. It's a genetic condition, you understand, and it's found almost exclusively among the Negro race."

Any halfwit could see Mr. Riddel was nervous about the turn our meeting was taking, but he needn't have worried. At this point I was interested only in the aesthetics of my condition—not its origins.

"Well, whatever," I answered rather shortly. "Are they going to go away?" Threats to my vanity overrode anything so trivial as racial singularities.

"I hope so, Mrs. Kinsman," he said, looking ever so slightly past me. "I certainly do hope so."

As he grew older, John's soft gold curls became less soft and less golden. The unwritten dress code at Eton College includes the requirement that the boys' hair not be allowed to grow below their ears nor touch their collars. John complied, but without ever having to cut his hair. It grew ever upwards and out until eventually it stood wider than his shoulders. The best natural afro on any white man you ever saw, it seemed to defy one or two fairly rigid laws of nature. When he turned his head, the hair would follow.

Soon after coming down from Eton, John grew a full beard—one that you could see from the back—and cut his hair. I understand he even shaved his head at around that time, and he insisted that the bald effect had been "generally very well received." When his new hair grew back, its texture had taken on a certain vibrance—not unlike Brillo—and the colour had darkened perceptibly. By the time he was 25, it was very nearly black. He says he owns a comb, but I'm not sure why; his coiffure is now clipped neat and short. And it never, *ever* becomes tousled.

The family saga continues some more. Not so long ago, two friends came to my house for a drink after work one Friday afternoon. Cookie Emery is a Cajun from Biloxi, Mississippi, and Gayle Bustraan is a light-skinned black woman from St. Stephen, South Carolina. As we were mixing our drinks in the kitchen, they admired the black-and-white photographs over the counter of my three children. The pictures are grouped together in a single horizontal frame. People always comment on them. My heart swelled for the 100th time.

In the one of Blake, he's 14 years old. It's a nostalgic shot. He's leaning against a tree in the garden at The Mossings. Blonde bangs hang over straight dark eyebrows and he wears a calm direct expression. He is beautiful. The photograph has been cropped, but you can still make out a ragged denim-covered leg and a bare foot hanging over a branch just above Blake's head. They belong to 10-year-old John.

The picture of Emmeline was taken when she was about 18, in her minuscule ground-floor flat on Wentworth Street in Charleston.

She is sitting with her cat Cream on her lap, in a shabby wing chair, the wings of which are obviously the cat's scratching post. Emmeline is trying to hold onto Cream—her fingers deep in his fur—who doesn't want to pose and is leaning away from her, trying to get down. Emmeline's longish curls are held back loosely by a thin ribbon that ends in a feather and sunlight shimmers through the strands. She is looking down at Cream, showing us a three-quarter profile of her smile and her fine Roman nose. Though the photograph is black-and-white, you somehow sense her wide-set eyes are gray-blue behind the lowered lashes.

I'm not sure how old John is in his picture. Twenty-four, perhaps. It was taken in Zimbabwe, and John is in a rowboat on the Zambezi, which he says is full of hippos. There's a wooded shoreline in the background, and John sports a T-shirt with a pink fox on it—I've seen the actual shirt, so I know the fox is pink. A patterned kerchief is tied around John's neck, and a straw hat shades his bearded face—exactly like Daddy's routine getup, except for the beard, when he used to fish in the Carolina surf.

Unanimous on the merits of these keepsakes, Cookie and Gayle and I repaired to the drawing room, lit the fire, and settled down with our drinks and snacks. And since that moment, none of us has been able to remember exactly which part of the ensuing chitchat led to my suddenly making an electrifying connection between Judge Lane, the keloids on my wrist, and John's hair. A connection that struck me with the effect of a blow to the solar plexus.

First, after her pilgrimage to Tennessee, Totsy had referred to George W. Lane as a "brass ankle," carefully explaining to us that such a person was the offspring of a Caucasian and an American Indian. As I said earlier, she felt that being a judge amply qualified

Lane as a member of the family and that there was even a certain eminence in having a Congressional Indian Chief somewhere in our distant past.

I have since learnt, however, that Totsy was much mistaken. I now know that a brass ankle is a person who carries Caucasian, American Indian and *African American* blood. And if Totsy had ever become aware of this expanded definition, she would have moved heaven and earth to expunge all records of Lane's very existence—let alone any family fable suggesting he might be one of us! Judgeship and chieftain be damned!

Second, there were the beastly keloids that had formed on my ganglion cyst scar.

And third—what about John's hair?

By God, I thought, as my mind slammed shut, *We're black!*

First thing the following Monday morning, I telephoned the Medical University of South Carolina. When I finally tracked down a professor in the Genetics Department, I introduced myself and gave him a condensed version of Friday's revelation before asking the $64,000 question.

"I wonder, could you tell me, please, is there some sort of test that could determine whether there's any Negro blood in my veins?"

I sensed that my not-altogether-American voice threw him a bit at first. Remember, I'm now divorced and using my thoroughly Anglo-Saxon—not to mention distinctly Lowcountry—surname of Middleton again. And this certainly wasn't the sort of common-or-garden inquiry he was likely to get on a common-or-garden Monday morning.

"The only definitive proof of this would be if anyone in your family ever contracts sickle cell anaemia, Ms. Middleton," he said, managing an admirably neutral tone of voice. Then he coughed politely. "But since both you and your son ... uh, in other words ... uh, since two consecutive generations carry these specific genetic characteristics ... well, uh, there's almost certainly African blood somewhere in your ancestry."

Book XXI
Better Than Fortune Cookies

I remember Totsy's saying there had to be compensations for growing older—she just hadn't come across them yet. It's beginning to be my own experience, though, that she was right, and I've recently begun jotting down some of the very real benefits—or unsung rewards—of bidding our salad days adieu.

Stretching before you get out of bed in the morning is a luxury, not a jumpstart.

The best gifts these days hardly ever come in wrapping paper.

Your house echoes your history; you wouldn't dream of replacing the faded upholstery on your grandmother's chaise-longue.

You'd rather feast your eyes on your pet's face than on a lover's.

In retrospect, your parents' idiosyncrasies seem rather charming; in fact, they bear an uncanny resemblance to your own.

To hell with three-inch heels; you wonder why it took you so long to value comfort over chic.

You dab on your best perfume after a bath—even when it's just you at home.

Your letters used to be a means of keeping people up to date; now, when you write to those people, it's usually to tell them how much you love them.

Fear of loneliness becomes the luxury of privacy.

You look with interest at the face in the mirror—and feel a certain wry satisfaction.

You begin remembering your parents as if they were your contemporaries and wish you could compress time accordingly.

Your siblings are, of course, still your siblings; unlike you, however, they still don't get it.

You don't have to "make" friends anymore; you simply recognize them.

You used to assume that age would jade and fade you; so it's a pleasant surprise to find that the perspective of added years rejuvenates and liberates you.

You look back at your family's old dynamics and marvel that any of you survived.

It's easy now to walk into a room full of strangers—and to walk right back out again if you don't like what you see.

Never mind that your waistline is no longer the middle of an hourglass; people seem more interested in what you say than in how you look.

You stop being afraid to die; now you're afraid only that you might not have lived enough by the time you fall off your perch.

You think how useful it would have been at 30, to have had the self-confidence you have at 60, even though you still don't feel a day over 20.

You used to suspect you were your family's black sheep; now you know you are—and feel as if you won the prize.

Someone politely suggests you bleach the age spots on your hands; you hadn't even noticed them.

Annual physicals are just as loathsome as they ever were, but a good report is like money in the bank.

If you used to be a Republican, you begin to think twice; if you used to be a Democrat, now you know why.

You bask in the sun for its warmth—not to get a tan.

You begin to feel kindly toward your old mistakes; they're part of that person whose company you've come to enjoy so much.

On the rare occasions that you shed a tear, it's probably because your heart is singing.

Fancy dinner parties are a thing of the past; you'd rather spend long easy evenings with a couple of old friends and a big bottle of wine.

You relish talking about your past; and you try very, very hard not to repeat yourself.

You review your former ages with a certain charity and eagerly await the ones that lie ahead.

You remember an old love and thank God for having managed to leave him far behind.

You remember another old love—and miss him.

Occasionally you think of updating your 40-year-old haircut; but why, when it still suits you?

You're gradually sorting out which of your inhibitions are the ones that really inhibit you, and begin to shed them with gay abandon.

Slowly but surely, you are acquiring the elusive virtue of patience—and relish the delicious power it brings.

You're also learning when you should draw the so-called line, and are usually brave enough to go ahead and draw it.

You wonder how you happened on the sense of well-being that accompanies you almost everywhere—and then quickly remind yourself of the folly of trying to analyse happiness.

Come what may, you usually look forward to tomorrow.

Book XXII
And There Were Shepherds Abiding in the Field

Totsy came back to England almost every year, and each of her visits involved a major enterprise. On one such trip in the early 1970s, she stepped off the plane and presented me with Ma and Pa's 12 silver julep cups. She had held them on her lap, in a padded container, all the way across the ocean.

"This is to be The Year of the Mint Julep," she announced, and went on to explain that as I was of Southern descent, she had decided my summer parties at The Mossings should feature the Southern specialty.

Totsy was herself a feature—and very popular among our friends—and we asked a few of her favourites to come over after church on Sunday. With Pa's julep recipe as reference, we began our preparations early in the week.

Blake talked our nextdoor farmer out of a burlap bag in which to pour the ice before crushing it with a mallet. Emmeline picked and trimmed lemon mint from the herb garden and left it in the fridge to crisp. John cut drinking straws in half so people's noses would be buried in the mint bouquet as they sipped. Francis went off to Halstead to find bourbon, which he managed to do, but only because the presence of American Air Force personnel at nearby Lakenheath *[an RAF-USAF base, which was still active]* influenced the local off-licenses to stock it. I filled the silver cups with the crushed ice and stored them in the freezer along with the container of julep mixture, which would eventually congeal.

Incidentally, Daddy's *Middleton Modified Method of Making Marvelous Martinis* matched, in killer quality, Pa's julep and eggnog formulae. The eggnog was so strong that an inebriated victim once quipped that the potion couldn't possibly contain anything other than "maybe a beaten egg white or two and a quart of bourbon." Both Pa and Daddy insisted that neither of these drinks was "worth a nickel unless you can carve your initials in the frost on the glass." It should also be noted that Daddy's answer to Prohibition had been to "make the gin and let it age while [he] shaved."

But back to the juleps. Totsy's Sunday drinks party took place on a stifling August afternoon. At least "stifling" by English standards. And with typical disregard for the unseasonal heat, the men were all wearing Harris tweed jackets—as if *not* sweating were merely mind over matter.

It soon became apparent that everyone assumed a mint julep was the American version of the Pimms No. 1: a long, relatively benign English summer concoction, made by mixing in a tall glass pitcher a measured portion of a gin-based concentrate with sparkling lemonade and slices of fresh fruit. It's sharp and refreshing and goes to your head only after drinking more than a few.

The same cannot be said, however, of the mint julep. The julep is *not* intended to slake a raging thirst. You are supposed to nurse a julep. You are supposed idly to jiggle the frosted cup and let the treacly mixture dilute—even *slightly*—as the ice melts. You are supposed to *taste* it.

But, no. Our parched guests gulped it down to the dregs and then reeled as the Angostura and neat bourbon hit their unsuspecting, unfortified bloodstreams. English brows were studded with damp little beads. And English eyes stood on stalks of somewhat indignant surprise. We were standing about on the terrace outside the drawing room, and everyone reached for a wall to lean against as they waited for their sea legs to return. And I looked on with great satisfaction. Of course, I hadn't actually planned my guests' discomfiture, but I did allow myself to gloat a little. The British still condescend to their American cousins from time to time, and here—for once, though briefly—one of those unsophisticated kin definitely had the advantage.

I am reminded of a Sunday luncheon at Dabbie and David Weston's house during one of Totsy's visits to Essex. Seated next to her was the Weston's unusually self-possessed, prep-school-age son. In a world where Totsy expected always to dominate centre stage, the boy yanked the mat out from under her with the timing of an experienced stand-up comedian.

"Mrs. Middleton," he began politely, neatly inserting himself into a gap in the adult conversation, "do you by any chance know the difference between the Watergate and the Profumo scandals?"

"Why, no, Dear, tell me."

"Well, one is Nixon and the other is knicks off."

On the first morning of her last trip to England, Totsy awoke to the smells of breakfast drifting through the quiet house. She assumed Francis had already left for the office and that everyone else was down in the kitchen. After putting on her dressing gown and slippers, she opened her door into the hall and headed for the stairs.

It was a fair spring day, and she paused at a window to look out at the orchard at the back of our property. Beyond the flowering apple trees, Mr. Newton's hazy green wheatfield stretched up the slope of a hill to St. Giles Church—England at its loveliest. As her gaze returned to the terrace beneath her, Totsy found herself looking at the rear view of a baby's perambulator. It had been positioned facing away from the house so its occupant would feel the warmth of the early sun rising behind the church beyond. Totsy was puzzled. John was her newest grandchild, and was nearly seven years old. She was almost certain he didn't still take morning naps. In a pram.

Her interest piqued, she hurried downstairs and pushed open the swing door from the dining room into the kitchen. I was prodding eggs in a frying pan. My friend and helper, Joyce Paulin, was emptying the dishwasher. And Blake and Emmeline and John were seated around the breakfast table, eating their fruit and cereal.

As Totsy and Mrs. P greeted each other fondly, I noticed Totsy cast a quizzical glance in John's direction. She helped herself to a cup of coffee and approached the children, who turned their faces to receive their grandmother's noticeably absentminded kisses. Adjusting the sash of her robe, Totsy then walked past me toward the terrace door and stepped outside into the beautiful April day. Carefully sipping her coffee, she strolled over to the pram. Then, with transparent nonchalance, she peeked in—and instantly sprang back, nearly spilling hot coffee all over a smiling black infant of about a year old. Totsy stood stock still, staring foolishly into the pram.

Watching her through the window and anticipating her reaction, Mrs. P and I had followed her outside and witnessed this little pantomime. The two of us fell about with laughter. The explanation was simple enough, but I hadn't thought to brief my mother ahead of time that Mrs. Paulin was participating in a Government-sponsored foster program. Dozens of Nigerians immigrated to England in the 1960s and '70s, and by providing reliable home care for the pre-school children, the authorities were making it possible for the parents to attend trade school, full-time, until they learnt to make their way within those very foreign shores.

The child in the pram on my terrace was named Addie, and he was the third child, so far, to benefit from Mrs. Paulin's splendid civic-mindedness. He was not the latest Middleton grandchild.

<hr />

"Blake, why don't you go to England and see the children?" some friend or another would ask my father from time to time.

"I've been to England," was his standard reply, inviting no discussion.

I knew he loved us, so it was hard to understand how his dislike of travel—or, more exactly, of being away from home—could outweigh his desire occasionally to visit us and his old English comrades. To be fair, he did accompany Totsy one time. It was 1966 and our first Christmas at The Mossings. The visit as a whole was an unqualified success, but it's the memory of Christmas Eve itself that lies most snug in my heart, and that recalls that other perfect Christmas Eve 20-odd years earlier, when Daddy came home, unexpectedly, from Naples.

Totsy and Francis and I had trekked up Lucking Street—a fairly steep incline that was now coated with snow and ice—to St. Giles Church for the midnight service, leaving Daddy at home with the children. Church wasn't his thing, even when there was likely to be some good music. I'm almost sure that the only two services he attended in the years between my birth in 1938, and his own death in 1986, were my Confirmation at Heathfield, and my wedding at the Grosvenor Chapel.

Walking home after the carols and Lessons, the night was intensely cold under a black starlit sky. Shivering and linking arms for warmth, we chatted and hummed as we inched our way down the middle of the hill, our breath hanging in the frosty air around us, our footsteps crunching on the ice. Approaching the house, we saw that all was in darkness except for a faint glow that washed over the diamond-flecked grass under the study window. The curtains were open, so we stopped and peered inside before opening the front door.

The scene within embraced us in its ineffable tenderness. We held our breath, spellbound. The soft illumination came from the string of white lights threaded throughout the bushy little Christmas tree and from the fading orange embers in the grate. Our three cats were nestled together on the hearth, blinking serenely into the fireplace, mesmerised by the hissing sound of the wood as it burnt through and fell into the ashes beneath.

Facing the tree and the slowly dying fire, Daddy was leaning back into the cushions at the end of the sofa, his eyes closed, his arms loosely crossed; I could see he was snoring softly. Enfolded warm within his embrace was two-year-old John—also fast asleep— his thumb in his mouth, his cheek resting on Daddy's chest. And about to fall out of John's relaxed little arms was a brown teddy bear, almost as large as John himself—his main Christmas present.

The three of us standing outside turned and looked wordlessly into each others' eyes. Before us was the very essence of universal peace and good will. The hope of all the world.

Epilogue

I do not believe in a traditional god. I believe that godly influence comes uniquely and solely through the love of friends—which I suppose means I'm a heathen—in spite of the fact that the first tentative steps of my soul's journey were more or less orthodox. Since then, that journey has wandered from the comfortably straightforward, to the deeply religious, to the heated denouncement of any belief at all. To the epiphany of my mother's death today.

If I'd had to depend on Totsy to teach me even the rudiments of the Christian faith, it would have been an uphill exercise for us both. Totsy's concept of religion never reached beyond the grandeur of the literature and music and architecture inspired throughout the ages by Mother Church. She barely knew even the Lord's Prayer, and she listened to sermons for their editorial commentary alone. Her own religious experience, drawn solely from the melodrama of other people's ardour, was mawkish at best. That such a devout hedonist should have been allowed to illumine the mystery of death seems an oddly humourous kind of symbolism. And that I, long the angry unbeliever still mourning a child, should have been allowed at my mother's death to witness a bit of Divine comedy, is indeed God being most mysterious in His ways.

Totsy's mother, Ma, was the first person ever to take me to church. It was 1943, and I was five years old. And because Daddy had to travel on business regularly from New York to Europe,

Totsy and Brother Blake and I were living in Summerville, South Carolina, not far down the road from our Goodwyn grandparents. Ma was a God-fearing, or I should say a God-loving woman, and she warmed to her self-appointed duty of teaching me the basics—the Ten Commandments, the Lord's Prayer, the Apostles' Creed, and the 23rd Psalm—which I memorised until I could rattle them off as easily as my ABCs. She took me to Sunday School every day during Lent that year and, as the only child in the group who turned up on 40 consecutive days, I was rewarded with a small pale-blue enamel cross on a silver chain. Even then I knew I owed that lovely little prize entirely to Ma.

I liked milling around the big kitchen at Pinewood with my grandmother more than almost anything else in the world. She hummed Chopin nocturnes while she pottered about at the stove. I'd shell pecans, morsel by broken morsel, which she'd let me stir into fudge before pouring it onto a buttered plate to set. I learnt how to "make butter" by squeezing a capsule of bright orange powdered dye into a mound of anaemic oleomargarine in a thick plastic bag, and then kneading and blending it until it masqueraded as the real thing. I'd rub the silverware and carefully lay the dining table, folding the napkins and filling the salt and pepper shakers. I'd try my hand with mini flower arrangements—sprigs of honeysuckle and woods azalea, and the yellow Lady Banksia rose that climbed up the back porch. And we'd just talk. About things.

Ma showed me cunning card tricks and let me win when we played Canasta. She allowed me to dress up in her size four-and-a-half high-heeled shoes and her little mink cape—being herself of Lilliputian proportion, her clothes almost fit me. And she taught me to knit, my first project being a small yellow popcorn-stitch blanket to wrap around the white velour cat she gave me for my birthday that spring.

I loved her with a child's comfortable, pure love. I loved her smiling voice. I loved the heavy grizzled braid which she wound into a loose knot at the nape of her neck, where the hair underneath was still black. And I loved the way she called me "Daughter." Far and away the most important person in the world of my childhood, Ma's sweetness was transcendent—like the essence of a southern garden. Like the eternal and universal Golden Rule.

Sending me to Heathfield several years later was the most felicitous decision my parents ever made on my behalf. I thrived there and spread my wings in safety. And even now, half a century later, I'm still reaping unexpected benefits. The basic appeal of the school's strict religious overtones was short-lived, but the remaining apparently unshakable elements of faith seem to have been a quiet preparation for the infusion of life offered me today by my mother's death.

It was at Heathfield that I fell ardently, if briefly, into the thrall of Protestant doctrine and became almost immediately the typical child-woman, stalked and ensnared by the lure of demure piety, a mysticism that seemed to acquire substance through the glories of sacred music. Our venerable choirmaster, Charles Faulkner, believed that all children should be drilled in the heroic works of Bach and Handel, and, by the time we left school, every single one of us—whether musically inclined or not—had become intimately acquainted with the monumental arias and chorales of the 18th century. It is those great works rather than the fundamentals of the Church of England that became my rod and my staff. My comfort and my daily bread.

As Francis and I were still living in London when Blake and Emmeline were born, it was logical to have them both christened at the Grosvenor Chapel where we had been married. And later, after returning to England from Pakistan and settling in Essex, John was welcomed into the faith at the Round Church in Little Maplestead. Eventually, we undertook our children's admittedly sketchy Sunday morning attendance at St. Giles, the Norman church in Great Maplestead. And it was, ironically, at this ancient sanctuary—always redolent of dust and peace and candle wax and Harvest Festival—that a newborn champion of reason-at-any-price fluttered alongside my mindless devotion. Encountering only listless competition, it soon matured and soared past the complaisance of rote dogma, out into the unsatisfactory realm of skepticism.

By the time I returned to South Carolina in 1976, I had begun to equate Sundays with gloves and gossip, and sexless women sermonising, and unctuous laymen handing out the body and blood of Christ. Determined to avenge what seemed such repugnant sacrilege, I embraced my heresy with the zeal of a convert, and then congratulated myself on being wise at last to spiritual trickery by a God who spoke in riddles. Riddles whose answers He kept jealously to Himself.

So it was with a calloused heart, on November 17, 1983, that I learnt my Blake had died. And I continued defiantly to live by that bitter creed—the waste and tragedy of his death seemed irrefutably to justify it—until this afternoon. Until this jubilant April afternoon, when riddles became axioms, death confirmed life, and doubt burst into exultation. Until this soft warm April afternoon when God took my hand.

Take a deep breath, Lane, and open your eyes, He said. *There. Now you'll begin to understand.*

MY UPCOMING OBITUARY

LANE MIDDLETON grew up in Grosvenor Square, London, where her father was Director of the English branch of the Mobil Oil Company from 1950 to 1960. During that time, she attended Heathfield School in Ascot, England; Riante-Rive in Lausanne, Switzerland; and La Sorbonne in Paris. She married in 1959 and lived with her young English family in London, East Pakistan, and East Anglia until her divorce in 1976, when she returned to Charleston. She became a docent there for several years at the museum houses run by Historic Charleston Foundation and worked for Charleston County from 1985 to 2009 in the Legal Department and the Administrator's Office. Ms. Middleton is now retired.

CPSIA information can be obtained
at www.ICGtesting.com
Printed in the USA
BVOW10*1917170217

476236BV00001B/1/P